PRIVATE LABEL MARKETING IN THE 1990s

The Evolution of Price Labels Into Global Brands

by

Philip Fitzell

Global Book Productions
New York, NY

Published in the United States by
Global Book Productions, Suite 1006, 54 West 21st Street, New York, NY 10010.

Library of Congress Cataloging in Publication Data # 92-97124.
ISBN #0-9632920-1-3.

Cover Design by
DRA Graphics, 171 Madison Avenue, New York, NY.

The
Evolution
of
Price
Labels
Into
Global
Brands

A

Comprehensive
Guide
For The
1990s

Contents

Preface

A frequent question encountered whenever I bring up the subject of private labels is: 'What are they?' or 'What do you mean?' People generally are confused about private labels.

The term 'private label' is unfortunate, because it is so vague. It means many things to different people around the world. That may be its strength, too, because those different meanings tie together under the umbrella term, private label.

The British perhaps have a more precise term, 'own label' or 'own brand.' A private label is owned by somebody who usually does not manufacture that item. It is contracted out to some manufacturer, who makes the product to that customer's specifications, then puts that customer's own label on the product. There are, of course, branded manufacturers who contract work on their products out to other manufacturers, but they end up putting their brand on that finished product. In this case, the product is manufactured privately, but still owned by the manufacturer. This points up a distinction between private label and a manufacturer's brand. The latter is most often sold to the general trade. While it may be an exclusive brand, that is, owned by a particular manufacturer, it is not sold exclusively by a retailer, for example. A private label, however, is generally sold exclusively by that retailer. It also may be licensed to other non-competitive retailers in other markets under a similar exclusive deal arranged by the label owner. The difference here is that the private label owner is in control, not the manufacturer. Anyone principally involved in manufacturing branded products cannot be a private label owner, because their branded products are not necessarily produced on an exclusive basis for trade customers. Manufacturers may attempt to 'private label' their brands, that is, pack them for someone exclusively. That 'someone,' however, is not the exclusive owner. He or she usually has no control over how that branded line is made. This distinction gives private label its meaning: Products exclusively owned and/or licensed by the label owner.

Since there are so many different private label owners, this business is complex. Each label owner can market their products differently. Under license, the products also can be marketed differently. Private labels also involve almost every market segment in retailing and foodservice.

This book puts private label activities into focus. There is no other text like it. No one can truly describe the complexity of this business, especially on an international scale. Even this author is humbled by the task.

With some 13 years research and writing experience in the private label field, working under contract for a trade publisher who covers private label on an international scale, I do have an advantage in providing a better perspective. Hopefully, this book will help clear up some of the mystery surrounding this complex subject. The focus is placed on marketing, because that is the point where private label has evolved today.

In an analysis of the past decade—"The 1980s in Retrospect"—this author wrote in *Private Label Magazine's* 10th Anniversary Issue (March/April 1989):

"Tracking private label developments over the past 10 years—the life of this magazine—is nearly impossible in this multi-faceted industry. So many different factors have had an impact, things like: an improving economy; the increased consolidations, acquisitions and mergers of companies; the dominance of national brands with their forceful entry into incentive marketing strategies (couponing, giveaways, etc.); the takeover battles; the emergence of generics; the entry of new product categories for private label; the debut of *Private Label* magazine and then the Private Label Manufacturers Association, both opening opportunities for communication, education and selling; and changing consumer perceptions about private label. There has been an overall shedding of the 'price only' image of private label, replaced by one of equal to or better than national brand quality standards. With less 'knock off' activity, there has developed more originality in private label programs, specifically more calculated and creative efforts put behind private label packaging to reflect the upgraded quality of the products. Both merchandising and marketing strategies have become more aggressive. There also has been some start-up private label programs and much reemphasis or revamping of private label strategies by retailers and wholesalers in all market segments. Additionally, there has been a significant growing interest in private label by major wholesalers, introducing programs to independent grocers and druggists who on their own would be reluctant to invest in the effort. A surge has come in specialty retailing with private label representing a good portion of all the business, particularly in the apparel industry. In this decade, generic prescription drugs, too, have grown to become respectable alternatives to branded drugs. And trends are now developing in upscale or gourmet private label, in store-made private label foods for both deli and take-out business, and in a general move to branded status, including the licensing and exporting of private label products."

Quite a mouthful!

Private labels are a fascinating story, touching on all aspects of life—the packaged consumer goods associated with food, clothing, shelter, health and grooming. They are especially exciting because they have taken on a life of their own, striking out in new creative and innovative ways. True, there are still some copycat private label products around; but that stereotype image is quickly fading from the picture. Today's marketplace for private label is ever-changing. Even that three-year-old analysis, quoted above, needs an update. This industry is becoming more sophisticated.

CURRENT TRENDS

- More major media attention now being given to private label (i.e., *The New York Times*, *The Wall Street Journal*, *Business Week*, *Forbes*, *Ad Age*, etc.

- More involvement by major national brand manufacturers in private label, where firms like Campbell Soup in packaged goods or Ralston Purina in pet foods are rethinking private label quality with a new mind-set that allows for their expansion into this area.

- More topnotch brand-only package design firms entering the business.

- More interest expressed in private label manufacturers and retailers/wholesalersdistributors by stock brokers and Wall Street analysts who track different product segments or industries.

- More boasting about their own private label programs by the label owners, who actually flaunt these products or highlight the subject in their annual reports—for example, mid-Atlantic food wholesaler Richfood Holding, Inc., Richmond, VA, in fiscal 1992 (ending May 2) reported that "during the year, products packed under the IGA label increased from 350 in 1991 to more than 500 at year end. The redesign of our Richfood label and packaging prompted increased demand for diversity in this line which resulted in a total of 1,414 Richfood brand items being offered at year end, up 18.6% from last year. Matching a consumer trend toward lower priced items in tough economic times, our neo-generic Econ line experienced substantial growth. During the year, the Econ line grew to 200 items, with a sales increase of 178% over last year."

- More export opportunities opening throughout the world for private label by wholesalers and cooperatives in particular.

- More openings in peripheral market segments like the military, convenience stores, deep discount drugstore chains, membership club stores and the like.

- More influence on private label programs in the US by European and Canadian retailers/wholesalers, who have established a strong stake in that market.

- More co-ventures or partnerships formed by retailers and wholesalers worldwide, where private label represents an important, if not the most important factor in their activities.

That's what this book is all about.

Not too long ago, private label was criticized harshly for its imitation of leading national brands. The argument simply put was that consumers are confused and/or tricked into buying a private label because it looks like the brands' packaging. Today, private label acts like the brands, that is, its product quality matches or exceeds the brands. The crutch of imitation packaging, while not completely gone, has been almost cast off.

The private label industry has grown mostly through networking—an exchange of ideas by its participants. Most of this exchange has been on a one-on-one basis. Companies today, however, are introducing educational programs for their management and employees to help them better understand private labels. Companies,too, have shared ideas, visiting their peers or participating in the industry trade shows or its publications. Hopefully, this book is properly 'wired' into this network to help others better understand just what private label means today.

Acknowledgements

The private label world opened for me in April 1979, when I joined *Private Label Magazine* in its launch as a new trade publication. Ever since, under contract with this magazine, I have almost daily been exposed to private label developments. I wish to thank Ed Williams, its publisher, for opening this fascinating world to me. Also, I would like to thank the magazine for use of some of the photographs appearing in this book.

I would also like to thank the industry people, who helped me write articles about the business and guided me in producing the first private label textbook, Private Label: Store Brands & Generic Products, in 1982. It literally would take another volume, filled with names and affiliations, to properly give credit. Everyone in this industry has been learning the business as it grows. From the major retailers and wholesalers to small regional or local grocers to drugstore operators, they all have played a role in shaping this book while educating this author.

A special thank you must go to the Private Label Manufacturers Association, New York, its president Brian Sharoff, and his staff, including the irascible Lewis Sterler, all of whom have played an important behind-the-scenes role in helping this industry mature. PLMA has shaped my perception of the business through its numerous meetings and trade shows conducted since 1980.

A personal thanks also goes to Carolyn Dunn, who helped to clearly type and organize the book material—not realizing the detailed, time-consuming effort required, when first making the commitment. I also would like to thank my family, which has had to literally live without me as I pieced together this book in my home office, neglecting important house work as well as our quality time together.

Permission for use of market research data in this book has been granted by: Nielsen, Information Resources (SAMI), and Towne-Oller in the United States; Euromonitor and Mintel in the United Kingdom; and SECODIP in France.

As for the major part of the material in this book, I must directly and indirectly credit *Private Label* and *Private Label International* magazines, particularly since I have been associated with both publications since their start-ups in 1979 and 1985, respectively. This experience has helped to focus my perception and interpretation of developments in this industry.

Philip Fitzell
Bloomfield, NJ

Introduction

At ALL I.G.A. STORES YOU CAN BUY FROM THE INDEPENDENT *without sacrificing anything*

..... Your Ideas, Mrs. Homemaker
built this perfect new shopping service

THE outstanding success of the I.G.A. can be traced directly back to YOUR ideas, Mrs. Homemaker—yours and millions of other American women's.

You made it clear that you preferred to trade with the Independent grocer—*but* that you wouldn't do so *at Your Family's Expense!* You insisted upon buying wholesome quality foods at prices which would make your food dollar buy more.

You demanded that the store where you bought your foods should be as clean and sanitary as your own kitchen.

Because you value your time, you chose to trade in a store where your marketing can be done quickly and easily. In order to serve "different meals" you asked for a wide variety of foods.

You showed your preference for the courtesy and interest of the store owner. And finally, you wanted the dependability of a National organization.

These are the things you demanded of your grocery store. And I realize that in order to merit your patronage, I MUST live up to the things you have a right to expect of me.

Because you wanted finer foods at lower prices, I pooled my buying with thousands of other I. G. A. Grocers and shared with you the savings of our $500,000,000 purchasing power.

To answer your demand for cleanliness, I made my Ivory and Blue Store spic and span from front to rear.

To save your time and energy, I plainly priced and arranged my merchandise on open shelves, where you can help yourself quickly and easily, or have my personal service if you prefer. So that you may have a wide selection of delicacies to choose from, our food experts search the world for the finest of foods.

To meet your desire for the courtesy of an individual owner, I maintained my Independence. And because I own my store, I am naturally interested in keeping your confidence and in proving my sincere desire to help you meet your family's needs.

Those were your ideas, Mrs. Homemaker—your demands. In order to meet them and assure you of the power of a National Organization, I allied myself with thousands of other Independent I. G. A. Grocers throughout the country. The fact that I have succeeded can be traced directly back to you. As a result you can now shop at my store without sacrificing anything in value, service or quality, have money left over to spend for other things—and in addition make your money buy parks, playgrounds and schools for your children, and prosperity for your community.

INDEPENDENT GROCERS' ALLIANCE *of America*

My I. G. A. Brand of Food Products—as well as other nationally advertised brands—guarantees known quality at budget beating prices—at my I. G. A. Store.

NATIONAL HEADQUARTERS
176 WEST ADAMS STREET, DEPT. 11
CHICAGO, ILLINOIS, U. S. A.

"The I. G. A. is dedicated to the maintenance of America's Priceless Heritage—the Principle of Individual Opportunity and Ownership"—*Independently yours*, J. FRANK GRIMES, President, I. G. A.

IGA 1931 Consumer Magazine Advertisement.

A History Lesson*

Prosperous days for private label are documented throughout its history, stretching back into the 19th century, when mail-order houses first were established in the United States. That's how A&P got started early in the 1860s, evolving into a retail business from its expertise in importing and wholesaling teas plus grinding coffees in its stores. Eight O'Clock coffee and Our Own tea were two of its first private label grocery items. Both are still around today. Eight O'Clock, in fact, is now the fourth largest coffee "brand" in the US, according to A&P.

A&P itself grew to dominate the grocery business in the US, late in the 1920s operating more than 15,000 stores—a retailing empire built on low price, low profit, high turnover and, of course, a strong private label presence. During the 1960s -70s, those private label sales represented 35% of A&P's total store volume, while its total sales as early as the 1940s surpassed $1 billion. With its own strong manufacturing support, A&P aggressively promoted private label up to a point where the stores in its chain were force-fed private label at the expense of stocking national brands. Meanwhile, competition and resistance developed on all fronts—other grocers, brand manufacturers, the Government, and even consumers (denied a choice in the A&P stores), all opposed to the "A&P monopoly." Eventually, A&P was hit with an anti-trust investigation, which proved to be costly, plucking the company out of its leadership role.

As a result, A&P had to trim back its retail operations through the 1970s and virtually eliminate most of its manufacturing capacity, because it was too excessive or burdensome with fewer stores in its chain. The emphasis was placed on branded products; so its private label program suffered. In fact, private label share of its sales dipped to a low of about 15%.

This A&P private label story has become a classic tale in the trade, symbolizing what can happen to a retailer who promotes private label over the national brands. The interpretation has been that it's wrong to promote private labels. This overstates the reality of the situation. A&P's private label sales took no more than 35% of its total volume. In fact, A&P's private label share in recent years has climbed back to 23% of sales within its successful US operations. The problem was its continual push on its own manufactured products, giving them top billings in the A&P stores. National brands were considered a competitor and not so much another choice for the consumer. In effect, A&P lost its identity, acting more like a manufacturer than a retailer. The lesson here really is that the retailer can emphasize private label—but not all of the time. Consumers should be given a choice between private labels and national brands.

Throughout this century, private label actually has found strong support in retailing, both from the chains and independent operators. A group of independents banded together in 1926 as a matter of survival up against the giant A&P chain. They formed the Independent Grocers Alliance (IGA), rallying around a food wholesaler in Poughkeepsie, NY. Originally, 25 retailers signed on as IGA retailers. By the end of the 1930s, IGA had some 10,000 IGA food stores in 37 states. Their private label program grew right in step with a top quality philosophy. IGA Inc., Chicago, innovated with its program and walked away with grand prize gold medals and honorary diplomas for its quality private labels at international expositions. IGA brand products received endorsements from Babe Ruth, the legendary baseball slugger. The group developed its own IGA radio show. IGA cooperated with *Parent's Magazine* on a canned food promotion for children in its formative years. IGA products were advertised on CBS radio network. There also was a tie-in poster stamp promotion for IGA products with Walt Disney Studios—real big-time stuff, but decades ago—activities that IGA today would find prohibitive in costs. There is talk today, however, about scheduling TV ads for IGA, including its private labels, on a cable TV network nationwide, which would recall its strategy of the 1930s.

In a 1931 advertisement (see reproduction on previous page) in a national consumer magazine (*Life* or *Colliers*), IGA states: "My I.G.A. brand of food products—as well as other nationally advertised brands—guarantees known quality at budget beating prices—at my I.G.A. store." That brand perception of private label fired entrepreneurs in the early part of this century. IGA was considered another nationally-advertised brand—on an equal footing with the brands in terms of quality.

In the grocery business, pioneers like George Hartford at A&P and Barney Kroger who started The Great Western Tea Co. in 1883 (19 years later adopting its owner's name) and in the department store segment, Rowland Macy and John Wanamaker, all set high quality standards for their own labels. The same strategy was adopted by Aaron Montgomery Ward and Richard Sears, first in the mail-order business, then in retailing. Within the first 10 years of this century, both the latter entrepreneurs had their own fully-operational testing labs, working to ensure that quality.

In 1902, in Kemmerer, Wyoming, James Cash Penney opened the Gold Rule Dry Goods Store. Some 16 years later, he launched his own brands, starting with Pay Day work clothes. In 1930, he set up a research and testing lab, which became one of the largest and best-equipped facilities in the country for consumer end-use testing of textiles. You could say that his 'Gold Rule' about delivering the best quality merchandise has produced uninterrupted 'Pay Days' up to the present. JC Penney today boasts that it has been the number one seller of private label soft goods in the US for decades. More than 60% of its stock is estimated to be in private label. Its private label suppliers are ranked among the finest brand manufacturers in the country: Hart Schaffner & Marx, Johnston & Murphy, Bally, Bugle Boy, etc.

Unfortunately, not every retailer or wholesaler has kept the same quality standards in private label. It may be somewhat of an oversimplification, but from the 1920s on into the advent of radio, going forward into the 1940s with TV's debut, plus the emergence and growth of more nationally-advertised brands, a majority of grocery retailers reassigned their consumer trust to outside manufacturers and food processors. There also was the introduction of supermarkets, which offered multiple selections of brands. At the same time, canners proliferated in the Midwest and with them many more regional and national brands came on the scene. The frozen food industry grew up, adding still more brands to the marketplace. Other product categories emerged as well. Of course, private label benefitted with its own entries into these categories, growing considerably. One of the most successful recent growth categories for private label has been the health and beauty care business.

This brand madness, feeding off media advertising, infected private label retailers and wholesalers as well. They, too, went brand crazy: At one time, Safeway Stores had more than 100 different private label identities; while food wholesaler Fleming Companies had 40+ private brands. Even department store merchant JC Penney fell into this trap, carrying up to 60 different, poorly-named-and-designed store brands that made its private label products look cheap.

More than competition, economics came into play, starting in the 1960s, when consumer boycotts plus other factors eventually led to inflation and unemployment, coupled with a recession started in the 1970s. (That recession also spilled over into Europe, impacting on retailers there as well.) Consumers started to get smarter about shopping for value, especially when their dollar was shrinking in value. Those jingles on radio or TV just didn't sell products as effectively. Brand loyalties began crumbling. Then something significant happened to retailers. They began to perceive themselves as being more than just merchandisers of national brands. Their commitment to private label was revitalized.

Actually, this has been a renewed commitment, but now with smarter marketing strategies. Initially, retailers had the idea that they had to grow nationally, just like the so-called national brands. Almost from day one, A&P stood for Atlantic & Pacific Tea Company, suggesting a national presence. IGA was pushing in that direction, too, early in its history. When independent wholesalers formed the Shurfine-Central cooperative in the Midwest some 40 years ago, it wasn't long before that same mentality took hold. Throughout its growth into the 1960s and 1970s, moving eastward and westward, Shurfine was purchasing national TV commercials, sponsoring national TV shows, featuring celebrities like the rising singer, Wayne Newton, and so on. Suddenly, that co-op smartened up by zeroing in on local markets, buying local media, supporting local promotions and in-store demonstrations, etc.

Since 1965, Fleming Companies had been outgrowing its mid-US origins via acquisitions; but rather than create a national brand presence, the country's second largest food wholesaler today has concentrated on its top-quality private brands being positioned as regional brands, overall encompassing more than 30,000 items in all product sizes and varieties.

In fact, commitment to private label in the US has been most noticeable in the wholesaling sector in recent years, probably because their private label involvement in the past was weak versus grocery chains that had a long history of private label activity.

There has developed an openness in communications, sharing ideas through national private label trade shows. The trade show concept has developed into localized private label shows as well, many of them sponsored by groups of wholesalers and retailers. There has been a cross-fertilization of ideas: Retailers at first coming from Europe and other parts of the world to tour US stores, then reciprocating by inviting US retailers to see their operations.

US wholesalers and retailers also have been helped considerably in private label by brokers like Daymon Associates in New York; Federated Foods in Arlington Heights, IL; Marketing Management in Ft. Worth, TX, and others. Additionally, independent laboratories have supported private label development, giving retailers and wholesalers better quality assurance guarantees over their private labels...enough assurance, in fact, that they now willingly put a guaranteed 'seal of quality' on their private label packaging.

Two important influences have helped to shape private label in the recent past. One influence is a new retailers' attitude that took root when Jewel Food Stores in Chicago introduced generics into the US market. Closely tied to this development is the European influence on US retailing and wholesaling. Generics was inspired by the French hypermarket operator Carrefour, which introduced its no-frills private label program in the 1970s. Jewel was responding competitively to the Aldi limited assortment store concept with 80% private label stock, first developed in Germany. Today, there is more than 25% ownership by the Europeans in US retail and wholesale operations overall.

At a 1982 private label trade show, sponsored by the Private Label Manufacturers Association (PLMA), Jewel's president James Henson credited generics with changing the US marketplace, giving "retailers (the opportunity) to rethink shelf allocation and warehouse arrangements. We have realized," Mr. Henson said, "that we can change the way we promote the grocery department. We no longer are required to invest our margins on branded items to maintain category velocity which we control, price, and allocate. That core is different from the branded products: and unlike the old private label, this private label is a real alternative that our customers understand, respond to, and want."

Dave Nichol, president of Loblaws Ontario (Canada) at the time, picked up on this trend as well. Loblaw really didn't have much of a private label program; so Mr. Nichol programmed "No Name" generics as his private label strategy, helping to differentiate Loblaws from its competitors. Mr. Nichol, who traveled extensively, knew early in the 1980s that the European retailers had capitalized on a strategy of creating unique families of products, available only at their stores. So he developed the upscale President's Choice program, which lately has caught fire in the US and even inspired the country's largest retailer, Wal-Mart Stores, Bentonville, AR, to adopt its own Sam's American Choice private label program.

EUROPEAN DEVELOPMENTS

Private label history in Europe can be traced back to its roots within the cooperative movements, started by retailers, wholesalers, and consumers in the last century. Its evolution into the 20th century has been more diverse with a few key countries like England, France, The Netherlands, Germany, and Switzerland, taking the lead. England in particular—especially its Marks & Spencer phenomenon, that is, a 100% dedicated private label retailer—is now directly or indirectly influencing private label trends around the world.

When the Resale Price Maintenance law—where suppliers to the grocery trade decided and imposed the "proper price" for their products—was abolished in the United Kingdom in 1963, grocery retailers there began to exert influence over their product mix. In tracing these developments, the London-based market researcher Mintel notes: "The late 1960s and early 1970s spawned the first major generation of own label products from the leading multiples. These initial products aimed to be functional, simply presented versions of the brand leaders and priced as far as necessary to attract consumer spend from the brand leaders." Mintel in its 1991 analysis notes that with private label the retailers came to realize better margins up against stiff pricing competition among the brand leaders, while their private label pricing did not have to match a competitor's pricing.

It's interesting to note the attitude at that time, as reported by another London researcher, Euromonitor, in its 1986 "Own Label Report." Euromonitor indicated that "research carried out in 1970 by J. Walter Thompson concluded that: 'Own label per se is not an important element in the housewife's judgment of a store or a group. She is much more likely to be concerned with value for money, the overall quality of the products—especially perishables—and the physical aspects of the store, such as layout and hygiene, or the giving of trading stamps. Own label is a minor element in a consumer's assessment of a store or group."

In today's marketplace, where the top five grocery multiples command 60%+ of sales, that attitude has completely changed. Market leaders like Sainsbury and Tesco have a private label presence that exceeds 60%+ of their sales.

Across Europe, in fact, private label growth is spreading, even into the less developed countries like Spain and Italy, according to recent research by SECODIP, Chambourcy, France. These trends are discussed in the market research chapter of this book.

In the past 20 years, private label in the US has evolved first with emphasis placed on upgrading its quality standards and assuring its consistency. Then packaging enhancement has been addressed, along with more attention paid to in-store merchandising efforts. Lately, attention has focused on marketing support as well. Also, the idea, sparked by generics, that retailers can control their own product velocity has opened private label opportunities in the perishables department of supermarkets. Retailers like Tesco in England, Carrefour in France, Migros in Switzerland, Albert Heijn in the Netherlands, etc., have been doing this for years.

The idea that retailers can take control of products from the product development stage right through to incentive marketing activities in order to sell the product is now growing significantly in the US. The upgrading of private label products is more than cosmetic surgery, it's a serious undertaking to ensure the best quality for consumers. The Vons Companies in Arcadia, CA, for example, three years ago started to change its private label packaging. The job has only recently been completed. Private label director Raymond Swain literally has had to become a packaging expert, working almost daily with graphic houses on color separations, coordinating decisions on symbols, legal issues, regulatory requirements, computerized mock-ups, lithographers hook-up, and so on. The goal, says Mr. Swain, is not to have an expensive packaging look, but one that projects a quality product with a value message.

The private label quality issue itself is never completely resolved. Gail Drew, who now is president of the relatively new Quality Assurance Association, which addresses private label issues, and heads up the quality assurance department at Spartan Stores Inc., Grand Rapids, MI, describes her private label product line as "one of the top 10 private label brands" in the country. Ms. Drew elaborates:

"We monitor product quality with continuous retail sample audits, production audits of new/problem vendors, supplier audits, and plant tours. Samples that are sent in for evaluation from a vendor are looked on very cautiously and samples are picked up from retail to be compared to those sent in...Regular product evaluations are conducted such as consumer panels, product cuttings on existing products, new items, category review of all viable suppliers, and product improvements or changes..."

The players in this business now include "recruits" from top branded companies, who have joined in the private label supplier-or-trade-user segments. Consumer awareness of private label also has grown considerably. The general consumer media has helped in this education. Retailers and wholesalers have worked to educate their customers, too, through consumer contact, in-store product demonstrations, information booklets, and the like. Recent Gallup Polls, sponsored by the PLMA, confirm this growing awareness and trust in private labels.

The private label business by its very nature has traditionally been a follower of the brand leaders. Private label today now follows the brands' lead into a global presence as well. Private label also is striking out on its own through product innovations and new category developments.

This book charts these waters.

---

* *The US portion of this history is based partly on a speech given by the author at the ROFDA (Retailers Owned Food Distributors Association) Fall Conference, held Nov. 3-6, 1991 in Orlando, FL.*

I

An Orientation

1

Defining the Subject

This book addresses the marketing of all types of private labels today throughout the world, showing how many of them continue to evolve more into private brands. It is intended to serve as an orientation to an enormously complex subject, which by its private nature, growing number of diverse players, and new product category openings becomes more blurry everyday.

There are practically no rules limiting private label, which covers almost every product category imaginable. The labels are privately owned by different retailers, wholesalers, distributors and others; so those owners dictate what their private labels will be in terms of product quality, packaging, marketing strategies, and so forth. No one really has a crystal-clear idea about the size or parameters of this industry, because of its overwhelming presence and continual changes. It is ubiquitous, its products found in our food, clothing, and shelter needs. Definitions for private label in the general business world, throughout the media, and even into the private label industry itself fall short of its true scope.

Private labels, established regionally or nationally in many countries, are rapidly growing into a global brands business. Wholesale marketers in the United States are now expanding abroad with private label. European cooperative marketing-buying organizations are now developing standardized private labels for their partner-members throughout Europe, attracting the market leaders from every country. The recent collapse of communism in Eastern Europe and the former Soviet Union has opened new opportunities for private label as well. Japanese trading companies, investigating investments on an international scale, are now forming co-ventures with US private label marketing organizations. Unfortunately, the overall perspective of these dynamics remains superficial, myopic, or basically misinformed. This book hopefully will help to better focus the subject, showing the extent of as well as the power exerted by private label products on the world market today, not to mention their potential for growth.

Store brands...bargain brands...price brands...house brands...private brands...controlled labels...corporate brands...signature brands...copycat products...distributor labels...knockoffs...generics...no name...white labels...own labels...own brands... These are a few descriptions given to private labels. So many different identities—each carrying multiple or sometimes unrelated meanings to one another—suggest how elusive this subject can be. In fact, with widely diverse standards of quality assigned to private labels, a dichotomy exists in the marketplace. At retail, some generics still maintain only satisfactory, acceptable, or Grade B or C quality standards. The strongest private labels are positioned as first-tier or first-label, top-quality products—as good as or better than leading national brands—sold as an alternative and often lower-price choice, thus providing value to consumers. Other private labels—such as St Michael brand by Marks & Spencer, London; some of the corporate brand products under Loblaw Companies' President's Choice program available in Canada and the US; or items in the upscale Master Choice private brand distributed as a corporate label through A&P's supermarket chains in the US and Canada—deliver unquestionably superior quality, or unique, innovative product features unmatched by any national brand in the marketplace. Because of these wide differences in private labels generally, more and more retailers and wholesalers as well as foodservice distributors like ComSource Group or Sysco in the United States and restaurant operators like McDonald's on a worldwide basis insist on identifying their exclusive label products as brands. Different private label 'philosophies,' however, do not erase their common linkage: label exclusivity for the owner and built-in value for the consumer, delivering quality well worth the price. It's not uncommon for a private label in one segment of the market to cross over into another segment, but more as a brand in the latter segment. In the foodservice business, for example, restaurant chains like Nathan's, A&W Root Beer, Benihana, Marie Callender Pies, etc., sell their own branded products at retail outside their chains. This makes their identity a brand, because usually any retailer can sell the products. Retailers also may sell their private label items in institutional-size containers or so-called club packs, which foodservice operators may buy for use in their operations. When those operators redistribute the product, it's not really their private label.

These are the parameters set on the grocery shelf: the market leader in cold cereals, Kellogg's competes against a generic line literally surrounding the brand.

Here Kmart compares its own "brand" price to the national brand price, offering consumers a $5.25 savings.

2

The Label Owners

In the retail marketplace, private label identities cannot be sold by just anyone in the business. They belong to the label owner, who can sell them through his own retail outlets and/or assign them to members of a cooperative, a wholesaler, or to independent retailer licensees on an exclusive basis. The label owner does not manufacture or process all the products under his private label program. He frequently prices his private labels lower than the market's comparable brands or any specialty imported brands. The private label price, however, does not always sell "cheaper"; in fact, retailers like Harrods in London, Tiffany's in New York, or Neiman Marcus in Dallas can offer very expensive private label merchandise with no alternative choice branded items available in their stores.

The best way to identify a private label is through its exclusive ownership by any company that is not primarily a branded products manufacturer. That label owner will not sell his label products to just any trade customer in a given market where he competes for business. There must be an exclusivity assigned to the label in order to keep the products "private." In other words, competitors in a given market do not carry the same private labels. Many of them may carry private label products supplied by the same manufacturer, but not under the same label. (Close-out private label products may turn up in another retailer's operation—someone who is not under license to sell that label — but that is an exception to the rule.)

Private label owners may occasionally sell their own label products to non-competitive retailers or wholesalers, that is, in markets where they do not operate stores. This licensing arrangement is practiced by A&P, for example, with its coffee bean program, Eight O'Clock brand. There also are some retailers and wholesalers who export their private label products to other countries, where those items end up as brands, usually sold to anybody in the marketplace. But some label owners can control this distribution, too, keeping the label exclusive.

This analysis leads to a general definition: Private labels are products that are owned and/or licensed exclusively by retailers, wholesalers, restaurants operators, foodservice distributors or caterers for distribution in their respective segments of the marketplace. Other types of label owners also get involved in this business. Brokers, buying cooperatives, marketing/procurement organizations, mail order houses, the military, exporters, multi-level marketers, and others can manage their own exclusive private label programs. To a lesser degree, private label foods, cleaning supplies, toiletries and the like can be picked up under exclusive labels owned by firms in the services area, such as hotels, airlines, amusement-entertainment complexes, schools, hospitals, nursing homes, and prisons. The foodservice business, of course, also provides private labels to this market segment.

The diversity of players is complicated more by the variety of participants involved in the different market segments. In retailing, for example, every type of store can carry some private labels—supermarkets, drugstores, department stores, discount mass merchandisers, specialty outlets, Do-It-Yourself (DIY) retailers, membership warehouse club stores, convenience stores,

Albert Heijn's Brouwers brand beer holds its own against the international brand, Heineken in the Netherlands.

neighborhood grocers, etc. There, private label programs can appear in almost every product category imaginable—food, clothing, health and beauty care, household cleaning and repair supplies/furnishings/appliances, general merchandise, hardware, jewelry, auto parts, and so on.

Loyal brand-oriented consumers in the United States, however, have made it difficult for private label, except in specialty retail chain store operations that adopt their own label identity on merchandise (i.e., Victoria's Secret, the Body Shop, and others). Private label has had more difficulty in significantly penetrating some product categories, such as electronics, cosmetics, baby food, beer, etc. Mothers, for example, insist on having only "the best" food (the top national brand) for their babies; while most beer drinkers bow to the "King of Beers,"

Budweiser, leaving little market share for numerous domestic and imported brands. In Europe, where brand monopolies are not as strong, private label baby food and beer are quite successful. Boots The Chemist in the United Kingdom has offered its own label baby food for years; while Kesko in Helsinki has just recently introduced baby food under its Prikka label in K-stores (food outlets). At the same time, the identities for private label become more obscure in the perishable foods area—produce, fresh meats, deli items, chilled prepared foods. Own label beer in the UK is commonplace, while Dutch supermarket retailer Albert Heijn for years has promoted its Brouwers beer effectively against Heineken, the market leader. Attitudes are changing, however, as certain label owners are now organizing controlled labels for produce, while retailers are paying more attention to their quality meat programs with special sub-branding strategies.

It's noteworthy to mention one "untouchable" product category for private label: automobiles. While retailers like Sears and Montgomery Ward in the US and Tesco in the United Kingdom have attempted to put their own identities on cars in the past, their inability to establish dealerships to support these lines doomed the effort.

Often, private labels are incorrectly associated with activities that are unrelated to this business. When a product, for example, is produced "under contract" by one manufacturer for another manufacturer, the former calls it a "private label," because that product is not his brand. In this case, that product is still made under one manufacturer's brand specifications and assigned its brand identity. This happens frequently in the cosmetics field, where a manufacturer cannot meet consumer demand for his branded line of products, so he seeks outside production help. Similar "private label" contracted work occurs in the electronics and automotive fields, as well as in other industries, for various reasons: Soliciting outside production to meet market demand for a particular brand, seeking buying expertise from abroad, realizing lower labor costs or economies of scale from another manufacturer, and so forth. There is confusion here because private labels are placed under contract with a manufacturer by the label owner. The private label owner, however, cannot be primarily a manufacturer.

Another area of confusion occurs with the term 'generic.' Generic products can appear either as a private label or as a manufacturer's packer label. The latter is not a private label because it is a brand owned by the manufacturer. Sometimes the manufacturer will control its distribution and grant trade customers an exclusive on the packer label; but it still remains a brand, because of its ownership. Generic prescription drugs (products identified by their generic name) also are confused as being private label, when in fact they are remote to this business—if not non-existent, because they are strictly regulated by the Food and Drug Administration in Washington. All manufacturers, distributors and even packagers of these products in the US are subject to this scrutiny. They cannot set their own quality specifications. In contrast, manufacturers of over-the-counter (OTC), drugs like aspirin, acetaminophin, antacids, etc. are not required to report adverse side effects or other information to the FDA as in prescription drugs. Private label OTC drugs, therefore, are a viable business. Even the term 'generic drugs' itself is considered inaccurate, because these products really deal more with bioequivalent prescription drugs that are made by manufacturers after the original manufacturer's patent on a brand-name drug has expired. The Generic Pharmaceutical Industry Association, New York, tells this author that prescription drugs in general are rarely, if ever, sold under a "house label" or "private label" in any US pharmacy. Sometimes generic prescription drugs are manufactured on a contract basis for another manufacturer or distributor; but this is rarely if ever an exclusive basis and the exclusivity never extends to the retail level. In these instances, furthermore, most states require that the actual manufacturer's name be on the label along with the distributor's name.

In the grocery business, as well as in other industries, the term generic itself has never been clearly defined. As will be seen later, it has taken on many different meanings.

Private labels first grew out of a need by entrepreneurial retailers in the last century to beat the system, that is, overcome inflated product pricing created in the distribution system by too many middlemen between the manufacturer and the retailer. These enterprising retailers wanted to offer their customers top-quality merchandise, but at a lower price. For decades since, they have exercised control over their own product mix—less so in the United States because of national brands' growing dominance in the marketplace, secured by huge advertising budgets designed to establish a premium brand image at a premium price. In fact, lower pricing became private label's major weapon against these powerful marketers. More recently, retailers, helped along by private label manufacturers, have sharpened their weapon, putting on a new edge—marketing support. The retailers and wholesalers, too, have come to realize that they can differentiate themselves from being just another brand name distributor. In this process, they now know that private labels help them:

- BOOST profits with high-volume, basic grocery items (canned goods, paper products, household cleaning products, and the like) at a lower price than the name brands,

- EXPAND into lower volume categories as well, where the key to success is the comparative gross profit contribution,

- PROJECT a low-price image for their stores with private label pricing across different product categories below the name brands,

- DRAW in customer traffic and create customer loyalty by offering exclusive lines under one or several labels not found in competitors' stores,

- PRESENT value to their customers by offering quality private label products at a lower price or better quality at the same price as the name brands,

- DEVELOP their own promotions and nurture excitement in their stores with special displays, super pricing deals, lost leader (giveaway) items, etc.

- REINFORCE their store name both on the store shelves and in their customers' homes, especially when their own label carries the store logo, serving as a mini-billboard.

Competition from so-called advertised brands has not been as fierce in Europe, where retailers have adopted much less subservient private label strategies. One example is the Migros cooperatives in Switzerland with 95%+ private label stock. Its policy involves stocking a large range of articles, but without product overlapping; that is, Migros does not stock "identical" articles from different producers in a range. In fact, most of the European market leaders in grocery retailing emphasize private label stock, carrying 30% or more of their volume in private label. The US grocery retailers usually stock private label at under 20% of their volume, but with some exceptions.

This comparison is especially significant in the 1990s, since many more US industry spokesmen in food retailing are predicting a trend toward European retailing. In a "State of the Supermarket Industry" speech, delivered in October 1991 at the Food Marketing Institute (Washington) General Merchandise/Health and Beauty Care Conference in Denver, CO, FMI's senior vice-president Tim Hammons said: "America has fragmented into (a) mosaic of very different ethnic, life-styles, and demographic groups, market-by-market. It's tougher to reach fragmented consumers with national media advertising." The fragmented market has resulted in more promotional dollars spent in stores, helping to "transfer some power to the supermarket operator. In Europe, the balance of power is much more with the retailer-wholesalers group and much less with the manufacturer than has been the case here. This trend, flowing from a fragmenting consumer marketplace, is going to shift the balance of power in the US to look more like the way it looks in Europe. That is, closer parity with the manufac-turer." In this change, Mr. Hammons added, the supermarket assortment of products will change, as consumers become less brand loyal. "(And) if you're going to pull down the assortment in the supermarket, one of those products that's likely to survive is upscale private label. By 'upscale,' I mean private label that really is competitive with national brands...I think that private label in the 1990s is a different kind of animal that is not going to come and go the way perhaps generics would come and go. This is a new way of marketing in the supermarket environment of the 1990s that is not going to be simply another cycle in what we've all been used to. For many of our operators, upscale private label has become their frequent shopper program, a way to build loyalty for the store."

What Mr. Hammons neglects to mention is the fact that this trend is not just a retailer-driven activity, but involves private label manufacturers, who only within the past 10 years have come to realize that they can market private label like a brand.

Customer loyalty of a different sort exists in the foodservice business. In fact, national brands are not considered as 'sacred' at the foodservice level in the United States. Private label for foodservice distributors commands a larger share of their business — estimated at 40%+ of the total stock distributed. In fact, private label can be more expensive for them to buy than brands; but the distributors purposely join foodservice distributor groups, preferring their private label programs, which give them the exact quality level they want (fancy or choice down to standard grade) on a consistent basis with a guarantee of supply, plus national advertising support provided by the group. Their private labels provide integrity across many different product categories: canned or dry goods, frozen foods, perishable foods, nonfoods, etc. The local distributors also can claim exclusivity for these labels. They don't have to haggle over national brand pricing or be squeezed out by a competing distributor who buys the brand cheaper. While private label in retailing has traditionally put its focus more on pricing, its counterpart in foodservice was evolving as restaurant operators and foodservice distributors grew with the emphasis mostly on quality. The groups provided a different private label identity for each quality level ordered. The groups also provided expertise in sourcing these products, in controlling their quality specifications, in marketing the different grades of quality, in building customer acceptance, and in the physical and logistical distribution support needed to get the products through distributors and on to their commercial or institutional foodservice accounts. At that point, consumers do not see the group's label, since the product is prepared in the kitchen in the back of the house. But the foodservice operator, such as a fast food chain, can take pride in buying quality products by preparing and packaging them in-house for take-out under his own store brand identity. The focus on quality has in recent years picked up momentum in the retailing segment as well. Price is still important for private label in retailing, but not the one and only consideration any more for private label buyers.

The diversity of private label products and players is illustrated here: (Top) the US retailer-owned co-op Topco with generic fabric softener sheets under its Valu Time label; Canadian drugstore retailer Jean Coutu's Personnelle multi-vitamins and minerals for seniors; England's Marks & Spencer with its St Michael brand in a single-serve chilled lasagna dish; and US food wholesaler Fleming Companies Rainbow brand moist cat food.

3

Sourcing Private Labels

Private label products in the retail segment usually are sourced from outside manufacturers working under contract for the label owners, who establish the quality specifications for their own products. Some label owners also can be involved in manufacturing their own private label products, but that is not their principle business. These products, of course, can be imported as well. In fact, some of the pioneering food retailers in the US first entered into business by roasting their own coffee beans as well as importing teas for sale through their outlets or off wagons or trucks on the road. They also stocked different commodity items like flour, sugar, salt, etc., selling this merchandise by bulk out of barrels. Other staples, including dairy products, bakery items, and general dry groceries were added as they moved from bulk sales more into packaged goods, some of which eventually came to be identified under their own private labels.

Initially, top quality was the watchword. In those formative years, the retailers, who produced their own private labels, delivered the very best quality that they could muster. As entrepreneurs, they put their own name and reputation behind those labels. Merchants who couldn't manufacture or process goods sought that same high quality from outside suppliers. When good reliable sources were located, long-term relationships were established between the trade customer and the manufacturer. Developing in this century, however, private labels generally have had to bow before an onslaught of brands. Retailers, especially those in the grocery trade, began to emphasize brands more, relegating private label to a secondary role. Grocery buyers began to purchase brands first, then private label, if they had the time or interest. It was at best an afterthought. Usually buyers were assigned to different product categories—their areas of expertise. So there was virtually no control over or any structure to a private label program. As a result, private label quality standards either slipped, were neglected, or were never fully established in the first place, depending on the retailer involved.

Under the shadow of the brands proliferation, private labels, too, proliferated upward literally into hundreds of different labels, first in the canned goods business, then into other major product categories such as frozen foods and health and beauty care. Usually smaller manufacturers supplied private label stock. If a larger, mostly branded manufacturer supplied private label at all, it was strictly on a low-profile basis, done more to satisfy large trade customers, who expressly asked for private label, or to increase plant efficiency. The brand market leaders were not a bit interested in developing private label business. Today, that attitude has changed somewhat, but not dramatically.

Private label really became orchestrated as a marketing strategy in the late 1950s, when influential, powerful private label brokers entered the picture, promoting canned goods and then other products. Their customers, the retailers, sometimes used to adopt a broker-owned label or use a manufacturer's packer label on an exclusive basis. Overall, there was very little confidence built around private label.

The situation at Ralphs Grocery, Compton, CA, illustrates how this scenario has changed. Back in the 1960s, this grocery chain had virtually no structure to or very little commitment for private labels. Graham Lee (now vice-president of the Grocery Division) recalls: "When I began buying private label products (early in the 1970s), our quality was usually handled with a handshake. As you got to know the packer, you'd say, 'This is Ralphs and we only want good stuff. Tell me what you've got...'" But Ralphs Grocery at that time also got better oriented to private label, when Daymon Associates, a New York-based marketing broker, specializing in private label, began representing suppliers to Ralphs. In 1981, the grocer set up its own, independent quality assurance department for private label products. A couple of years later, the company retained an outside design firm to redesign its Ralphs label, which became one of the industry's most sophisticated private labels, featuring vignettes so attractive that it has been sold by Ralphs to non-competitors for their own private label programs. In the past 20 years, Ralphs' private label commitment has soared from 70 up to 1,500+ skus (stock keeping units), accounting for an estimated $115 million+ in sales or 15% of its total sales in 1991. Today, its program continues to grow via new sub-branding strategies under the Ralphs logo. (See Chapter 26 of this book.)

In this century, retailers outside the food area have courted major brand manufacturers—i.e., Sears with Whirlpool appliances and Kmart with Admiral TVs, Benjamin Moore paints, or Jonathan Logan apparel, adopting their products under private labels. But major brand manufacturers in these segments of the market also captured most of the business. Some retailers like Sears and J.C. Penney have kept their private labels viable over the years, but the brands overall did capture most of the market share. In the past, Sears with its nearly 100% commitment to private label or Marks & Spencer still 100% dedicated to own label merchandise, both could virtually take over the production capacities of certain manufacturers. And they did.

That activity, however, was an exception to the rule. Actually, a manufacturer can commit to private label production anywhere from below 1% up to 100% of its capacity. Their involvement can switch on or off, it can be converted from private label to brand-only production, or vice-versa. Private label product manufacturing attracts them because it is often less costly to produce products, requiring little product development work (private label often targets the leading brand as the quality standard in the marketplace), and no national advertising support (that left up to the brands). Some manufacturers, including major brand manufacturers, use private label merely to fill in downtime on their production lines, to reactivate production lines or plants that might have to be closed or sold because of lower market demand for their branded products, or to sell off products in an over-production run of their branded line. Major brand manufacturers also will take on private label business when the retail account is a major customer who specifically asks for a substantial private label order: The business is too good to turn away. The brand manufacturers do not solicit that business. They merely respect an unwritten law in business: The customer is always right. Still other manufacturers, who do not command a major market share in their product categories, stay competitive by also supplying products to private label accounts. Marriages like this can end in divorce especially when their branded products begin to look much better in terms of market share.

A good example of a manufacturer who straddles this fence is H.J. Heinz Co., Pittsburgh, PA. Heinz brand ketchup is the market leader in its category; so Heinz makes no private label ketchup—period. The company also makes canned soup, having marketed its line since the turn of the century. But about 15 years ago, Heinz decided it was no match for Campbell soups in the retail market, so Heinz pulled its brand out of the US, selling only Heinz brand soups in the foodservice segment. In retail, Heinz began supplying private label soups more aggressively. Today, Heinz commands some 83% of the private label retail soup business in the US, where no Heinz brand exists. But its brand does continue in foodservice in the US as well as in retail and foodservice in Canada, the United Kingdom, and Australia—some of its major markets.

Sometimes, private label business becomes such a growth area in a particular product category that the brand leader enters this business, too. A recent striking example is Ralston Purina Co., St. Louis, a 65-year-old brands-only pet food supplier, which in 1991 announced it has targeted up to 30 private label accounts for business. The company made its formal entry at the November 1991 Private Label Trade Show, sponsored by the Private Label Manufacturers Association, held in Chicago, as a first-time exhibitor.

As mentioned previously, manufacturers also apply their packer label to private label strategies, too. Sometimes, these packer labels are licensed exclusively to retailers as "private labels." In the United Kingdom, this practice is called "surrogate" own label. These packer label, however, still belong to the manufacturer, who establishes their specifications, packaging, and other product requirements. They are only licensed to the retailer or wholesaler in the retail business. In the definition suggested in this book, private labels cannot be owned by someone principally involved in manufacturing. The licensing agreement for a packer label also can be non-restrictive, allowing players in other segments of the market to use the label or even permitting non-competitors the use of this "exclusive" label. Perhaps all these packer labels should be called surrogate labels, since they only substitute for a real private label, which is owned and originates from a non-manufacturing source. Some manufacturers, however, have begun to call these labels 'value brands' right in step with today's trend toward better quality private brands.

Quite often, a retailers will use a manufacturer's packer label as a 'test product' in a product category not covered by his private label program. If that packer label proves viable, it can then be switched over to the retailer's private label program.

One interesting packer label twist involves Wal-Mart, Bentonville, AR, the largest retailer in the world. Wal-Mart has purchased exclusive marketing rights to the Equate packer label from Perrigo Co., Allegan, MI, now the largest private label manufacturer of health and beauty care products. Under its licensing agreement, Wal-Mart has been able to build a surrogate label program under the Equate identity, using different suppliers to fill out the line. Interestingly, Wal-Mart has chosen to put only the manufacturers' names on the distribution clause of the package—at least seven different manufacturers (including Perrigo) for a growing line of products.

The strategy for European manufacturers generally has been to become dedicated private label suppliers or branded houses. There has been a trend during the 1980s for some brand manufacturers to keep their brand presence within their own country, but to include private label outside that marketing area. As Europe breaks down trade barriers in the 1990s, this private label export business promises to grow substantially.

4

Label Identities

The owner of a retail private label doesn't always directly identify himself on the package. While his logo on the package can be the same as the store name, other private label identities can be used as well. Supermarket General Holding Corp., Woodbridge, NJ, for example uses the Pathmark label for its first line of private label products, a No Frills label for its generic products, and a Chef Mark for deli items, fresh pizza, and other items of that kind—all within its Pathmark supermarkets. A retailer like The Vons Companies, Arcadia, CA, operates different store concepts, each with its own first line private label program: Vons at Vons supermarkets, Pavilions at Pavilion supermarkets, and Tianguis at Tianguis supermarkets. Vons also exercises its option to use these labels throughout its operation, wherever they fit, almost like a corporate label strategy. The company additionally operates the Jerseymaid Milk Products Co., Los Angeles, using the Jerseymaid Dairies private label for different dairy and ice cream products. While Vons identifies Jerseymaid Dairies as the source on the packaging's distribution statement, Vons additionally lists itself as 'The Vons Companies' on the packaging within the product guarantee statement. When a retailer operates many different manufacturing facilities, label identities can grow more complicated.

While Winn-Dixie Stores, Jacksonville, FL, has cut back on the number of its own manufacturing and processing plants—a current count of 20 operations—the company still maintains more than 25 private label identities in

A sampling of Winn-Dixie's different label identities, covering foods to pet foods to health and beauty care plus its generic label, Price Breaker.

different product categories, using its own facility names on the distribution statements. For example, under its Astor Products Inc., Jacksonville, FL, operation, the retailer stocks Astor dry soup mixes, Prestige brick-pack coffee, WD Brand steak sauce, Kountry Fresh ready-to-eat cereals, Dixie Home tea bags, Dixie Darling cake mixes, Prestigio pasta items, Sun Belt paper products, Arrow fabric softener sheets, Kountry Cookin charcoal lighter fluid, Lilac liquid dish detergent, plus a number of private label pet products—Feedin' Time soft cat food, Vita Pep soft dog food, Slick canned dog food, etc. Under its operation, the Monterey Canning Co., San Mateo, CA, the chain processes Thrifty Maid canned fruits and vegetables and Price Breaker canned goods as well as other items (i.e., Quick grits). Its Deep South Products, Inc., Orlando, FL, produces Sta-Fit thirst quencher, Chek soft drinks, Deep South peanut butter, Superbrand spread (made in the Gainesville, GA, plant), etc. W-D's Crackin' Good Bakers, Inc., Valdosa, GA, makes Crackin Good crackers and Deli chips. The Winn-Dixie Stores identity does appear on the distribution statement for different health and beauty care items: Ultra Fresh mouthwash, Fresh' n Gentle panti-shields, Nite-Time cold medicine, Kuddles baby wipes, etc. The chain also puts its name on other products outside that category, for example, Fisherman's Wharf seasonings.

Private labels often appear as controlled labels in the marketplace. It may be difficult to identify the label owner, since that company may have no direct relationship with its trade customer, the retailer or wholesaler. Basically, the owner controls the label, using it in his own operation and/or licensing others to use the same label. The other users get exclusive rights in their marketing area. So in the case of Loblaw Companies, Toronto, Canada, its President' Choice range of upscale private label products is sold in the Loblaw stores in Canada but also is licensed to retailers and wholesalers in the US as well as being adopted by Loblaws' own U.S. divisions. Through its Intersave Buying & Merchandising Services, West Seneca, NY, Loblaw is now helping Wal-Mart source product in the US for its new Sam's American Choice program. A number of US retailers meantime have begun picking up licensing rights for President's Choice, one being Jewel Companies, Inc., Chicago, which began integrating the line early in 1992, first announcing its presence to the public in April. Jewel continues to maintain its own Jewel private label program as well as its No Frills generic program. Other licensees of the President's Choice program in the US include: D'Agostino Supermarkets, New Rochelle, NY; wholesaler Harris Teeter, Matthews, NC; Peter J. Schmitt Co., West Seneca, NY (a wholesaler); Fred Meyer, Portland, OR, and Smitty's Food & Drug, Phoenix, AZ. At this writing, others like Acme Markets, Philadelphia, also are considering the line.

Controlled labels are private labels since their owners are not primarily manufacturers and continue to maintain exclusivity for the licensee. A wholesaler, broker, or cooperative will sometimes refer to their private labels as controlled labels. It's all a matter of semantics.

This distinction of ownership in private labels is critical, because the label owner doesn't just buy ready-for-sale products for his program. He can do that readily with branded or so-called off-brand products sold by the manufacturers. But for private labels, the owner instead must establish a program around his products and literally bring them into existence within his operation, while continually supporting the effort to ensure their success. Working closely with the manufacturers, the label owner, on his own or through a broker (account specific or independent), a wholesaler or distributor, must do all the legwork that the brand manufacturers do to make his private label program 'fly' in the marketplace.

Private labels work successfully when the label owner identifies with the program not only in a figurative sense (placing a store logo on the label) but literally (an operations effort) by securing top management support and commitment to the effort. Then an experienced team of managers must be assembled to coordinate this program. That team and its support staff must properly source products from reliable manufacturers, specify the product quality desired, establish attractive and protective packaging, address legalities like copyright and trade dress issues as well as government regulations, assure that product quality is met through both in-house and outside laboratory analysis with spot-checks and follow-up inspections, support marketing efforts to better educate consumers about the price, quality, and value of the products, and grow the overall program as an identifiable profit center. The program must be continually reviewed and updated to meet product/ packaging technological changes, government regulation changes, market changes, and so forth. There must be 100% commitment by everyone in the company from board chairman down to stock clerk or store cashier. In the not-too-distant past, many label owners identified only figuratively with their program, letting manufacturers or brokers handle the program support. Today, private label programs succeed with strong support from both ends, where a partnership forms among the participants—retailer, wholesaler, broker, manufacturer, ingredient/packaging supplier, package designer, market researcher, etc.

Anyone who makes this investment in the private label program can truly identify their private labels as brands. Yet these products, especially in the United States, still carry the stigma of being 'second best' up against national brands, which continue to dominate market share in most product categories. Call it brain-washing, call it conditioning, the national brands over the years, through TV advertising, have convinced consumers that their brands are the best quality available in the marketplace. Anything sold cheaper is just that—cheap. In some product areas, national brand quality may be the best available. But as a generalization, it doesn't make sense today. Private labels have positioned themselves to be as good as or better than the leading brands. Their maturing programs back up this claim. Consumer taste or test panels and market research reports now verify that fact.

Since brands are less dominant in Europe, private label market share is stronger, particularly in countries like England, Denmark, the Netherlands, Germany, and France. The international emergence of generic products in the late 1970s and early 1980s impacted significantly on the quality image of private labels. Generics debuted in food stores as low-price, no-name/no frills products that offer acceptable quality or performance. They have since been upgraded in packaging with more of a secondary private label look, while offering more consistency in product quality and performance. Even the instigator of generics in the US, Jewel Food Stores, Chicago, has this past year finally switched from its dull, all-white label with black lettering and a distinctive green and black stripe motif, to a secondary private label Econo Buy label, developed by its parent company, American Stores Co., Salt Lake City, UT. Econo Buy products feature more colorful packaging with graphics and some photography or vignetted product illustrations, as well as nutritional data and a recycled symbol where appropriate. Of all the private label descriptions mentioned earlier, generics perhaps is the most commonly used term by people who have little knowledge about this business.

Interestingly, while the inferior product quality and packaging of generics generally have dragged down the private label quality image, generics (as will be seen later) also has liberated retailers and wholesalers, so to speak, giving them more control over the product mix in their stores. Up until the 'generics revolution' of the early 1980s, national brands really controlled shelf space, especially in US supermarket—up to 90% or more of the sku count. Private label's liberalization came with the emergence of generics, because the retailers and wholesalers themselves introduced this phenomenon into retail stores. In the foodservice segment, generics, too, became a factor, but more as another quality level option in distributors' color-coding schemes—top quality or premium quality down to standard grade (generics).

The generics concept was originated by Carrefour, a hypermarket retailer in France, positioned as a distinctive private label identity. Carrefour previously had no private label program. The chain put its own logo on the label, but not prominently. The packaging for its "produits libre" line was very simple with no fancy wrapping. Carrefour's idea was to present products that were "brand free (and) as good as the best, but less expensive." These quality products were free of the costs of name-brand marketing, advertising, and packaging. The look of the packaging was a plain white background, with black lettering to identify the product category and a single narrow red-and-blue strip with a tiny Carrefour insignia in its center.

Since Jewel in the US already had an established private label program, it adopted the same plain packaging look, but with the quality set below that of its first-line private label range. Jewel called its new generic line "a no brand name alternative" of basic bargain products of standard grade quality. While Carrefour's "produits libre" really meant free from the brand costs, Jewel took this meaning literally to mean no brand name at all. It wasn't coincidental that Jewel at that time (1976-77) was competing against no frills box stores (limited assortment stores) in its Midwest marketing area—the Aldi store concept, which featured 80%+ private label stock displayed in cut shipping boxes in a no frills setting. Jewel responded with what it felt was similar plain-looking merchandise displays in a no-frills generic aisle. This strategy, in fact, caught fire in the US, spreading rapidly. It gave other retailers and wholesalers a sense of power or freedom, which eventually was flexed as well in their private label lines, and more recently with new upscale private labels as well as a move into private label perishable programs today.

5

Private Labels are Brands

Private labels, in effect, are becoming more like brands. But just what is a brand? The dictionary defines it as a 'sign of quality' or 'a proof of ownership,' which could apply as easily to many private label as it so commonly does to the manufacturers' brands. "There really is no legal definition for a brand," according to Arthur Handler of the legal firm, Whitman & Ransom, New York. Mr. Handler, who has been legal counsel for the Private Label Manufacturers Association, this industry's only trade organization, since 1986, says that "a brand is really a fact-driven concept, best described by a grouping of characteristics." Those brand characteristics can include: consumer recognition, trademark/copyright protection, product research and development support, product/packaging innovation, advertising/marketing support, top-quality specifications from first-class quality control manufacturing procedures, beautiful package design, and so forth. Perceived value derives from the equity built into a brand name over the years. While more of an intangible characteristic, it still is very viable.

In today's marketplace, so-called national brands do not have a monopoly on any one of these marks of identity. In fact, some private brands today exceed the manufacturers' brands in many of these area. First-line private label products traditionally have set high-quality standards to meet or exceed the brands, which because of their market dominance became the target or acceptable standard in a product category. Private label competes against these popular or best-selling products by attempting to duplicate those standards—and sometimes even exceeding the brands' standards—through product testing, follow-up enforcement of the specifications, and auditing of the products in the field, spot-checking on product taken right off the store shelf. This activity centers around the label owner's in-house quality assurance department, including laboratory facilities, as well as outside lab support. Quality assurance also includes consumer panel testing of private labels against the brands as well as competing private labels, where the test results often favor private label over the top brands in a number of product categories. So-called brand quality in private label is not a new phenomenon by any stretch of the imagination.

When this industry was less structured, back in the 1950s and early 1960s, Topco Associates, Inc., Skokie, IL, a buying cooperative for medium-size grocery retailers, developed its Food Club label with quality standards based upon the minimum standards set by the US Department of Agriculture. Topco then would send its own quality control people into its suppliers' manufacturing plants to assure that those standards were met. The cliché at that time for competitors, building their own private label programs, was: 'Give me what you give Topco.'

This co-op was truly a trend-setter. As its product line evolved away from just commodity items into paper goods, formulated products, and various nonedible items, Topco, having no basis for a quality comparison, had to target the leading brand leader in different product categories for its quality standards.

Today, Topco is one of the top companies in this business with private label sales exceeding $3 billion, generated from a stable of more than 16,000 skus. Some major US food retailers today have become members of Topco: Kroger's Dillon Companies, Dominick's, Meijer, etc. Topco also has helped some of its members to develop their own private labels as well as supplying them with Topco generated labels, such as Food Club, World Classics, GreenMark, etc.

In addressing particular needs of their customers, private label owners have actually innovated or opened new product business in their own lines. Stop & Shop Companies, Boston, MA is generally credited with introducing no salt, no sugar private label canned vegetables and fruits under the Stop & Shop label to the supermarket trade during the early 1980s. Today, both brands and private labels copy this strategy in many food products in response to growing consumer consciousness about healthy foods. The generic cigarettes boom, occurring about the same time, also triggered a competitive response by the brand manufacturers, who introduced value brand cigarettes like Alpine and Richmond, or repriced the Doral and Viceroy brands as value brands. Private label also can claim a first with environmentally-friendly products, introducing so-called green lines well before the brand manufacturers, working off their large inventories, could address this important issue. In June 1989, Loblaw's in Canada debuted its President's

Choice G.R.E.E.N. range, the first such program in North America. In fact, it is not uncommon today for private label retailers and wholesalers to embark on product development and research projects. Good examples are Loblaw in Canada and Tesco in England—two strategies outlined in Part VI of this book.

One of the oldest private labels in the US, A&P's Eight O'Clock coffee, dating back to 1882, has proven to be such a success that its owner since 1979 has been selling it also as a "brand" to non-competitive customers, that is, supermarkets operating outside A&P's marketing areas. The eight A&P regional chains, however, still maintain Eight O'Clock coffee as their own corporate brand, a descriptor that lately has caught on as retailers and wholesalers grow and diversify in this business. A&P also distributes its Master Choice upscale products throughout its chain system.

Most of the private label brand characteristics mentioned earlier, in fact, have been adopted by retailers such as Sears Roebuck & Co., Chicago, or J.C. Penney, Dallas, TX, for decades. In the US, Sear's Kenmore appliances and Craftsman tool lines, for example, have commanded a strong consumer following since being introduced years ago. In 1918, Penney's began selling Pay Day work clothes; today, as one of the top 10 US retailers, this chain boasts about its Hunt

Not too long ago, A&P attempted to extend its strong brand equity in Eight O'Clock coffee into the tea category; but the effort was short-lived, proving unsuccessful up against A&P's Our Own brand tea products.

Club, Jacqueline Ferrar, St. John's Bay and Stafford soft goods and shoe lines as being "exclusive J.C. Penney national brands." (Annual Report, 1991)

In Europe, private labels are perceived more as brands, because the retailers there take more initiative in introducing their own new product. London-based Euromonitor's "Own Brands 1989" market research report states that own brands account for 30% of packaged grocery sales, nearly 50% of menswear sales, and 50%+ of footwear sales in the UK. By 1992, Euromonitor predicted own label will account for 27% of total retail sales in the UK.

Grocery market leader J. Sainsbury, London, maintaining more than two-thirds of its turnover in own brands, now has more than 7,000 product lines under its Sainsbury brands, having added 1,300 items in one year (1990). This total range is said to command 40% of its non-perishable grocery sales and up to 100% of its perishable sales, according to an "Own Label Review," published by the trade magazine, *Super Marketing* (Feb. 28, 1992).

At the first International Private Label Show, sponsored by the Private Label Manufacturers Association in Paris (Feb. 24-26, 1986), speakers from two major European grocers outlined their private label marketing strategies. From Switzerland, Francis Rigotti, director of marketing at Migros, talked about the early history of Migros, when it attempted to shorten the distribution chain by cutting out middlemen and therefore reducing retail pricing by as much as 40% below the competition. Opposition rose everywhere, including a boycott by all the major brands because Migors refused to sell at their suggested retail price. But the Swiss loved Migros' pricing, so the company itself became a manufacturer/processor of certain products. Eventually, some of those products under its private brands grew to become the "biggest brand names in Switzerland," according to Mr. Rigotti.

In the 1950s, Sainsburys of England faced similar pressures from the branded suppliers, who dictated pricing at retail under the Resale Price Maintenance law. M.I. Samuel, advertising/ marketing manager, noted at the PLMA meeting: "Not surprisingly, we sought ways of getting around this absurd idea. We chose, like Migros, to extend out own brand into every area of our business to give better value than the recognized brands and still to offer everything that our customers had come to expect from us in the way of quality. Thus we were commited.

"The philosophy of today's own brand products is very simple, it has not changed from the early days. It is totally consistent with the corporate ethos. In broad terms, a Sainsburys own brand product must offer our customers something they would not otherwise get from us, either in terms of a better product or a better price. This is extended and elaborated to say that a Sainsbury own brand must be as good in quality as the brand leader, but at a lower price, or be at a better quality at the same price."

Mr. Samuel held no punches when distinguishing between brands and own brand..."The successful brand is judged by its customer to offer something extra, to have an added value over and above the sum of its constituent parts. That may vary from person to person. So I may be a person to whom the aspirational properties of a brand are particularly important—the Gucci watch, the Porsche, the Sainsbury champagne. You, on the other hand, may be people for whom price is the be all and end all. That is what sets the brand apart from the commodity, and thus all so-called own brands are truly brands—even generics.

"We do not see own brand as parasitical nor do we have to wait for the major brands to pioneer a market before we introduce a product ourselves. We have Vitapinit, a pasteurized skimmed milk but with added skimmed milk solids plus Vitamins A and D. These additions make it taste like full cream milk and feel like full cream milk in the mouth, yet have only two-thirds the energy-value and 28% the fat content. We introduced the product in 1981 against considerable resistance from the dairy companies. We did not allow ourselves to be deterred by the fact that the product did not constitute milk under UK law, and some nimble footwork was required to get it on sale at all. We felt that the consumer need was there and have been proven very right. Now the dairies have followed on behind us and nearly one-fifth of all fresh milk sales in the UK are fat-reduced."

That same success was realized with fruit-drinks—not the syrups found on the Continent and unrelated to fruit juices. Mr. Samuel indicated that research told Sainsbury that children can become hyperactive from drinking fruit juices fill with preservatives such as sodium benzoate and artificial colors..."So we took them out and instead used real orange juice...The product is (now) the largest single orange drink line we sell."

Sainsbury also has introduced voluntary programs that show exactly what nutrients are in the own label products: measures for calories, carbohydrates, protein and fat as well as added salt, sugar and nutrients where they are significant. Also, levels of fiber and fat content are included—even when there is no statutory basis required—and long before the majority of brands did this.

In the UK, Marks & Spencer with 100% own brands commitment has established a strong consumer franchise for its St Michael brand in the clothing market as well as in foods. In recent years, the firm has added upscale fashionwear, which now is featured at its own fashion shows. This chain of clothing/home fashions/fine food stores prides itself on developing hundreds of new products yearly, while expanding into new ranges of products. Marks & Spencer also has pioneered the chilled prepared ready meals category, utilizing high manufacturing standards and an excellent sales distribution network to get the product into its stores "very fresh" daily.

On the Continent, ASKO Deutsche Kaufhaus AG, Saarbrucken, Germany, since May 1990 has been building its Isabelle O'Lacy's private label program as a brand, not only in Germany, but through retailer partners in the Netherlands and in Sweden. O'Lacy's range of 500+ products, covering foods, health products, cosmetics, etc., is supported with strong marketing, including TV commercials programmed internationally just like the brands.

Back in the US, retailers' brand orientation in private label has not been restricted to the large chain store operators. As far back as the 1930s, IGA grocers, under the Independent Grocers Alliance of America in Chicago, carried IGA brand food products that guaranteed their "known quality" just like the "nationally advertised brands" which they also carried. The IGA brand stock was offered at "budget beating prices." Small mom-and-pop grocers across the U.S. had their exclusive IGA brand, which was winning grand prize gold medals for quality, picking up endorsements from Babe Ruth (the famous baseball home run 'slugger'), advertising on CBS radio network, sponsoring its own radio shows, tying in with Walt Disney Studios on a Pinocchio promotion, etc.

Partly through the brands gaining market share dominance, partly through fault of their own management, private label programs at IGA and also at A&P (as will be discussed)—both major market forces early in this century—did falter. Yet, private label over the past decade (including programs at IGA and A&P) is gaining strength and respectability. Not all private labels can make this claim, but the ranks are growing, especially as larger and more powerful players enter the industry.

II

The Players

6

A Who's Who: The Retailers

In most of the leading retailers' stores in the United States and in the northern countries of Europe, there is a private label presence. As a result of consolidations in the marketplace, chain store operators and independent retailers supplied through large wholesalers or buying cooperatives now dominate the market versus the single-store or mom-and-pop operators on their own. The retailers with the strongest back-up support (large quantity purchasing and more efficient distribution and inventory controls) are better equipped to handle a private label program.

In some cases, their private label business can be very significant, taking up to 100% of the stock. For others, it can be barely noticed, merchandised as just another brand in a few product categories or stocked without any identity or label. Of course, there are retailers who do not carry private label at all. Brand manufacturers who operate off-price discount specialty stores look to sell only their own brand name merchandise, i.e., a Van Heusen shirt outlet or a Sassoon clothing store. Specialty outlets owned and operated by retailers also can have a strong private label commitment. Examples are found in numerous product categories: the Scandinavian furniture store chain, IKEA, with 100% private label stock; Mothercare baby-and-small children clothing and merchandise outlets now with an estimated 90% of own label commitment in the UK; General Nutrition Centers, Pittsburgh, PA, with 65% private label stock in vitamins and supplements; The Body Shop, Littlehampton, West Sussex, England, with 100%

own label skin and hair care products; the Limited, Columbus, OH, which through its Limited and Victoria's Secret clothing chains stocks close to 100% private label merchandise; Radio Shack, Dallas, "the world's largest electronics retailer" carrying 100% private labels...The list continues. The Gap, Inc., San Francisco, CA, a $2 billion+ specialty clothing retailer, which sells all private label stock in its Gap stores, was credited in 1991 for its Gap-labeled clothes with having the second-largest selling brand name in the US, after Levi Strauss (*The New York Times*, Aug. 23, 1992). Additionally, there are some leading food, drug, or general merchandise retailers who have been dedicated to a brands-only strategy, such as the deep discount drugstore chains Phar-Mor Inc., Youngstown, OH, and Drug Emporium, Inc., Columbus, OH, or the cut price grocer, Kwik Save in the UK.

Overall, retailers who choose not to stock any private labels are more the exception than the rule. The rule is that it does help retail sales to carry an exclusive, top-quality private label line, offering consumers value: a lower price product with comparable quality to the leading brands—as an alternative choice. Most top retailers recognize this fact. Indeed, some of the brand-only retail leaders in different segments of the market are becoming more receptive to the private label idea. Drug Emporium is a case in point.

The recent emphasis by US discount retailers on lower-price brands has challenged but not destroyed private labels. In fact, this competition has drawn private label retailers into strategies adopted by the membership club stores, i.e., introducing club pack size products at a discount price, under both brands and private label. Top discounters, operating membership warehouse club chains or discount mass merchandise outlets, emphasize low-price brand name merchandise. But within their ranks, there are some retailers who adopt private label, not only because of its complementary low-price image, but also because of its higher profit margins over the brands and its exclusivity feature. Discount retailers have been able to build profit margins on low-priced brands, too, by limiting their stock, buying in volume lots, buying on deal, and by buying directly from manufacturers to avoid middlemen costs.

The largest US discount mass retailer, Wal-Mart, Bentonville, AR, (sales of $43.8 billion from 1,720 Wal-Mart and 208 Sam's Club stores) late in 1991 announced it would no longer buy through brokers or manufacturers representatives, but only deal directly with the suppliers. Wal-Mart has built its success on selling low-price brands along with a sprinkling of private labels in different product categories, such as paint, clothing, household cleaners, health and beauty care items, plumbing fixtures, dog food, paper items, and the like. This merchandising strategy is changing, however, as Wal-Mart moves more aggressively into food wholesaling and retailing. In November, 1991, the company shocked the industry—without saying a word publicly—by introducing its first private label food program, the upscale Sam's American Choice line, first into Wal-Mart stores and now reportedly also into its Sam's Wholesale Club Stores. It was a tacit, forceful reminder that private label does have its place even within a discount brand-oriented retailer's operations. Wal-Mart, however, did announce its existence in the fiscal 1992 annual report, indicating that its fall 1991 introduction of "a growing line of premium controlled brand products made in the USA exclusively for Wal-Mart," Sam's American Choice, does not mean an abandonment of "our branded merchandise strategy... However, we believe an opportunity exists to enhance value and further the trust we have established with our customers through a control-label program executed the Wal-Mart way."

While Wal-Mart remains silent about the size and success of Sam's American Choice, New York financial analyst, Goldman Sachs, referenced in an article in *Brandweek* magazine (Sept. 7, 1992) projected Wal-Mart's private label sales (in hard-line and consumable merchandise), now at $875 million, to grow to $2.6 billion by 1995.

The strongest private label retail commitments in the food segment occur mostly in Europe, the most cited example being the successful "high street" retailer, Marks & Spencer, a London-based chain of combination food and clothing stores, which carry 100% own brand stock under the St Michael label. Many other retailers follow closely behind in their private label commitment. Zurich-based Migros, an organization of a dozen regional cooperative in Switzerland, operating food/clothing/hygiene/home furnishings/leisure time goods stores, has an estimated 95% of its stock in private label, while processing more than 25% of those goods out of its own manufacturing plants. The same 95% private label commitment is shared by Irma a/s, Rodorre, Denmark, one of that country's top three food retailers. Spreading across Europe and into the United States, Aldi, a limited assortment, low-price, no frills food retailer, based in Germany, has an estimated 85% of its stock in private label. Aldi has its imitators, too, such as Paris-based Carrefour's Ed, l'épicier budget stores, stocking just 500 items, mostly "exclusive" packer labels or the Ed brand; and wholesaler Wetterau, St. Louis, MO, which owns the Sav-a-Lot chain of so-called box stores, stocking up to 700 items with about 80% of its product mix in different exclusive labels, all selling at "everyday low prices." Monoprix variety stores, a subsidiary of Galeries Lafayette, Paris, stocks some 60% of its products in food, while selling an estimated 80% of its items in private label. The three largest multiples (supermarket chains) in the United Kingdom—Sainsbury, London; Tesco, Chestnut, Hertfordshire; and Waitrose Ltd., Bracknell, Berk. (part of The John Lewis Partnership plc, London)—each maintain own brand packaged goods approaching or in excess of 50% of sales; perishable goods, such as meats, produce, deli items and the like, bring Sainsbury and Tesco own brand commitment closer to 70% or higher. Britain's largest retailer, Co-op stores (4,000+ units), organized through CWS, Manchester, England, and its wholesaling and manufacturing federations, reports its retailer shareholders carry up to 80% Co-op brand merchandise.

Across Europe, mostly in the northern countries, food retail leaders for years have featured significant private label stock. In France, Casino has more than a 40% commitment. Numerous other examples could be cited. But in the United States, food retail chain generally have kept their private label share of sales to just under 20% on average, because of a national brands dominance in the marketplace. A retailing/wholesaling neighbor to the north, Loblaw, Toronto, itself greatly influenced by European private label commitment, has pushed its private label stock to 35%. Loblaw is now influencing US retailers, as will be seen.

Had A&P, a pioneer in private label food retailing in the US, been based in Europe, its private label story might have evolved more like the European market leaders. But A&P, Montvale, NJ, faced tough competition no only from the brand manufacturers, but also from jealous and/or frustrated competitors, from angry consumers limited in their selection of brands in A&P stores, and even from the US Government (pressured by lobbying groups), which took legislative action against this growing "monopoly" on the basis of its "coercion" over pricing tactics. At one time, A&P was the biggest food retailer in the US with 15,645 stores in 1927 and with the country's largest food manufacturing operation. Its need to build production volume and manufacturing profits led to an overemphasis on private label in A&P stores, estimated to have climbed to 35% of its retail sales in the 1960s. That strategy forced its stores to carry company-produced private label stock, cutting back on the selection of national brands. Its manufacturing muscle has since been trimmed to a few plants, its store count reduced to 1,100+ units, while its private label presence, after being reduced to a low of 15% of sales, has picked up recently to its present level, estimated at about 23%+ of sales. Ironically, A&P's private label retail sales today, estimated at $2 billion+, are higher than in its so-called heyday private-label- dominated years, since the company has pulled back into becoming the country's fifth largest US food chain retailer ($9 billion+ in sales in addition to another $2 billion in Canada).

It could be argued that A&P was victimized by outside forces, by its own greed, as well as by neglect in keeping up quality standards for private label, which together spelled its undoing as the largest US food retailer. Private label itself cannot be blamed—as so many observers have stated—but rather the way it was force-fed to A&P stores and the manner in which its quality standards were compromised, after years of maintaining the highest standards. A&P admits that its quality grew slack. If those earlier standards were maintained—as they now are today—and if A&P had had more marketing savvy in dealing with branded merchandise, the company might have developed a dominant private label presence as Sears did in the department store segment of retailing.

Market changes dictate a shifting of position by the major players. Sears, Roebuck and Co., Chicago, which built itself into the largest department store retailer in the US, with a private label stock approaching 99% of total sales, has over the years diversified into other businesses. More recently, Sears has had to face the challenge of discount retailers, particularly giants like Kmart, Troy, MI, and more recently, Wal-Mart, now the biggest retailer. Sears today follows Kmart in third place with sales of nearly $28 billion. As recently as 1989, Sears had to make major adjustments in its marketing position just to stay competitive. Sears, in fact, has become more of a discounter, having slashed the prices on more than 50,000 of its stocked items. This retailer also, after having slowly introduced national brands into its product mix over several years, has opened the floodgates to brands, plunging its private label commitment down to an estimated 80% of retail sales. In the company's 1990 annual report, chairman-president-CEO Edward Brennan said: "Our strong private label brands with many national brands (combine) to provide customers with a wider assortment of products and prices." Sears, in effect, remerchandised its different departments—appliances, hardware, furniture, apparel, etc.—with brands.

A company spokesperson reports that these brands now actually complement its Kenmore appliances, Craftsman tools, Sears apparel, etc.

To stay on top, the market leaders must change. One of the oldest variety store chains in the US, S.S. Kresge Co., started the Kmart discount store concept in 1962. Today, the Kresge name is gone with Kmart left as the country's second largest retailer, having relinquished its top spot to Wal-Mart in 1990. Kmart, like Wal-Mart, built its leadership around discounting national brand merchandise. But Kmart also has courted private labels more aggressively than Wal-Mart, recognizing that top quality goods, no matter what the label says, sold at a discount will give consumers value for their money. Kmart positions itself as the price leader with low-price brands and private labels. An educated guess on its private label commitment is about 40%+ of sales. The company does not release these figures.

Another major department store player, J.C. Penney Co., Dallas, TX, has maintained more of an equal balance between private label and national brand stock, slightly favoring the former: An estimated 60% of its merchandise under its own brands—"exclusive J.C. Penney national brands," such as Hunt Club, Jacqueline Ferrar, St. John's Bay, and Stafford—all supplied by respected national brand manufacturers like Hart Schaffner & Marx, Johnston & Murphy, Bally, and Bugle Boy. Penney also claims to be the country's largest private brand distributor of soft apparel.

Private labels can appear in the most stark retailing environment, such as an Aldi store in a downtown, blue collar Chicago neighborhood or in a fashionably elegant setting claimed by a Neiman-Marcus store—a mall or downtown shopping center in Dallas. Private labels can be found as Fortron men's watches or Avignon women's watches displayed in glamorous jewelry showcases in a Fortunoff store, a regional specialty store retailer serving the New York and New Jersey markets. Private label also can be found as a generic label toilet paper in many supermarkets around the country. The retail settings vary as much as the range of items available.

7

A Wholesaler Phenomenon

Welcome to the multi-layered world of private label procurement.

Private label products can be purchased directly from manufacturers by the retailers themselves. Very often, independent food brokers (manufacturers' representatives) become involved, buying for their customers (the retailers/wholesalers) from their principals (the manufacturers). Sometimes an account-specific broker like Cal Growers, San Jose, CA, can work right inside a retailer/wholesaler operation on an exclusive basis for that customer—100% dedicated to private label buying. There also are master brokers, such as Federated Foods, Arlington Heights, IL, or Marketing Management, Ft. Worth, TX, who form their own private label sales/procurement/marketing organizations, serving the entire food distribution network—vendors, retailers, wholesalers, and even the groups or alliances formed by the latter two. All these players (retailer, wholesaler, broker, or group) can start up their own private label programs. Perhaps the most ubiquitous, multifaceted player in this industry is the wholesaler, who buys (and sometimes produces) product, transports it, stocks it in his distribution centers, and sells it to independent grocers as well as other customers. Wholesalers are evolving into one of the most powerful marketing forces for private label in food distribution today.

There are many variations of wholesalers throughout the United States and Europe. Of course, numerous wholesalers concentrate on distributing food and non-foods, primarily to the grocery trade. (Wholesalers also serve the drugstore trade, which will be discussed later.) Some of the larger one also get involved in retailing, that is owning and/or franchising their own private label products as well as providing other services (training, financing, real estate development, etc.) for a wide variety of trade customers. There are food wholesalers who join together into a cooperative buying group, either like the member-owners of Shurfine-Central Corp., Northlake, IL (30 shareholder wholesalers serving 10,000+ retailers with more than 9,000 private label skus including produce, deli and bakery items) or the volunteer members of Spar International, Amsterdam (117 wholesalers, serving 20,300+ shops in 24 countries on four continents with its own Spar brand program). There are food retailers, too, who adopt wholesaling (such as Canada's largest food distributor, Loblaw Companies, Toronto), who band together to own and operate their own wholesale business (such as WestPac, Lathrop, CA, started in 1990 by three regional retailer partners with some 750 private label skus), or who join as member-owners of a marketing/procurement organization like Topco, Inc., Skokie, IL (25 "blue chip" retailers with access to 16,000+ private label skus).

Thanks to food wholesalers, US independent grocers have been able to survive competitively against huge food chain store operations throughout this century. IGA, the largest voluntary group of independent grocers (3,750+ today drawing from a private label program of some 2,500 items) is licensed by many of the largest U.S. food wholesalers; while the second largest voluntary group is Foodland International (500+ stores), owned by wholesalers, Wetterau Inc., Hazelwood, MO. (Overall, Wetterau manages 6,000+ private label skus in different programs, including Foodland.) From a humble, subordinate role, these wholesalers, especially over the past decade, have taken control of their own destiny. They also have come to realize the power of private label, revitalizing their programs out of what had been for many the doldrums. Some of their labels had been untouched—neglected—for up to 20 years or longer.

They have been strengthened in part by their own consolidations, acquisitions, and mergers. The latest is the marriage of the second largest US wholesaler, SUPERVALU, Minneapolis, MN, with Wetterau, fourth largest, still being finalized at this writing. A growing customer base has snowballed this effect. Also food wholesalers have benefitted from a weakening of the major US food retail chains, themselves victimized by leverage buyout and corporate raiders or major acquisitions which have saddled them with heavy debts and forced significant divestiture of some of their operations. Meantime, wholesalers have caught up where their own sales organizations now rival the biggest U.S. retail chains. While the latter are on the mend, but still busy 'licking' their financial wounds of the recent past, the major food wholesalers are focusing their attention on international expansion.

These wholesalers service not only independent grocers, but also their own corporate-owned food stores and some of the regional operations of major chain retailers, providing: dry groceries, meat, produce, frozen foods, deli and dairy products, health and beauty care, and general merchandise stock. They also distribute product to growing markets such as the military, convenience stores, and foodservice accounts. Independent food stores, their biggest customers, now represent 64% of total retail food sales in the US. The independent food store count is impressive: In 1991, the top three chain retailers—American Stores, Salt Lake City, UT: Kroger, Cincinnati: and Safeway, Oakland, Ca—operated a total of 4,600 food stores; while the country's second largest wholesale food distributor, Fleming Companies, Oklahoma City, OK, alone serves more than 4,800 stores. Those three top food retailers together sell almost 12,000 private label skus total, but Fleming alone manages 30,000+ private label skus. Someone might argue that the trend has been to fewer and larger stores for the retail chain operators; but the wholesalers, too, are moving their independent grocer customers in this direction with full start-up support.

What is significant about the wholesalers and their growing sales volumes is the fact that they are becoming more committed to private label. This commitment varies, because of their diverse customer base. Some of their retailer customers have very little or no interest in private label, because of their particular market needs; others are quite aggressive in promoting this profit-maker. Of course, wholesalers, too, can differ in their handling of private label. Some keep a big chunk of the profits for themselves, while others pass along the margins to the retailers, providing them with more incentives to support the private label program. Some of the geographic markets they serve are national brand strongholds, where customers are not receptive to private label. Also, the type of trade customer can determine the private label commitment: smaller store operators cannot accommodate space for an extensive private label line or spare any space for an extra, upscale private label program, let alone guaranteeing that the sales volume needed will be delivered. As a result, US wholesalers average a private label share of sales at about 10%*; but their commitment continues to intensify from its initial spark in the early 1980s right into this decade.

One catalyst contributing to the wholesalers' private label commitment is the recent growth of IGA, Inc. Chicago—an independent grocery alliance of 3,750+ food retailers located in 49 states plus in Australia, Japan, Canada, Korea, and Papua New Guinea. The 'timber' of this organization is the wholesaler: 21 major food wholesalers who own and drive the IGA system, purchasing and delivering goods to the small IGA retailers and supporting them in their marketing and merchandising activities. Of the top five U.S. food wholesalers, four service the IGA stores as IGA owning wholesalers. IGA's retail volume today exceeds $16 billion. The retailers can choose from some 3,000 IGA brand skus as part of their stock. On average, their private label commitment is about 6% of total sales—not as high as the chain operators, but growing significantly. In 1991, IGA reported its private label sales were up 16% or $675.9 million versus the previous year.

The IGA wholesaler owners, who have their own private label programs, too, support the IGA brand because of their vested interest in IGA, Inc. One outstanding example is Wetterau, Inc., Hazelwood, MO, the fourth largest food wholesaler with sales at nearly $6 billion. Wetterau is one of IGA's biggest houses, where many independent retailers in its 15 divisions adopt the IGA store identity and its private label program. Some of them, like the Portland, ME, division report that private label takes 22.6% of their sales on average. Overall, controlled label activity at Wetterau—its IGA brand business plus six other controlled labels, all together accounting for some 6,000 skus—takes about 11% of sales. Wetterau actually allows its divisions to pick and choose among its own programs—the IGA program covering 2,567 items is the largest. But the biggest IGA house is found at the second largest wholesaler, Fleming Companies, which handles 3,315 skus in the IGA program alone. When you take measure of Fleming's other controlled labels (more than a dozen), that private label sku count skyrockets to 30,695—one of the largest private label sku in the food distribution industry, in terms of number of items.

In recent surveys of the food distribution business, at least a dozen food wholesalers each now have sales exceeding $1 billion, ranking them in the top US companies in that business along with the retail chains. These wholesalers all support private label because of the demands of their customers, the independent retailers, who are asking for their own exclusive labels. The wholesalers really are participating in a universal awakening of private label's potential in the United States.

---

* *An exclusive survey by "US Distribution Journal" (Sept. 15, 1992) found that private label represents 12.2% of overall sales for the top 50 grocery wholesalers in the US. That amounts to $9 billion+ in private label sales. This report also indicated that "wholesale grocers as a trade class account for about 55% of the $27 billion private label industry."*

Photographic
Album

This new pin-stripe packaging look for Vons Companies, Los Angeles, conveys a quality look with its combination of the raw ingredients on the left and the final product spilling over to a side panel. The frozen peas and carrots are contained in a microwavable carton that carries Vons Quality Assured guarantee.

Charlie Garcia, director of world trade and special marketing at Shurfine-Central, Northlake, IL, shows new smaller count diaper packaging designed especially for the convenience store market.

Shurfine-Central addresses its customers' needs to compete with membership club store larger-pack sizes with this version of its diapers in higher diaper counts — 66 and 102.

Chicago-based Jewel Stores sub-brands its refrigerated pizza under the Chef's Kitchen logo, featuring mouth-watering graphics on the packaging.

London-based Sainsbury's Homebase House and Garden Centres carry a range of sundry decorating items under the Homebase brand.

The retailer-owned cooperative, Topco Associates, Skokie, IL, debuted this green line under its GreenMark brand in July 1990, which continues as a viable and growing program today.

Carrefour of France for the past several years has been developing its own label in South America, this particular line carried in Brazil.

Aldi GmbH of West Germany purchased the 24-store Benner Tea Co., Burlington, IA in 1976, converting the latter to its format of low-gross margins and high-volume sales. Competition triggered reaction by Jewel Stores in that market to introduce no frills generics. This store in Chicago stocks product in cut cases, but neatly displayed with price signage overhead. Its 70%+ private label stock includes numerous "brands," such as Best Wash laundry detergent and Vogue no phosphate detergents (shown here).

A sampling of the quality products that appear under the Spar brand available for years in different European countries.

The 120-year-old Grand Union Co., Wayne, NJ, not too long ago upgraded its 1950s packaging to a more modern, appetizing presentation.

In that same packaging change, Grand Union created a billboard effect on the shelves with divided images, such as on its pet food line.

That same treatment was applied to its disposable diaper line.

National brand cookie makers now face these formitable competitors: Loblaw's President's Choice, The Decadent cookie, Wal-Mart's Sam's American Choice cookies, First National's The Sensational cookie, and Kmart's Nature's Classics cookies.

At a recent trade show, one supplier showed its generic cigarette line, including selections from Safeway's Scotch Buy, Vons' Slim Price, Fleming's Rainbow, and Federated Foods' Better Valu lines.

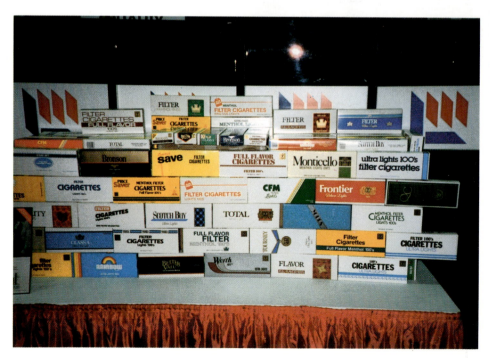

8

The European Market

Throughout Europe, as a matter of survival, independent grocers, wholesalers, caterers, and cash & carry operators have relied on buying consortiums, cooperative, or buying-marketing groups. These joint efforts have resulted in the creation of multibillion-dollar sales groups. Private label has been very much part of their marketing strategies as well.

For upwards of 150 years, Europeans have realized the benefits of joint purchasing efforts through the cooperative—owned by retailers, wholesalers or consumers. Today, that same thinking is being applied to the new European buying associations being formed to address trade in Europe as a single market in 1992 and beyond. These groups, involving both the independents or private sector as well as the giant retailing market leaders in different countries, also are developing private labels for their membership.

The cooperative movement probably first got started in England in 1844 in the small Lancashire textile town of Rochdale, when workers there formed a retail cooperative society to supply food and other goods to their families. Some 19 years later, CWS was formed as a non-profit wholesaling and manufacturing federation with different retail societies becoming its shareholders. CWS, Manchester, is positioned as Britain's largest retailer in terms of number of food stores—some 4,000+. It also is one of Europe's top 50 food processors, supplying own brand food products from 12 manufacturing plants that realize combined sales of nearly £650 million yearly. It exports private label and exclusive brands to 32 countries. The factories also provide the CWS retailing side with products. CWS operates its supply business as FE Barber Ltd. The co-op brand itself encompasses some 2,500 lines, worth about £750 million at retail. Some 85 independent retail societies participate in the co-op, adopting its store logo and own brand program. In fact, the societies take up to 80% of the goods available and usually stock their stores with about 33% own brand goods. Co-op membership is about 8 million people, but non-members can shop their stores (as they can in other co-op organizations).

Switzerland has traditionally been a stronghold for the cooperative movement ever since the idea first took root in 1883. Coop Switzerland, formed in 1890, has become the country's second major retailing force. Migros, the market leader today, started as a corporation in 1925, but was formed into a cooperative in 1940. In 1990, three holdout retailers in the country—Hofer-Curti, Denner, and Usego—united as a "third force" in retail trade by signing a cooperative agreement, too.

Migros, Zurich, today operates its cooperative like a stock company, but with a "democratic management." Its "Federation" consists of 12 regional cooperatives in the country whose retail turnover totaled 11,148 Sfr. in 1990. Some 28% of its total retail sales are accounted for by products produced in its own 13 manufacturing plants. The Migros food selection in its own 541 Migros stores covers some 5,000 items, while non-foods comprise 25,000 articles. As mentioned previously, Migros maintains some 95% of its stock in private label. The cooperative also operates some 91 stores on wheels. Its membership at the end of 1990 totaled 1,520,940 people.

Coop Switzerland, based in Basle, Switzerland, celebrated its Centennial in 1990 with a retail turnover at 8,582.8 million Sfr. Its 28 Coop societies operate through 19 distribution centers, supplying 1,252 shops (excluding its petrol stations, restaurants, cafes, and hotels). The operation has 18 manufacturing and trading firms. Its Co-op private brand, estimated to take about 50% of sales, has a history tracing back to 1914.

Both Swiss cooperatives have in recent years joined the new European groups in their joint sales efforts: Migros, an associate member (its company charter preventing full membership) in Associated Marketing Services (AMS) and Coop Switzerland with Eurogroup S.A. AMS, Zug, Switzerland which operates as a service company on behalf of the European Retail Alliance (E.R.A.), a co-op of 11 retail companies in different European countries, works to develop cooperative efforts and strategies of both suppliers and retailer partners. Its other partners include: Argyll Group in the UK, Allkauf SB in Germany, Dansk Supermarked Indkob AS in Denmark, Groupe Casino in France, Grouppo Rinascente in Italy, Hagen Gruppen in Norway, ICA Partihandel AB in Sweden, Kesko OY in Finland, Koninklije Ahold NV in the

Netherlands, and Mercadona SA in Spain.

Eurogroup, Cologne, Germany, is a strategic alliance of retail partners, who together represent a 1990 turnover in retail sales of 72.6 million DM ($48.4 billion). Like AMS, all of its member have some interest in their own private label programs as well as looking to develop synergies through the partnership. Eurogroup explains that its partners market their own label either as store brands (the store name), umbrella brands, monobrands for specific products, or generics for the low-price assortment (competing against discounters). Together, they are now adopting a common private label assortment, whenever there is an opportunity for such a "Eurobrand." Several national markets already have been started for Eurobrands. Joseph Bastin, general manager at Eurogroup, reports that "within the context of the private label business of our partners, we are focusing on the standardization of qualities and packaging, enabling joint-venture activities. In this field, huge volumes already have been placed either in Europe or in overseas countries." The beneficiaries of this activity include: Coop Switzerland, GIB Group in Belgium, Paridoc Group in France, Rewe Trading Group in Germany, and Vendex Group in the Netherlands.

The co-op movement inside Germany started first with hundreds of independent consumer co-ops, which finally consolidated into Coop AG in 1974 as eight regional companies. The consumers and trade unions then wanted centralized purchasing and "rationalized" distribution to compete against the emergence of supermarket chains, which were taking more market share.

It could be generalized that the co-op movement has succeeded in most countries, but not everywhere. In Germany, the co-op concept was unable to compete effectively against strong retail chain competitors in that country, perhaps because of the nature of that market. Private label was well established with the discounter Aldi, almost holding a monopoly on discounted private label in Germany, while elsewhere the brands dominated the marketplace. Even though the co-ops there united their purchasing, production, and distribution efforts, they were not as effective against giants like Metro Group, Rewe AG, Edeka, Tengelmann, and of course Aldi.

It's interesting to note that the independent retailers and wholesalers in Germany also for years struggled against this competition from the public sector. As far back as the 1920s, they joined forces in "Einkaufskontors" (central purchasing offices). But in 1951, after WWII and just before German currency reforms, their "first food trade chain," A&O, was founded on a voluntary basis, involving not only trade members in Germany but also members from other European countries. As competition intensified, A&O in 1983 merged its Selex and Tania operations into one trade group for greater strength in the private sector. In 1988, this group set up Markant AG in Pfaffikon, Switzerland, to coordinate a partnership—just like the giant chain retailers were doing across Europe—among its European trade members with product manufacturers. Markant began drawing support from its group of German service partners: Selex Handelsgesellschaft GmbH, Offenburg, handling food, commodities, household cleaning products, cosmetics, etc.; Tania Handelsgesellschaft GmbH, Wiesbaden, for non-foods (hardware DIY, textiles, leather goods) and other service companies, handling the partners' accounting, sales marketing, data processing, training needs—based in Offenburg. Affiliates of A&O also were drawn in as Markant's European partners: B.V., Bilthoven, The Netherlands; Selex Iberica S.A., Barcelona, Spain; S.E.V. GmbH & Co., Vienna, Austria; as well as more than 100 Markant customers (including retailers and wholesalers) in Germany.

Private label business from Selex and Tania represents an important part of this operation. The partners in eight countries (Germany, Austria, the Netherlands, France, Italy, Spain, Portugal, and Switzerland) today represent sales in excess of 40 billion DM. New partners recently have joined from Great Britain and France. This united effort, therefore, is not dwarfed up against the giant German grocers. A German correspondent for the trade magazine *Super Marketing* (April 17, 1992), based in the UK, reported 1991 grocers turnover for market leaders in Germany as follows: Metro Group at 35.9 billion DM, Rewe AG at 32.6 billion DM, Aldi Group at 25 billion DM, Edeka Group at 23.1 billion DM, Tengelmann Group at 20.4 billion DM, and Asko Group at 19 billion DM.

It is truly amazing that another such independent voluntary group of retailers and wholesalers members from 24 countries met in May 1992 in Amsterdam to celebrate its 60th anniversary with very little fanfare from the press. What's amazing is that Spar International, Amsterdam, is one of the largest voluntary chains in the world. In fact, this group recently joined with the German buying group Gedelfi to form a joint trading company, BIGS (Buying International Gedelfi Spar) to harness the buying power of its membership—some 117 wholesalers who serve 20,300+ shops in 24 countries. This venture reportedly has a combined turnover of £61.5 billion, as reported by *Super Marketing* magazine.

All the members of Spar are committed to display their affiliation to the group by using a uniform Spar image. In fact, "the biggest single asset" that this organization has is its Spar brands—giving quality and value to consumers and profits to its independent retailers and wholesalers. The Spar brand sets Spar above its competition. This attitude is now being reinforce with efforts underway to launch an international private label Spar range sometime in 1992. Completely autonomous, Spar independent members in different countries adopt their own marketing strategies, such as a white label Spar pack in Austria versus a premium Spar brand in the United Kingdom. Variations by country will be considered in the range, which will carry a recognizable international Spar identity throughout, according to the company. Private label share of business in the Spar stores (from convenience store, to grocery store , to supermarket, to a Eurospar format of up to 2,500 square meters) varies by country, reaching 20% to 24% in some of the stronger markets like Germany and the United Kingdom. Perhaps Spar is able to survive in Germany primarily because of its Spar brand.

The Spar formula started in 1932 in the Netherlands, when the independent food wholesalers united under the first voluntary chain, called Door Eendrachtin Samenwerken Profitern Allen Regeimatig, picking up the first letters in each word, "De Spar."

Independent retailers and wholesalers have survived with similar strategies within other countries. In the United Kingdom, for example, competing against the multiples, some independents formed their own buying consortiums, NISA-Today, a retail/wholesale buying and marketing umbrella organization. Since the 1980s, this group has had its own NISA label, now encompassing more than 800 products. Its 320+ retail members work through more than 2,500 branch stores, all under the National Retail Association. The 1990 turnover for the NISA own label program alone was expected to top £100 million. This group also includes 160 cash-and-carry operations, formed with some 70 members as the Today's Super Group—the leading independents negotiating group. The Today's own label range, launched about 1987, now realizes a turnover of £25 million out of total turnover of £1.5 billion, covering some 420 food, drink, household products, etc.

Another wholesale cash-and-carry operator, Booker, based in Wellingborough, Northants, England, covers a chain of 162 wholesale warehouses, serving grocery retailer, caterers, and licensed trade customers. Booker supplies own label like Family Choice and Chef's Larder ranges, covering more than 700 products in the total range.

Started in 1937 as a group to buy fresh produce, The Produce Importers Alliance has developed into a £3.4 billion business—one of the UK's leading umbrella buying organizations, representing 212 wholesale, cash-and-carry, and retail members. The bulk of its business is branded products, but work is underway on developing its new NOW own label range, as well as Basic Buy, another retail brand, and Maytree brand for catering, as well as other exclusive labels for wines, spirits, and beer. PIA is a non-profit organization, run by the members.

It is a fierce struggle for survival in the Danish market, representing a $10 billion grocery business. The independents hold some 40% market share, but are slipping up against giant retailers like FDB (Faellesforeningen for Danmarks Brugsforeninger), an association of Danish retail cooperatives, comprising retail operations like Brugsen, Irma, Kvickly, Obs, etc. or more than 1,000 stores. Its private label business accounted for about 33% of retail turnover in 1989, but has slipped to 28% recently, because of the introduction of commercial TV just three years ago in Denmark. Large foreign and multinational brands are buying most of the airtime, which is swaying consumers to buy the brands. But FDB plans to fight back with its own TV campaign. The operation has a strong stake in private label: Its Irma stores have 95% private label stock, giving over the remaining 5% to brands in such categories as tobacco, alcohol, soft drinks and the like to create a full-service store.

Meantime, Dagrofa, A/S, a wholesaling and marketing group, supplies Favor chains and other retailers, including a tie-in with the Spar organization, via its recent merger of 250 Dankob mini markets. Dagrofa works with some 1,000 member retail outlets with its private label business accounting for about 20% of turnover.

Denmark's main wholesaling cooperative, Oceka-NH, Albertslund, had a turnover of DLk 4.1.3 billion in 1991. It supplies some 600 retail outlets, but has a limited Supervare private label program. Over the past couple of years, mergers in Denmark have resulted in three main blocs of wholesalers forming: Superkoeb, Din Koebmand, Prima and Davli; Dagrofa, owned by grocery industrials such as Skandinavisk Holding, MD Foods and others; and Edeka from Germany, which merged with Denmark's Hoki wholesaling organization, serving retailers like Edeka, Trika and Ekstra. Edeka reportedly is now working to strengthen its private label program.

9

Rx-Oriented Retailers/Wholesalers

If you remove prescription drug products from drugstores, pharmacies or wholesale drug companies in the US, their business very likely would collapse. This core of their operation, which recently has undergone dramatic growth, really has had very little to do with private labels. So private label stock is not necessarily a significant part of their overall business. Its presence, in fact, is found mostly in over-the-counter drugs (analgesics, cough-and-cold remedies, antacids, and the like) as well as in health and beauty care products—hair-and-skin treatments, vitamins, diapers, etc. Overshadowed by the all-important pharmacy, private label nevertheless does effectively fit into the drugstore product mix, especially in health-related products. In the past decade, private label's share of sales in this market segment has edged upward close to 7% average in major drugstore chains. More recently, private label programs also have taken root in drug wholesale companies which serve the independent drugstore operators, taking an estimated average of 3% of their total sales.

Both chain and independent drugstore operators have come to recognize private label's value, riding on the crest of its acceptance as a quality product and as one that appeals to a more price-conscious and value-oriented consumer. These consumers also are smarter, knowing that aspirin is aspirin, ibuprofen (pain reliever/fever reducer) is ibuprofen, or chlorpheniramine (antihistamine) is chlorpheniramine—whether sold as a brand or a private label. Early in the 1980s, the drugstore chains were the first to react, upgrading their private label packaging and putting more marketing and merchandising support behind their programs, using them as a customer draw as well as a profit center for their stores. Interestingly, Rite Aid Corp., Shiremanstown, PA, has been more aggressive than most other drugstore chains with its private label commitment set well above 10% since fiscal 1984. At that time, Rite Aid reported total chain sales of $1.1 billion with 1,155 stores, making it the eighth largest US drugstore chain company. Eight years later, for fiscal 1992, that company is now the third largest drugstore chain in the country with sales of $3.5 billion from 2,452 stores. Its private label share of sales is now double the industry average—at 14%. By comparison, in 1984, Walgreen Co., Deerfield, IL, was the number two chain with $2.2 billion in sales from 941 stores. In recent years, Walgreens has maintained its number one position with $6.7 billion sales reported in fiscal 1991 from 1,646 stores; while Jack Eckerd Corp., Clearwater, FL, was number three in 1984 with $2 billion sales from 1,319 stores, while its current position is number two at $3.6 billion sales from 1,675 stores. Walgreen and Jack Eckerd each maintain estimated private label commitments of 7 and 8%, respectively. Rite Aid reports its private label stock of some 1,200 items, priced 30 to 50% lower than comparable national brands, has "developed a loyal customer following and outsell(s) the national brand equivalent in many product categories. These items are laboratory-tested while their packaging is updated regularly to maximize customer appeal." Both of the other two drugstore chain leaders remain very quiet about their private label activities, which the best estimates put at about 800+ skus in each program.

PRIVATE LABEL NEWCOMERS: DRUG WHOLESALERS

Meanwhile, private label appears to be taking on more significance with US drug wholesale companies as well. In fact, the market leaders are putting more effort behind programs not only for the voluntary groups of independent drugstores they serve, but for their non-group customers as well. The voluntary groups were started years ago mostly for advertising programs, but eventually picked up on an exclusive label program. Each of the four largest drug wholesalers have groups. McKesson Corp., San Francisco, ($9.8 billion) started the Valu-Rite chain of independents in 1977; today, it numbers 3,500+ stores, which can carry some 215 skus of Valu-Rite label products. McKesson also provides a Medalist program of 110 skus for its other drugstore accounts, as well as a Valu-Star program of 195 skus for its grocery accounts. The Good Neighbor chain of independents, totaling 990+ stores, launched by Bergen Brunswig Drug, Orange, CA, ($4.3 billion) has access to a Good Neighbor exclusive label program of 480 skus; while Bergen's other drugstore accounts pick up the Brite

Life program of 530 skus. Good Neighbor was started in 1983, the same year that FoxMeyer Corp., Dallas, TX, ($3.1 billion) started its Health Mart group which now includes 700+ stores, picking up on the Health Mart label of 460 skus. FoxMeyer provides its other customers with a Full Value private label program of 220 skus. Alco Health Services Corp., Malvern, PA, ($2.8 billion) began its Family Independent Pharmacies (now called Family Pharmacy) in 1968, which now covers 1,200+ stores, picking up on the Family Pharmacy program of 350 skus. Other wholesalers have similar programs, although some (just as in the chain drugstore segment) have no private label at all.

Altogether, there are more than 2,300 skus in private label handled by these wholesalers for independent drugstores. The interesting point is that these private label programs are expanding, while some drug wholesaler like Cardinal Distribution, Inc., Dublin, OH, and Durr-Fillauer Medical Inc., Montgomery, AL, have recently introduced programs: Cardinal's Leader program of 300 skus and CPS (Community Pharmacy Shopper) program of 67 skus; and the PriceGuard program at Durr-Fillauer.

The US drug wholesale industry itself has more than doubled in volume since 1983, growing to in excess of $34 billion. This growth has been spurred on by wholesalers (as well as by chain drugstores who are becoming their customers) and by an aging US population, where older people (over 65 years) are big users of prescription drugs: Only 12% of the population is over age 65, yet they account for one-third of all prescription drugs filled. Both the chain drugstores and the wholesalers emphasize this business more than over-the-counter drugs because of the higher retail pricing: On average, a 100-tablet container of a brand name prescription drug retails at $400 versus a 100-tablet container of private label aspirin, for example, selling at around $1.50. But both wholesaler and retailer appreciate the importance of having prescription and non-prescription choices. Additionally, many prescription drugs lately have come off patent as generic drugs and into over-the-counter formulations, which impacts on private label.

In Europe, there are literally thousands of independently-owned pharmacies or chemists, which traditionally have been able to sell prescription drugs or medicine only under license in different countries. These outlets also have dispensed non-prescription or over-the-counter medicines (including vitamins) as well as toiletry items and other sundries. Meantime, the non-licensed discount self-service drugstores usually have stocked an assortment of toiletries and personal care products. In some cases, they also have diversified into foods, household goods, baby articles, non-prescription medicinal products, hosiery, stationery, drinks, etc.

In the United Kingdom, where own label dominates many grocery multiples' operations and is strong in independent cash-and-carry operations, the £2.5

billion chemist and pharmacist, the Boots Company plc, Nottingham, England, is market leader, claiming to be the UK's largest outlet for baby foods, toiletries and nappies (diapers). Boots now maintains some 40% of its sales in own label—up from 35% in the recent past. The trend now is to push that share to 45% in the next couple of years and eventually to 50%. As part of its pharmaceutical division, the firm operates Boots Contract Marketing, supplying its own shops plus third-party contracts with a wide range of products: cosmetics, toiletries, and health care items—representing some £120 million in business.

England's largest discount drugstore chain, Superdrug Stores plc, Croydon, Surrey, also maintains 38% of its total sales of £559 million in own label. Superdrug distinguishes itself from Boots, describing the latter as a chemist with health and personal care products, while Superdrug operates without a pharmacy. On the Continent, there are numerous chains and independent pharmacists, but private label plays a smaller role in the product mix, ranging anywhere from 10 to 20% of total sales per operation.

Leading drugstore chains in other European countries include: Schecker stores in Germany; Etos (owned by Ahold NV, Zaandam, The Netherlands) in Holland; Matas A/S (Materialisternes Aktieselkkab), Copenhagen, Denmark, etc. Each of these chains carry a private label product mix. Etos, for example, a chain of 100+ health and beauty care stores, has in the recent past specialized with a successful Beauty Case format, which carries beauty and health items plus toiletries for women in combination with a hairdresser service, beauty parlor and solarium. With a freer market opening in Europe, there is now talk about ending the legal pharmacy monopoly to allow non-pharmacies to sell prescription drugs as well as more over-the-counter products, which could help this market segment develop. But existing laws will be difficult to surmount.

10

Brokers:
More than Middlemen

There are some unsung heroes in this industry—companies and individuals who many people outside the trade have heard very little to nothing about. They include four major account-specific brokers (those assigned to particular account(s) in a market) who have been dedicated to the private label business for decades—Alliance Associates, Daymon Associates, Federated Foods, and Marketing Management—as well as countless market brokers (those calling on all accounts in a market) who have handled both private label and branded business. For decades, these brokers have played a significant, but mostly behind-the-scenes role in helping private label develop into viable brands in the grocery marketplace. Acting as middlemen between their principals, the manufacturers of products, and their trade customers, the retailers, wholesalers or foodservice distributors, who buy those products, many brokers have created and/or helped to build successful private label programs for their customers. The account-specific brokers especially have evolved from strictly direct sales representatives for item or product categories into full-fledged sales and marketing organizations, providing package design and label inventory control, quality assurance lab support, data processing back-up, and marketing strategies in private label for their trade customers. They, in effect, have become more program- and marketing-oriented for both their customers and their principals. Some market brokers, too, have taken a similar initiative—especially the dedicated private label market brokers—going the extra mile or two in helping develop private label programs for their customers. In fact, two brokers participated in the first organizational meeting of the Private Label Manufacturers Association (PLMA) in 1979 in New York: Herb Pease Sr. from Marketing Management, Ft. Worth, TX, and Greg Phillips, representing his own firm, Gregory Marketing, which is now called Ashdun Industries, Englewood Cliffs, NJ. In recent years, brokers generally have become more specialized and enterprising in this field as well.

The brokerage industry today continues to change because of the consolidation of retailers, wholesalers, distributors, and manufacturers. In the past five years, the number of brokers has been reduced from more than 2,300 to probably less than 1,600 in the United States. This has caused almost all brokers to rethink their business strategy. Those brokers specializing in private label have each developed different ways of performing their functions. Some of these brokers rebate checks for more than 50%, sometimes as much as 95% of their brokerage to the customer. Other brokers act as the purchasing arm of the customer, while some try to add value by performing sales and marketing functions which their customer or their principal (the supplier) does not have.

Broker participation in the private label business was first triggered back in 1936 with passage of the Robinson-Patman Act, which independent grocers had lobbied for, alleging that manufacturers were giving favorable discriminatory pricing to the larger chains. The Act prohibits anti-competitive practices such as unfair price discrimination and inequitable quantity discounts, while also addressing brokerage and promotional payments. In part, this law additionally no longer allows wholesalers or retailers to act as their own brokers. So they were forced to divest their brokerage business or at least not allow their buyers to collect brokerage payments unless they functioned solely as a broker. This latter point recently has erupted into another controversy provoked by market brokers, who question the control that retailers or wholesalers exercise over brokers who work "in house." That term "in-house broker" lately has become charged,

Federated Foods' Red & White logo as it appears today

Under MacBeth lighting in Federated Foods' quality assurance lab, technologist Karen Whalen analyzes food ingredients from products in the Parade brand line.

controversial and confusing. All of these brokers now prefer to be called marketing agents or account-specific controlled brand brokers.

The 1930s situation is best illustrated with an example. To compete against the giant grocery chain A&P, a regional retailer, S.M. Flickinger in Buffalo, NY, in the late 1920s sold off his stores to the store managers and became their wholesaler. In a sort of patriotic gesture, he began supplying them with Red & White private label products. This group of independent grocers also used the Red & White logo as their store identity. These retailers had set up their own in-house brokerage to handle product procurement. But with the Robinson-Patman enacted, they were forced to spin off that operation, which was reformed on the outside as Busey, Maury and Wright. Over the next 20-plus years, this broker kept the Red & White private label business relatively small, up until the mid-1950s, when Don Albrecht joined the firm. It was then decided to branch out into more private labels, offered to customers other than just those in the wholesaler-sponsored Red & White program. In effect, the broker began creating other proprietary labels like Hy.Top, Fine Fare, Parade, etc., which were franchised on an exclusive basis to retailers and wholesalers around the country. As a result, the

Two labels from Alliance Foods show a yellow generic label for whole kernel corn and a Coop natural pack for whole tomatoes, the latter carring a refund guarantee and targeted to health-conscious consumers (no salt added).

brokerage was renamed Federated Foods, based in Arlington Heights, IL. Federated Foods also began handling private label programs already established by distributors like Wetterau in St. Louis, MO; IGA in Chicago, IL; and Malone & Hyde in Memphis, TN. Federated additionally entered the private label foodservice business, supplying Red & White, Parade, and Lead Way products to wholesalers and independent foodservice distributors.

The company credits itself with inaugurating the first broker-managed private label program belonging to someone else: Piggly Wiggly in the early 1960s. Different independent local brokers had been handling that program previously for the Piggly Wiggly grocery group, but without any continuity in their efforts. Federated also claims to have set up the first broker-operated private label quality assurance program. Its emphasis on foodservice business led to the sponsorship of that industry's first private label selling show, starting about 1977-78. Today, foodservice distributor groups run similar selling shows with a focus on their own private label programs.

Prompted by the success of these shows, Federated pioneered a similar private label selling show for its retail accounts, starting with IGA in 1983. These trade shows, one or two held each year for each account, today have become regular events in the retailing industry—copied by major wholesalers or co-ops on behalf of their own private label programs.

In the past decade, Federated developed into the country's third largest private label marketing/sales agent, building up its retail and foodservice business to total billings of in excess of $1 billion in private label. With some acount switching, its billings have reportedly fluctuated slightly. The company manages more than 200 retail/foodservice customers, overseeing more than 1,000 private label food and non-food skus. With all its different proprietary label programs combined, including different package sizes and product varieties, its private label skus count easily exceeds 30,000 items. Those products are sourced from its principals, some 400+ vendors. Its operation provides full service, covering quality assurance lab support and Management Information System back-up. Federated also has a Product Management Group of product managers plus support staff devoted to 'brand development' as well as creating marketing support programs. Today, the firm, acting through new investors from Europe, is looking to develop similar private label business internationally.

Another long-time private label brokerage house in the retail segment started into business in 1929 as Jobber Services. After the Robinson-Patman Act was enacted, this company evolved into Alliance Associates, Coldwater, MI, an account-specific private label broker. Some 20 years ago, the firm saw one of its employees, Peter Schwartz, leave to form another brokerage partnership with Milton Sender, called Daymon Associates, Inc., based in New York, which was set up pretty much like Alliance, handling only private label accounts. Both these private label brokers—keeping a low profile throughout the years—continue to leave an indelible imprint on the private label industry.

Alliance, in fact, still refers to itself as "the quiet company"; yet it has played a significant role in private label developments, tracing back at least to the 1970s, when it began instigating some of the trends for its private label trade customers that only now are being adopted by branded manufacturers: Solidifying partnering efforts between the manufacturer and the retailer. In the late 1970s, six months after Jewel Stores in Chicago introduced the generics concept in the US, Alliance helped its trade customers to start up black-and-white generic labels, too. Over the years, Alliance helped developed a non-exclusive Family Fare controlled label for its customers—an identity that has been dormant for some three years now, replaced by about a dozen other exclusive food labels, under development over the past five years: Nature's Classics, American Feast, Walton's Farm, etc. Alliance itself has changed in this period, diversifying from not only handling private label for grocery retailers, but also for mass merchandisers, drugstore chain retailers, warehouse club store operators, limited assortment store merchants, etc. Most people see the results of this work in the recent trend toward more private label activity in these different market segments.

In the early 1970s, one of Daymon Associates' first retail customers was Ralphs Grocery Co., Compton, CA, which since has acknowledged that Daymon has been one of its biggest confidence builders for the Ralphs private label program. Daymon still represents Ralphs today, while the latter's Ralphs brand sku count during this relationship has soared from 70 items up to in excess of 1,500 items, accounting for an estimated $115 million+ in sales. (Ralphs also sources private label from its own manufacturing and processing facilities—bakery, dairy-ice cream, deli—adding to those sales.)

Daymon's track record has been impressive in recent years, ranking the firm as the top private label marketing/sales agent in the United States. Its billings are substantial, and it probably employs more people under its umbrella companies than all of the other private label brokers combined. Daymon now represents suppliers to more than 40 large retail/wholesale customers, including accounts with Salt Lake City, UT-based American Stores, the Jewel Stores in Chicago, and Acme Markets in Philadelphia; Fred Meyer Co., a multi-department store retailer based in Portland, OR; Skokie, IL-based Topco Associates, a member-owned cooperative of 39 local and regional grocery chains and wholesalers; plus other grocery retailers like Bi-Lo in Mauldin, SC, and H-E-B Stores in San Antonio, TX.

Interestingly, Daymon is probably characterized as much by its policies which distant it from other private label brokers. For example, Daymon will not rebate brokerage to its customers nor will it perform private label purchasing from its suppliers. Daymon, on behalf of its suppliers, offers merchandising savvy, category analysis, new product development experience, label and shelf management and marketing concepts. The company, however, does not broadcast its existence at all—operating out of a four-floor headquarters in New York City, while its field staff works right in the customer's own operations.

Daymon remains publicity-shy, because it argues that its work is best reflected through its customers' private label programs. One exception to this silence rule—which actually surprised people in the Daymon camp—was an interview granted to the *Shelby Report of the Southeast* trade newspaper in its January 1992 issue, where David Abelman, Daymon's marketing director outlined some general industry strategies, such as "...the real challenge for manufacturers of corporate brands is to be more marketing and sales driven, and not have a co-packer mentality... The real challenge is for retailers to think like national brands, instead of just letting the national brands think for them... The industry has bred great buyers, not great sellers. They forgot what the business was about... The art of selling has to come back around." Mr. Abelman, not surprisingly, gave no specific information about Daymon—at least not in that published interview.

Daymon's positioning as a marketing agent rather than a broker points to a general trend in the industry, where brokers are becoming more specialized. That sophistication is evident in the March 1992 start-up of a private label sales and marketing company, called Pivotal Sales Co., Walnut Creek, CA, which does not source products from principals at all. Not coincidentally, Pivotal is located right in the neighborhood of Safeway Inc.'s Glencourt private label manufacturing headquarters. Pivotal was launched by Ed Dougherty, its president, who previously worked at Safeway as marketing services manager in grocery. Mr. Dougherty's firm acts as a sales and marketing coordinator between packaged goods suppliers for the Oakland, CA-based chain (including its own 38 manufacturing facilities in the US) and some 850 Safeway stores in the company's wholly-owned divisions. Pivotal, in turn, has retained the services of Professional In-Store Advantage (PIA), Irving, CA, for retail merchandising field support. Up until 1992, PIA serviced only branded manufacturers like Procter & Gamble, S.C. Johnson and others, providing them with field support as well as shelf-schematic development and other services. That expertise is now being directed into private label, via Pivotal, where PIA's retail personnel (one assigned to every 20 Safeway stores) call on the store to insure that private label is properly displayed on the shelves, tagged, and not put out of stock or cancelled (not carried at all). This sales and marketing support now provides Safeway with a staff of 50 people (42 of them in the field) looking after private label interests in the stores. A PIA spokesman notes that such supervision impacts quickly on the higher-velocity products, lifting sales to 7 to 9% per item. Pivotal is expected to extend this private label service to other private label customers in the future.

Sophistication in the private label broker area, of course, is nothing new. It is just becoming better tuned. The second largest account-specific broker organization, Marketing Management Inc., Ft. Worth, TX—its private label billings estimated at $1.5 billion+—was started by Herb Pease Sr. in 1966. Mr. Pease served as an item broker at first for retailers and wholesalers like Handy Andy, Fleming, H.E.B., Albertsons, and Safeway, all in Texas. As the industry evolved, MMI became more of a program broker. In 1976, its Generics Products Corp., subsidiary was launched. That function continues today, developing and marketing generic canned and packaged products under yellow and black, black and white, or white with various color strip labels, depending on what its customers want. In this connection, Mr. Pease, when he first spotted generic cigarettes in a Jewel Store, got together with Brown & Williamson Tobacco Co., to develop an MMI value brand called GCP Approved Brand cigarettes, which today capture close to a 2% market share in the total cigarette market, ranking number 10 of all brands sold.

Over the years, MMI has developed a number of exclusive private label identities for both its retail and foodservice customers: Real Value, Hyper Value, Budget Buy, and Best Way in food and non-food lines. There are now some 20,000+ skus overall, which MMI can program, for example, like the Real Value label—as a first- or second-quality private label or as a generic label, depending on a customer's needs.

Developing as a program-oriented broker, MMI in April 1981 signed wholesaler Fleming Companies, Oklahoma City, OK, as its first member in a pioneering service, called the Service Purchase Program. This program is designed to guarantee MMI's principals expanded private label sales. MMI then reinvests a sizeable portion of the commission collected from those sales into the accounts assigned to the program, giving them merchandising and marketing support materials to help build their private label sales. More than a dozen retailers and wholesalers now belong the Service Purchase Program today, including the co-op Shurfine-Central, retailers Bruno's and Thriftway, wholesalers Fleming and Thriftway, etc. This program, MMI says, was developed to conform with and operate within the guidelines set out in Section 2(c) of the Robinson-Patman Act.

Also over the years, MMI has provided support to the private label industry in a number of ways. In 1989, Mr. Pease, for example, invited key quality assurance technologists from top retailer and wholesaler companies to his headquarters to investigate the organization of a quality assurance association for private label. He then helped fund the actual formation of a national private label Quality Assurance Association, now consisting of companies in both retail and foodservice. QAA, however, has no ties to MMI.

MMI also has provided leadership support for private label through its research and involvement in Voluntary Industry Guidelines for shipping containers. Today, the company is positioned as a total marketing company rather than an account-specific private label broker, providing both its principals and customers with full support in quality assurance, data processing, graphics design, and so forth.

Although not totally dedicated to private label, Continental Companies, Concord, CA, deserves special mention as an account-specific broker. Started in 1963 as a specialist in both branded and private label frozen foods, Continental kept a low profile over the years. About 12 years ago, the firm began innovating with its Continental Coordinators concept, combining private label and branded frozen product into pooling warehouses, then consolidating the orders for shipment via its massive computer capability into full truckloads at minimum cost and maximum time savings for its trade customers. About the mid-1980s, however, Continental found that private label frozen dinners and entrees were taking a beating from the higher-priced branded products. So the company decided to take on dry grocery private label business as well, actually adding to its overall volume, when it began serving mostly wholesaler customers that picked up on Continental's frozen food program, too. Continental also began managing the packaging and labeling aspects of its customers' private labels, while working with top retailer and wholesalers on new product ideas, innovative selling techniques, effective packaging strategies, helping to develop private label business for them.

Another account-specific broker, Cal Growers, San Jose, CA, has come into its own only recently, thanks in part to its relationship with its biggest customer, SuperValu Stores, Minneapolis. In fact, Cal Growers can be credited with being at the right place at the right time with this customer. SuperValu, the second largest food wholesalers in the US announced in June 1992 its acquisition plans for the country's fourth largest US food wholesaler, Wetterau Inc., Hazelwood, MO, which would make the renamed "SUPERVALU", once the acquisition is completed, the country's largest food wholesaler with sales exceeding $15 billion. With this association plus new customer accounts added in 1992—Purity Supreme, West Pac, Food For Less and Alpha Beta—Cal Growers expects to double its private label billings in 1992 to $800 million+.

Started modestly in 1968 by Clem Perrucci, Cal Growers first handled commoditities as a field broker for California canners—hence its name. But in 1982, things changed for the broker when it purchased the rights and trademark to the Thorofare label from Farm House Foods Corp., Milwaukee, WI, which was pulling out of its Thorofare Markets chain. Cal Growers developed a full corporate-owned, first line private label program around Thorofare, licensing it on an exclusive basis to different trade customers. This activity grew to represent 60% of its billings by 1985, Rights to another label, Grocer's Pride, were acquired from another Cal Growers' account, Super-Rite Foods, Inc., Shiremanstown, PA. But the broker's business really began sparking when it developed private label programs for Charley Brothers, Pittsburgh, PA, a division of SuperValu. The parent organization especially liked a secondary private label program, Shoppers Value, which it eventually purchased from Cal Growers, while picking up the broker as its sales and marketing representative.

"That put Cal Growers on the map in May 1990," says Dave Dougherty, vice-president of the broker's Chicago office. But the association with SuperValu did not include handling procurement, quality assurance, and packaging services—things that the wholesalers wanted to handle itself. SuperValu at the time merged its controlled label activities into Preferred Products Inc., Chaswick, MN, which handles manufacturing/repacking of products for the wholesaler's private label program. Soon afterward, Cal Growers besides handling dry groceries started also working with private label dairy and frozen products as well (about February 1992).

Cal Growers places some 120 people for the SuperValu business. The brokers hire local brokers as part of its retail sales force, so-called sub-brokers. Results of this effort show SuperValu's private label sales in the first full fiscal year of the association climbing by 30%, while case sales jumped by 44%. Cal Growers also helped SuperValu organize its first National Buying Show in August 1991, followed by another show this past February (1992) in Orlando, FL. Both shows produced 12 million cases of private label product moved—an entire quarter's movement for the company compressed into two shows. Cal Growers projects private label sales in the current fiscal year will jump another 31%.

These major account-specific brokers are becoming more dominant in the private label business today. So where does that leave the market brokers, who are not part of this activity? For the larger market brokers, private label remains a small part of their overall business, representing no more than 5 or 10% of billings. The country's largest market broker, Merkert Enterprises, Canton, MA, which acquired The Boerner Co., Roslyn Heights, NY, in April 1992, bills more than $2 billion through its multi-divisional structure: six branded divisions, a private label division (Dorann Food Brokerage), marketing and packaging divisions, a biological products manufacturing division, and a supermarket supplies division. This employee-owned broker has less than 5% of its business in private label.

Another 100% employee-owned market broker, Bromar Inc., Newport Beach, CA, estimates that less than 5% of its $1.5 billion billings is in private label. In the late 1970s, the firm did set up Customer Sales Co., expressly to develop private label business, but that function has since been absorbed into the company.

Similar in billings size, Sales Force Companies, Inc., Shiller Park, IL, handles business in some 10+ Midwest states, but has most of what little private label business it handles centered in the Chicago market. Manufacturers really dictate whether the broker will sell private label along with the branded products they produce, but this broker has focused most of its attention on the branded side of the business.

As for the smaller market brokers, especially those who have been dedicated to or specialized in private label, they are slowly being squeezed out of the picture by the account-specific brokers. A case in point illustrates this development.

Started some 19 years ago with the acronym, Placo (Private Label Associates Co.), Dick Nicholson, president, has seen his dedicated private label broker business rise and fall in what he says is a scenario now being duplicated around the country. Blame it on competition; more specifically, blame it on the acquisitions/consolidations in the grocery industry and its growing reliance on account-specific brokers. Mr. Nichol reports that 20 years ago there was "virtually an army of specialized private label brokers out there. Now there are barely 15% of us guys left."

Placo Inc., Salt Lake City, UT, a market broker 100% dedicated to private label, at its peak billed some $550,000. But its customer base began eroding first when Fleming Companies took over American Stravell in its market, putting that customer into Marketing Management's hands. More recently, Placo's customer, Smith's Food & Drug Centers, Layton, UT, a member of Topco, has moved its business away from Placo, thus cutting Placo's billings by about 20%. Now Mr. Nicholson looks warily at one of his last big customers, Albertsons, in that market, which has contemplated its move to an account-specific brokerage system. This situation, he indicates, "gives Placo at best 24 months of business life left." In fact, the owner is now talking with some larger branded brokers about selling out.

Worse than the demise of the dedicated private label market broker, Mr. Nicholson points to an even "scarier trend"—the move by some large account-specific brokers toward diverting, that is, picking up branded business from the principals that already are being served through the brokerage for private label.

Alarmed by the increasing growth of account-specific private label brokers and the emergence of "power buyers" in retailing and wholesaling who use this service, a group of some 100 food market brokers and suppliers have formed a national Food Marketing Coalition, supported by the National Food Brokers Association, Washington. They are now petitioning the Federal Trade Commission (FTC) to investigate the use of so-called in-house brokers and whether or not retailers or wholesalers who retain them are taking kick-back rebates of cash and/or services. The NFBA and the Coalition charge that this practice violates Section 2(c) of the Robinson-Patman Act, because it's anti-competitive, creating greater concentration in the food industry and harming suppliers, market brokers, and ultimately the consumer, since such arrangements "increase prices, stifle innovation, and limit consumer choices."

The argument over what's better for this industry really comes down to a simple determination of what the independent broker (account specific or market) brings to the table in terms of new negotiations and new market information, versus just collecting a commission on items already sold to a trade customer, according to Greg Phillips, president of Ashdun Industries, Englewood Cliffs, NJ. In the past, Mr. Phillips has been positioned as a dedicated private label broker, but recently has become more of a marketing consultant, who has helped trade customer develop upscale food programs for private label and more recently 'green programs' bringing environmentally-responsive products under a private label or controlled label program. In fact, his firm has worked closely with principals in new product development, helping to launch compressed paper towels (a source reduction of material used by eliminating air from the paper rolls) and perforated half sheet towels (waste reduction via smaller sheet usage). Ashdun additionally has created a number of controlled labels exclusively for retailers and wholesalers—C.A.R.E., Envirocare, Aware, Project Green, SAFE, Enviroquest, etc.

Mr. Phillips says: "About 95% of the brokers selling private label today are inept. In a market like Denver, for example, you now have only two or three big volume customers, while there are 54 market brokers calling on them. So there has to be a shakeout. But the problem arises over who customers should choose. The account-specific brokers serve just one customer in a given market, so they cannot provide all the specific market information that numerous market brokers do, collected from their work with many customers in that market. The market brokers have a better perspective on specifics in a particular market."

This controversy over account-specific brokers, he feels, could result in the FTC ruling them illegal, which will encourage more direct buying by trade customers, while still putting the smaller market brokers out of business. Something definitely will be lost in the competitive networking that now goes on when working through many different market brokers, he feels.

11

Foodservice: A Distributors' World

Like apples and oranges, the retail business and the foodservice business are different. There are similarities, of course, such as both have retail outlets, both use brokers, both in some cases source products from the same manufacturers, and both do get involved in the other's business—a supermarket featuring sit-down or take-out foodservice and/or stocking institutional size packs or a restaurant packaging and selling products under its own identity through an on-premise retail outlet or licensing its name for products sold in retail stores. Yet there is at least one important difference: Consumers buy packaged goods in a retail store, using price points for comparison (private label versus national brands), while consumers in a foodservice environment make no such pricing comparisons when purchasing food as part of a total service concept—delivery of products, unpackaged or packaged, already prepared for on- or off-premise consumption. The latter business is more service-oriented, as its name, foodservice, implies.

In these terms, private label is more consumer-oriented in the retail setting, while it is more trade-oriented in foodservice. In the latter case, it is sold to back-of-the-house or kitchen personnel, the end users, so to speak. So private label can be tracked only up to a certain point where it is used in a foodservice facility. It may end up as part of a recipe, but not necessarily be noticed in the finished product consumed by patrons of that establishment. Consumers may see a foodservice operator's proprietary label on certain packaging materials used for take-out service or mentioned in a menu or on a menu board in a commercial restaurant or quick-service outlet. They also may spot a private label identity on a sugar pack, a coffee bag, a pie box, etc., in restaurants, hotels, institutional settings (schools, hospitals, jails, and the like), and sometimes may see that exclusive label used in a catered affair—airline foodservice, stadium concessions, etc. But these private labels, owned by the foodservice operator or controlled by a foodservice distributor—are not necessarily marketed to consumers: The Big Mac sandwich, the Hilton brand bar of soap, the CODE packet of sugar, all are positioned as part of a total service package.

As a result, private label's presence in foodservice is recognized mostly in the trade, appearing in larger institutional packs, usually sold by distributors to operators for use in food preparation, cleaning chores, or whatever. A problem arises, however in identifying private labels in the exchange. There are, for example, packer labels supplied by manufacturers that may be identified as private label by some distributors. There also are layers of label ownership. The foodservice distributor owns labels, but can also become a member of an independent foodservice distributor group, which supplies its own group labels. There also are foodservice brokers like Federated Foods, Inc., Arlington Heights, IL, and Taylor & Sledd's Pochanontas Foods, USA, Richmond, VA, each of which provides private labels to foodservice distributors.

Institutional Distribution (ID) estimates for 1991 that the foodservice distributors industry represents some $110 billion in sales in the U.S. *ID*, a 25-year-old trade magazine, covers this market exclusively. Its perception of the business is that it consists of two general categories: (1) broadline distributors, who handle food, nonfood items, restaurant and kitchen equipment and supplies, and cleaning products; and (2) specialized distributors, who serve a particular

The largest foodservice distributor, Sysco, has color-coded it brand under a four-tier quality classification system: Supreme, Imperial, Classic and Reliance. Photo from Sysco's Annual Report, 1991.

product category like bakery goods, meats, coffee, or frozen foods; a cash-and-carry operation; or a particular business segment like multi-chain operators, hospitals, convenience stores, etc. In its special Almanac Issue (May 15, 1992), *ID* reported on the top 200 distributors (114 broadline and 86 specialist), which accounted for only 38.3% or $42.1 billion of total market sales, meaning that foodservice distribution remains highly fragmented, represented mostly by smaller distributors.

As in the retail business, a foodservice distributor's private label commitment can vary widely. For example, the country's third largest broadline distributor, Rykoff-Sexton, Inc., Los Angeles, has 63% of its total $1.5 billion sales in private label, while the second largest broadline distributor, Kraft Foodservice Group, Deerfield, IL, uses the Kraft brand name in its program ($3.4 billion), which is not a private label.

ID reports that the top 10 US broadline distributors account for total sales of $19.3 billion or 17.5% of total industry sales. This author estimates their average private label commitment at 33.5% or $6.5 billion total, which illustrates another important difference between retail and foodservice: Private label penetration in the US is much higher in foodservice.

(*Private Label Magazine's* Supermarket Report, January 1992, showed the top 10 supermarket chain companies with 20% of their total sales of $98.2 billion in private label, while the top 10 food wholesalers had 14.7% of their $49.9 billion in private label sales.)

Nugget brand from the Nugget group has its Nutri-Gold label positioned as healthy food items, including this unsweetened juice fortified with Vitamin C. Other items include choice fruits in natural juice, white chicken in water (98% fat free), unbreaded veal slices, etc.

ID ranks Sysco Corp., Houston, TX, as the country's largest foodservice distributor, its sales of $8.4 billion in 1991 including 36% in private label. Sysco as a broadline distributor handles food, nonfood items, restaurant and kitchen equipment and supplies, plus cleaning products for some 230,000 customers— 60% of them restaurants. Its private label program, like others in the business, is tiered into quality levels (color-coded): Sysco Supreme (yellow), Sysco Imperial (blue), Sysco Classic (red), and Sysco Reliance (green), comprising some 25,000 items out of a total of more than 165,000 individual items offered in the firm's broad range of product lines. The company also offers customers a line of 36 Sysco Natural further-processed fruits and vegetables for use in salad bars and school lunch programs.

The specialized foodservice distributors, usually positioned as "system distributors," include players like Martin-Brower Co., Des Plaines, IL, taking $3.3 billion in sales, and Golden State Food Corp., Pasadena, CA, showing $1 billion in sales, according to *ID* estimates. Ranked as the number one and two distributors in this category, these companies, not surprisingly, are the number one and two largest foodservice distributors serving McDonald's, the world's largest restaurant chain. Martin-Brower has some two-thirds of its sales going to McDonald's, while 90% of its overall sales appear under its customers' proprietary labels. Incidentally, most of McDonald's product mix falls under its own labels, sold exclusively in its restaurants—except for a few licensing agreements.

THE DISTRIBUTOR GROUPS

There also are the independent foodservice distributor groups—about seven of them broadline and two specialized in equipment, as reported by *ID* in its Almanac Issue. These co-ops or buying/marketing groups actually list 36.8% or 1,287 of the total 3,500 distributors in the country as members, according to *ID*. The largest group is ComSource Independent Foodservice Companies, Inc., Atlanta, GA, which serves 135 independent distributor members in addition to their branches, raising the membership to 227 total distributors. *ID* estimates their members' total sales at $9.1 billion, of which 22% goes to private label. The total sales also include $849 million from 13 members in Canada, where a Sunshine private label is utilized. In the US, however, ComSource operates two private label programs: NIFDA (gold) top grade, NIFDA (red), Chef Pak (extra standard), Dandy, and Econo Pak (price sensitive). The North American program, however, is being phased out to be replaced by a ComSource program: Medallion premium quality, ComSource, and Insignia brand. Overall, the group handles some 14,000 products under private label, but its members' commitment can vary from 10% up to 40%+. A member like Tartan Foods, Philadelphia, PA ($148 million in sales), for example, has a strong in-house private label program that's supplemented with the ComSource programs. Overall, ComSource estimates the average private label commitment of its members at 22%, indicating that private label sales climbed by 20% in 1990, but registered a smaller gain ("in the low teens") in 1991.

Sysco brand products appear in this restaurant kitchen scene. Photo from Sysco's Annual Report, 1991.

TOP 10 FOODSERVICE GROUPS

Group	Member Companies	Member Sales-1991 ($ millions)	Percentage Change	Private Label Share of Sales*
1. **Foodservice Companies, Inc.**[1] Atlanta, GA	134	$9,103.2[1]	16.9%	20%
2. **EMCO Foodservice Systems**[2] Pittsburgh, PA	194	5,600	3.1	20-25%
3. **Nugget Distributors, Inc.** Stockton, CA	190	3,650	4.3	70%**
4. **F.Á.B., Inc.** Norcross, GA	79	3,715	11.9	N.A
5. **Federated Foods, Inc.**[3] Arlington Heights, IL	122	3,517	3.2	N.A.
6. **Pocahontas Foods USA**[4] Richmond, VA	119	2,585	17.1	N.A.
7. **All Kitchens Inc.** Boise, ID	108	2,250	9.7	30%
8. **Golbon** Boise, ID	76	1,900	26.7	25%
9. **Plee-Zing/Lil Brave** Glenview, IL	155	995	3.1	N.A.
10. **Allied Buying Corp.**[5] Chicago, IL	55	950	-1.6	N.A.

(Note: Underscored group indicates a co-op, where members pay a fee.)

* Private label data is provided by the author.

** 70% including equipment, 85% with just food distribution.

1. Data includes $849 million from 13 members in Canadian Associate Federated Foods Ltd.

2. Data includes $2.5 billion from 36 members in Canadian Associate AFD.

3. Federated is a sales/marketing organization, which includes retail brokerage business as well.

4. Pocahontas is a brokerage function of Taylor & Sledd.

5. Allied Buying specializes in equipment and supplies for distributors.

Source: Institutional Distribution Magazine, 1992

BROADLINE DISTRIBUTORS

Rank	Company	Number of Locations	Sales(% Change) (Millions)	PL Share of Sales*
1.	**Sysco Corp.** Houston, TX	104	$8,378 (+8.5%)	36%
2.	**Kraft Foodservice Group** Deerfield, IL	46	3,400 (+6.3%)	0%
3.	**Rykoff-Sexton, Inc.** Los Angeles, CA	29	1,500 (+3.1%)	63%
4.	**PYA/Monarch, Inc.** Greenville, SC	10	1,300 (-8.7%)	55%
5.	**JP Foodservice, Inc.**** Hanover, MD	9	1,070 (+7%)	25%
6.	**White Swan, Inc.** Euless, TX	9	793 (+6.4%)	45%
7.	**Food Services of America** Seattle, WA	18	775 (+6.9%)	20%
8.	**Gordon Food Service** Grand Rapids, MI	2	765 (+5.5%)	32%
9.	**Unifax, Inc.** Wilkes-Barre, PA	4	740 (+5.7%)	30%
10.	**Consolidated Foodservice Companies** Virginia Beach, VA	5	455 (+13.8%)	40%

*Private label estimates from Institutional Distribution and the author.
**JP is one of two licensees of Monarch label from PYA/Monarch. Other licensee is CP
Foodservice ($80.4 million), Ormond Beach, FL, which acquired PYA's Orlando brand recently.
Source: Institutional Distribution Magazine, 1992.

III

Going To The Source

12

A Cinderella Story for Manufacturers

In the United States for decades, the brands have dominated the food distribution system. Under the shadow of these brands proliferating throughout the 1930s, 1940s, and 1950s, private labels, too, proliferated first in canned fruits and vegetables, then into other product categories, such as frozen foods and health and beauty aids, as they developed. At one time, one grocery market leader Safeway Food Stores, Oakland, CA, stocked more than 100 different store brand names, many of them "disguised" as manufacturers' packer labels.

This industry really did not take shape or become focused until the 1960s, when many different product categories began taking on private labels. The private label manufacturers tended to be smaller in size, obscure, or mostly privately-held, none of them able to match the resources of the larger branded manufacturers. These private label players today represent sales volume anywhere from several million dollars upwards to a billion dollars-plus. Over the years—and up until today—some national brand leaders who supplied private label did so strictly on a low-profile basis, primarily to keep their large trade customers (the retailers) happy. Yet some of these branded manufacturers on their own or through acquisitions eventually came to establish a 'more respectable' private label presence of their own, too. They include such familiar names as: Bordens, Nabisco, Kraft, Ralston Purina, Heinz, Reynolds Metal, etc. There are also brand leaders like Procter & Gamble, Pillsbury, Coca-Cola, Gerber and the like, who have continued to remain adamantly against producing private labels.

Private label in grocery retailing came to be regarded generally as a 'second-class citizen' or stepchild of the brands. Actually, isolated pockets of quality for private label have existed in retailing for decades, examples being quality-oriented and innovative retailers like Sears or IGA in its formative years (mentioned earlier). But private label overall has carried a price image, often stereotyped as the 'price brand.' In the late 1970s, generics emerged to reinforce this perception, because of their generally lower or just acceptable quality standards. Inconsistencies in product quality and packaging ran rampant, where some producers of generic products literally scraped the bottom of the barrel. Others matched the best brand quality available in a product category: It was too expensive for a processor or manufacturer to switch to another quality level during a production run. So it was possible for the same product quality to appear under a brand identity, a private label, and a generic package identity.

Up against generic inconsistencies and a price brand image, private label manufacturers overall were not anxious to broadcast their participation in this business. In fact, for decades past, the private label manufacturers have remained secret, hidden or very quiet, primarily because the business itself has been retailer-driven. The private label products that retailers ordered or made themselves were identified on the package with their own name or designated identity. The manufacturing sources were really not given a presence. Consumers, therefore, often confused retailers as the manufacturer or thought that store brand products were 'leftovers' from the brand manufacturers.

In the 1980s, however, private label emerged like a Cinderella—its attractive features suddenly being realized and enhanced. Ironically, private labels have undergone this rags-to-riches transformation thanks partly to the emergence of generics. Generics gave both the retailers and wholesalers (willingly or unwillingly) more of a sense of power over what products they could stock on their shelves. The national brands had nothing to do with a generics aisle in a food store, or a generics in-store promotion, or a special generics advertisement in a newspaper circular. The retailers and wholesalers could push these products just like the brand manufacturers who pushed their products; generics gave these food distributors control over store merchandising sets as well as marketing efforts. As economic conditions improved through the 1980s, generics were slowly phased out or changed into more consistent quality as so-called neogeneric labels or secondary private label programs. The retailers' and wholesalers' control with generics was carried over to their first line private label, helping to buttress or push them closer to brand status. Generics filled the vacuum created when first line private labels vacated their 'price brand' quality level. As retailers and wholesalers pushed generics into private label's second quality level, their first line programs were made to compete more on an equal quality footing with the brands. Private labels became more respectable, so to speak, their lower price image retained but joined by a higher quality image, as the retailers and wholesalers more aggressively addressed:

- QUALITY SPECIFICATIONS (starting up in-house quality assurance labs or hiring outside labs for product analysis),

- PACKAGING ENHANCEMENTS (frequently retaining outside design firms to redesign and upgrade the private labels), and

- PROMOTIONAL MARKETING ACTIVITIES (introducing offers on-pack, coupons, more   print and TV advertising for private label, etc.).

These efforts gave trade customers along with their manufacturing sources (drawn into these activities as partners) a sense of pride in private label along with a better realization of its higher profit margins.

The generics phenomenon, however, was not well orchestrated. In fact, it was played very poorly with ugly labels and inconsistent quality levels, not at all in tune with what most consumers really wanted. There were exceptions to these procedures. One of them, Loblaws, in Canada—particularly, David Nichol—was years ahead of the US trade in its marketing strategy: To not only act as a "selling agent for national brand manufacturers, but become more of a buying agent for the consumers of the 1980s and as part of that role undertake to develop and market unique products and quality generics that meet the consumers' changing needs." Mr. Nichol's comments early in the 1980s about differentiating his company (like European retailers had been doing for years) show his foresight. Today, that strategy is impacting both directly and indirectly on the US grocery business, as a number of retailers and wholesalers sign licensing agreements with Loblaw for its President's Choice controlled label program, while Wal-Mart sources product similar to that program for its new upscale Sam's American Choice program, helped by Loblaw's wholesaling division. Additionally, others in the US are adopting upscale private label programs: A&P, Topco, Buffalo, NY-based Wegman's, Cincinnati-based First National, etc. Meantime, a majority of US retailers have since dismissed generics as a passing fad, while Loblaw's No Name generic program continues to be as viable today as it was when it was started back in 1979, because of its quality and orientation.

This rebirth of private label in the grocery segment also has impacted on retailers in the drugstore business. They saw the food retailers introducing pharmacies and full over-the-counter and health and beauty care sections into their larger combination food and drug stores or superstores. While the drugstore retailers' commitment to private label wasn't as strong as in the food industry, it nevertheless has picked up steam, following the same upgrade pattern in food retailing. The recent growth of warehouse club stores and deep discount drugstores has stirred up interest in private label as well.

In the 1980s, private label also benefited from the trend of an erosion of brand loyalty brought on by a number of complicated factors, such as inflated brand pricing, slotting allowance and product reclamation center charges by retailers, a buildup of brand promotional monies, etc. The recent US recession finally forced a majority of consumers to look for an alternative to these higher-priced brands—for something that delivered value: private labels. Evidence of this brand loyalty erosion is discussed in Chapter 18.

Meantime, those hidden private label manufacturers also were given an opportunity to come out of the closet. The door opened first with the start-up of a trade magazine, *Private Label*, founded by publisher E.W. Williams in April 1979, followed by the establishment of the Private Label Manufacturers Association (PLMA), New York, in October, 1979. Mr. Williams, acting on knowledge of the private label business through his work on another trade publication, *Quick Frozen Foods International*, which covered activities in private label frozen foods, called together a small group of mostly private label manufacturers from different product categories. They never before communicated with one another or even realized they had something in common. The PLMA, initially was organized and operated under the auspices of the magazine, but subsequently was spun off as a separate organization to avoid a conflict of interest. *Private Label* magazine itself literally brought these manufacturers out of the woodwork—most of them having never advertised their private label presence before. These new perfectly matched 'slippers,' the magazine and association, fit this industry as viable forms, permitting the manufacturers in concert with private label brokers to interact with their trade customers. In an early issue of the magazine, J.L. Prescott, So. Holland, MI, advertised itself as "the greatest unknown company in our industry." Prescott at the time announced that it was "one of the world's largest manufacturer of private label laundry and household cleaning products."

For its part, the PLMA brought the manufacturers together into meetings and trade shows—Cinderella brought to the masked ball—helping them to sell private label to the retail trade, particularly in the food and drugstore segments, as well as to the consumer. After the first organizational meeting, consisting of 20 people, PLMA held its first annual meeting in St. Louis in March 1980 with 39 companies as members. The show drew some 320 people, including the manufacturers, wholesalers, retailers, brokers, consultants, and guests. Its first trade show exhibition, held later that year in September in Chicago, hosted 58 exhibitors with 383 people in attendance. From this humble beginning, PLMA has grown into becoming one of the most successful trade associations in the US. Part of the credit for this success must go to Brian Sharoff, who was appointed full-time president of PLMA in 1982, a post he has held up to this day. A measure of PLMA's growth is illustrated by its latest trade show, held in November 1991 in Rosemont, IL (a Chicago suburb), where nearly 4,000 registrants came to see more than 400 exhibitors, occupying nearly 800 booths. PLMA's membership today now tops 1,000 companies.

Both the magazine and the association have served this industry well, not only giving it definition and direction, but more important helping to educate every player in the business about the nature of private label and its potential for growth. It has been a learning experience for everyone, including this author, who has had the good fortune to be involved in the pioneering efforts of both these industry forces since their inception.

Private Label magazine (today based in Ft. Lee, NJ) also has issued yearly directories of manufacturers and suppliers to the industry. In 1985, both the magazine and PLMA expanded internationally, the former introducing *Private Label International* magazine and the latter establishing trade shows and conferences in Europe and eventually opening an office in Amsterdam. From a modest 50-stand hotel show held in Paris in February 1986, PLMA's European shows have exploded up to 804 stands at the last exhibition held last May (1992) in Brussels. That trade show, in fact, surpassed the Chicago show, drawing exactly 4,000 registrants from 36 countries.

For everyone involved, it has been a maturing process. Private label marketing savvy has built up in different degrees by the retailers/wholesalers, by the brokers, and by the manufacturers. An anonymous chain grocery buyer, interviewed in an early issue of *Private Label*, claimed to have had years of experience in buying private label plus a "gut feeling" about what products fit into his program. As for the manufacturing sales people who called on him, he indicated that they left much to be desired, concerning their knowledge of the products: "They had the best intentions, until the bargaining began." But the private label grocery buyers generally, this buyer admitted, did sometimes compromise on quality when it came to price or a lack of product supply, settling for second best in their programs.

Many buyers had to settle for second best in the quality of sales people calling on them. Glenn Fischer, executive vice-president at Wetterau, Inc., one of the largest food wholesale operations in the US, remembers: "Going back 10 years, the thing that used to embarrass me the most was the quality of the manufacturers and brokers, specifically their expertise, calling upon us at the private label companies. Today, we have a much higher quality person making these calls. We don't have 'what's left' calling on us. This gives our overall private label program much higher visibility and importance within our own company. Ten years ago, we had just two people at corporate headquarters devoted to private label, now we've got five full-time staffers. And I think we've pulled in the very best talent with a cross-section of the industry—grocery chain, wholesaler, and broker backgrounds." Additionally, Wetterau works through private label coordinators and often private label buyers, at its 15 divisions.

This attitude and commitment to private label is best described by Fleming Companies, the second largest US food wholesaler. Through acquisitions, Fleming today manages some 30,700+ private label skus. In 1981, its private label division was handled by two full-time sales representatives, operating in Oklahoma City, OK, and Wichita, KS. Ten year later, that department, called Food Marketing Services, had 40 full-time sales reps. With the relatively recent acquisition of another wholesaling operation, Malone & Hyde, Fleming lately has restructured FMS as a category management function—just like the brand manufacturers—and at this writing is bringing at least 40 more sales representatives from the M&H division, now called its Mid-South Region, into FMS thus bringing the total sales force to 80+ reps—all dedicated to private label at Fleming. A spokesman notes that Fleming's private label growth has been close to or at a double-digit sales growth rate yearly over the past decade.

In the past 10 years, new private label manufacturers have emerged as the business grew; but a shake-out inevitably occurred, leaving only the successful manufacturers as survivors. Consultant Jerry Pinney, a former executive vice-president with IGA, Inc., observes: "A private label supplier use to be someone who basically packed a product, gave you a price, and asked you where you wanted it delivered and when. Anything that happened after delivery was the responsibility of the retailer or wholesaler." That has all changed today, Mr. Pinney adds, because the private label manufacturers now have become private label marketers. This has happened, he believes, because "the economics of procurement have become so complex, where retailers and wholesalers must now spend more time buying products (outside of commodity items like sugar, flour and cooking oil). So the private label manufacturers have had to step in with support such as marketing, advertising, merchandising—doing everything that the brand manufacturers do for their products." This changing role of the private label manufacturer was initiated by a few players in the business at first, but eventually began snowballing.

This new retailer orientation today, however, varies by the specific operator involved—especially by the people in charge. Some large retailers, for example, still emphasize the private label procurement function, while other larger and medium-sized retailers, are looking more to private label as a selling function first.

PRIVATE LABEL MARKETING CRUSADERS

At a PLMA 1988 conference, L. Perrigo Co., Allegan, MI, a private label manufacturer of health and beauty care products, reported on five years of company market research, which showed that price still was the number one factor cited by consumers (71%) for choosing a private label. (The very fact that a private label manufacturer was doing market research since the early 1980s was astonishing.) Its marketing director, Jim Tomschach, said that retailers were responding by marking down their private labels 25 up to 50% below the national brand pricing. But Perrigo also found that quality ranked high in consumers minds: 69% of respondents said private label delivered the same quality as the national brands. The speaker indicated that Perrigo was using this information in its own selling strategies, offering trial size packaging in baby care products, cough syrups, and analgesics, as well as bonus sizes (25% more product free or twin packs) and special display units (counter-top, floor stands, end-cap headers, etc.), all for private label.

Perrigo was ahead of most other private label manufacturers in this activity. The firm, started back in 1887 when Luther Perrigo hopped aboard his horse-drawn wagon to pedal medicinal ointments in western Michigan, progressed slowly through the first half of this century. It wasn't until the early 1950s that the modern Perrigo company took shape, when demand for private label started to grow. Eventually, the company evolved with 90%+ of its business in private label. The 1980s marked the beginning of its perception of store brands as a brand. Perrigo then started to tell retailer and wholesaler buyers to act more like brand managers—develop their products and provide support by "proactively" planning their marketing programs, versus just reacting to what the brands do in the marketplace—the old copycat mentality. This thinking has pushed Perrigo into a leadership role in the industry. Its fiscal 1991 sales topped $280 million. In December 1991, the company went public, and almost in the same breath, swallowed up a competitor, Cumberland-Swan, Inc., Smyrna, TN, a private label manufacturer of some over-the-counter drug products but mostly personal care items and 'wet' products (shampoos and the like). This acquisition signaled a restructuring of Perrigo into three separate divisions: health care/OTC, vitamins, and personal care products. Now the company handles about 450 products in 15 product categories. Some of its controlled labels have been signed under exclusive licenses to Wal-Mart for the Equate label used in different health and beauty care products and to the supermarket chain Meijer Inc., Grand Rapids, MI, for the Nature's Source label for vitamins. Perrigo mostly handles private label under its customers' own label identities, however.

It is interesting to note that Perrigo distinguishes itself from national brand manufacturers who focus on the consumer. Perrigo's strategy is to establish a close relationship with its customer, the retailer. So its marketing efforts are directed toward developing customized programs around its customers' store brands. This brand management approach, Perrigo believes, allows those customers to promote their own brand products in the stores. Since the store brand products are priced significantly lower than national brand products, the retailers can commit funds to promote the private label item through coupons, rebates plus other individualized promotional efforts while still realizing higher profit margin versus comparable brand products and, in many cases, earn more dollar profit per unit on the store brand products. This marketing distinction between private labels and the brands is important, because it underscores the loyalty that private label manufacturers can nurture toward the retailer versus a branded vendor who sells to any retailer without special attention necessarily paid to any one of them in particular.

Another early private label marketing crusader, Presto Products, Inc., Appleton, WI, began as a plastic wrap supplier in 1961 and eventually started supplying private label keyed into other plastic products as well—trash bags, kitchen bags, storage bags, etc. Today with some $250 million in sales (an estimated 40%+ in private label), Presto is neatly tucked into the Reynolds Metals Co., Richmond, VA, a $6 billion+ company with more than 100 different operations in 20 countries. That takeover occurred about 1988, but Presto has remained autonomous probably because of its private label orientation, specialization, and leadership.

When Tim Richardson (now working for a competitor, Mobil Chemical Co., Pittsford, NJ) joined Presto in 1975, that company dominated the private label plastic wrap business and was very likely the first to identify this category for private label. Some 50%+ of its business at the time went to private label, those products promoted via its sales force, but without any advertising support. As the big retail chains grew, their interest in private label increased. Mr. Richardson recalls that brokers like Federated Foods Inc., helped identify the fact that only larger customers could afford a private label program. So Federated stepped in, putting together its own private label program for some 500 to 1,000 items for the smaller retailers and wholesalers to adopt. The retailer- and wholesaler-owned co-ops like Topco and Shurfine-Central, respectively, as well as other private label brokers had adopted similar strategies. He notes that private label helped differentiate Presto in the marketplace, too. Before it became fashionable in the private label industry, the company offered its trade customers special shipper displays. Even when Coca-Cola Co., Atlanta, purchased Presto in the late 1970s, the takeover really had no influence on Presto's marketing efforts, except perhaps indirectly. The company did one tie-in with a Coke coupon promotion, working with the wholesaler Nash Finch Co., St. Louis Park, MN, where the latter got its customers to kick in some $600 to $700 each so that $5,000 was collected to pay for a roto advertisement featuring just private label products. This ad was backed with the national brand tie-in. "The effect of this," he says, "was that it told me that private label could merchandise itself; if it acted like a brand, it could generate sales on its own."

Mr. Richardson recalls: "There really was no national promotional effort of any kind for private label in 1983, because no one thought it would work. Private label relied on the national brands to do the promotions." But Presto started to put together a group of promotions that year, using stickers on cartons—an easy, inexpensive vehicle. All its customers of the 150-count sandwich bag got 'fun stickers,' for example, even the net pricing customers, since it was so inexpensive. These activities with their resulting sales gains inspired the national brand leader, Zip Lock, to start doing similar premium offers.

Presto today has more private label competitors; but the effects of these early promotions, Mr. Richardson feels, while not making the overall plastic wraps and bags the most successful private label category, has produced some of the largest market shares for private label by sub-category: private label trash can liners with a 43% share of the total $502.7 million market, private label tall kitchen bags with a 39% share of the total $420.9 million category, and private label garbage wastebasket bags with a 37% share of the $69.2 million category, according to SAMI (1/26/90) 52-week case sales data.

Only the leading brand, Zip Lock, remains stronger in reclosable bags, since private label was late in getting into that business. He adds: "The reason I wanted to create marketing plans for private label was to get our customers, the retailers and wholesalers, to pay a higher price for the products in order to help support those marketing programs—and sell more product." This strategy has been working ever since.

Both Perrigo and Presto illustrate two different routes often follow by private label manufacturers: (1) to remain self-sufficient and (2) to be acquired by a brand manufacturer and then...be converted more into the branded business (Procter & Gamble after its takeover of Ben Hill Citrus in Florida converted the latter from private label to a totally branded business), remain autonomous (Coke's then Reynold's acquisition of Presto), or become part of an agglomeration of companies under one company (the case of Borden, Inc., Columbus, OH). Over the years, Borden has purchased different companies, some with sizeable private label business, which the new parent recognized as an important and valuable part of the product mix. Private label helped the company remain competitive, while keeping costs down. So Borden today has a significant private label presence in pasta and ice cream, for example, which along with other product categories, also including private label business, makes the parent company one of the top private label manufacturers in the country with sales in this business alone exceeding $400 million.

Private companies continue to play a major role in the business. Their histories and their contributions for the most part remain undocumented or forgotten. One interesting example is the Penn-Champ Inc., Butler, PA, which early in the 1950s began developing A&P's first motor oil under the A Penn Label, which was expanded into other private label automotive products (antifreeze and the like) and then into household products, resulting in a fairly extensive range—available not only to A&P but other trade customers as well. The products were sold for the most part through independent brokers. In 1973, another private company, Bissell (The Barcolene Co., Holbrook, MA) acquired Penn-Champ in order to have a captive packager for home care products, primarily upholstery cleaner, to complement its carpet sweeper business. So the Bissell product range was expanded from 1979 onward from 10 to 15 skus sold to about four trade customers up to today's 500+ products in 50 different product categories sold to major private label customers.

Roger Taylor, former Penn-Champ president (now retired) recalls this business growing up from a marginal operation into one of the industry leaders: "We recognized that the key to success was private label and not a packer label strategy." Today, Barcolene Penn-Champ manufactures not just aerosols, but also liquids, lotions, and powders for private label. More than half its sales volume is in private label—a business that has grown tenfold through the 1980s up to a $50 million+ volume. The company also has worked with key accounts, providing all the sales-marketing materials necessary plus special and unique packaging. In 1986-87, Penn-Champ introduced its Arrowrap labeling system for aerosol products—first under private label—which allowed for production of smaller quantities of containers and greater flexibility in changing labels to accommodate bonus sizes, cents-off offers on-pack, etc., versus the standard lithographic can labeling method.

Another privately-held company—a 'sleeper' in the industry—Gilster-Mary Lee Corp., Chester, IL, was started up in the late 1890s as a small milling operation. After Don Welge, its president today, graduated from college, he joined the firm in 1957 and within a couple of years saw the company producing its first cake mixes for private label. That effort soon was expanded to brownie mix and pancake mix, then over the years developed into other product lines—potato products (scallop or flakes), dry sugar-flavored drink mixes, macaroni and cheese dinners, hamburger dinner mixes, microwave popcorn, breakfast cereals, chocolate drinks, syrups, and other grocery items. As a result, the company has grown to become one of the largest private label manufacturers, its volume estimated at "several hundred million dollars"—90%+ devoted to private label. Gilster-Mary Lee does have its own brands, too, such as Hospitality and Cinch, plus some foodservice accounts and does its share of contract packaging for other manufacturers; but its principal business is private label products, produced out of nine food plants and its own plastic packaging operation. Its efforts have helped build strong private label market share in some product categories, such as macaroni and cheese dinner, microwave popcorn, and some potato items. Lately, the firm also has developed some upscale private label dry mixes for pancake, muffin, and brownies, using formulas that match the best that the brands produce.

One of the most explosive private label categories in recent years have been ready-to-eat cereals. The largest private label manufacturer in this category is a branded company, Ralston-Purina Co., Specialty Foods, St. Louis, MO. The second largest supplier is a private company, called Malt-O-Meal Co., Minneapolis, MN, which began its business in 1919 with a 'copycat' version of the brand, Cream of Wheat hot cereal. Malt-O-Meal's farina-based cereal, however, was made differently with toasted malt, hence the company's name. That one product, sold as a regional brand, pretty much sustained the company right into the 1960s, at which time the first private label items debuted: puff wheat and puffed rice in bags. Then the firm moved its private label business into the five basic ready-to-eat cereals: corn flakes, raisin bran flakes, bran flakes, crisp rice, and sugar frosted flakes. Over the subsequent years, that line grew to some dozen types of cereals for private label, while the hot branded cereal market remained flat. Thus cold cereal products came to represent two-thirds of its business—primarily in private label. The company now estimates that upwards of 70% of its business is in private label. More interesting is the fact that this business has doubled every five years. In 1990, the company hit $100 million in sales, after doubling its business over the past three of its five-year plans. Malt-O-Meal is now right on target to pass the $200 million mark by 1995.

In this category, private label historically has stayed at about a 2.5% market share. When generics came on the scene, that private label share jumped past 4%, then later in the 1980s slipped below 4% until about 1989, when private label suddenly took off, helped by the US recession. Private label business in this category shot back up to a high of 8.5% share. But lately, Kellogg and other brands are fighting back for their lost market share and private label has slipped slightly. Malt-O-Meal throughout has established its private label presence up against the leading private label supplier, Ralston-Purina, which in the 1970s had over 90%+ of the private label cereal business.

Such growth in privately-held private label manufacturing companies is not uncommon. One small operation, Amolé, Dayton, OH, a producer of skin and bath care products, has been in business since 1848. Most of its history, however, is lost in relocations and ownership changes stretching back to when it was first called Mexican Amole Soap Co., named after the tropical plant, amole, which yields natural soap. Its present owner, Tom Isaacs, president, reports that the firm now does 80% of its business in private label and house brands—more than doubling its sales in the past five years, topping $13 million this past year. In the past three years, the firm has expanded internationally, exporting to the Far East, Middle East and South America, literally adding a new private label account every month. The company also credits itself with the creation of milk foam bath as a product in the mid 1960s, introduced first as a packer label, then a private label. Now the company offers more than 3,000 skus in a library of some 900 active formulations.

Private label in this category has evolved from a price item more into a top-quality product. The packaging, too, has changed from larger sizes to smaller packs, offering more variety of product. Amolé now positions itself as a "niche marketer" able to serve any size customer from a mini-chain operator with five stores up to a giant 2,000+ store operator. Mr. Isaacs still expresses some frustration in not knowing all the private label players or just who is the largest player in a fragmented market made up of large, medium, and small mom-and-pop manufacturers.

The industry is not only fragmented, but confusing as well. Manufacturers tend to overlap in their product category coverage. Also, they do not all identify themselves the same way, that is, as private label manufacturers. Some call themselves packer label producers, some refer to their product lines as controlled labels. Then there are cases like Lander Co., Englewood, NJ...

Starting out in the 1920s as a cosmetics supplier to variety and discount store chains, Lander over the years did produce some private label, but it wasn't until the period 1982-87 that the company got heavily involved. Then competition in the health and beauty care category became so crowded—everyone attempting to deliver quality equivalent to the brands—that Lander, which depended on volume business, couldn't carry the high inventory levels of product required in order to service smaller private label customers. So the company pulled out of private label and reposited itself by offering its branded line with a product quality not necessarily equal to the national brands, but "similar." Its products continue to be targeted to low and middle income consumers. The idea is to create price points around a full line of products (from 50 to 80 items, covering deodorants, baby products, shampoos, talcs, etc.) all retailing at an attractive price point. Says one company spokesman: "It's like a private label, because we do offer a program, but it's sold to anyone in the market. We sell more skus to a customer than most brands in this category." Lander has experimented with such prices points as one product for 59 cents or three for $2.

There is a tendency for some pioneering manufacturers to dominate private label share in a particular product category. A case in point is 3M Co., St. Paul, MN, the world's oldest and largest manufacturer of private label film with more than 150 retailers as clients worldwide. 3M's private label line of photographic film was started in 1964 with the acquisition of an Italian firm. At one time recently, 3M commanded 70% of private label film sales. This market share information today is proprietary; however, the company now takes about 10% of the total film market sales versus a 7% market share 10 years ago. Private label film actually now takes a 16.3% market share in the 110 film segment and about and 8.9% share in the 35 mm film segment. The leading five national brands (Agfa, Fuji, Kodak, Konica and 3M's Scotch brand) compete for the the bulk of the business.

Private label manufacturers often find themselves vying for private label business in a product category along with branded manufacturers. A good example is in the pet foods category, where brand leader, Ralston Purina Co., St. Louis,

MO—65 years a brands-only pet food supplier—jumped into to the private label market late in 1991, offering dry, soft-moist, canned, and snack cat/dog foods to some 30 accounts. But the second largest pet foods company in the U.S., privately-held Doane Products Co., Joplin, MO, now has some 95% of its estimated $400 million sales in private label—specifically dry dog and cat food, a category that takes two-thirds of the pet food market in the dog segment and up to 40% share in the cat segment. Some 36 years ago, Doane started into business with a small regional brand, but shortly thereafter began supplying private label to some Midwest retailers from its one plant. Today, Doane packs some 2,000+ different products in 10 plants. Some private label accounts now carry up to 40 of those items per program.

The third largest US pet food supplier, Heinz Pet Products, Newport, KY, got into this business when its parent organization, H.J. Heinz Co., in 1963 acquired Star Kist tuna, which included cat food brand business. Heinz over the years has maintained a small private label business and really didn't become committed to private label until its 1988 takeover of California Home Brands, a packer of canned pet foods. Now the company packs up to 65% of its 6-ounce cat food in private label and up to 40% of its canned dog food for private label. Yet private label share in the canned cat food market remains at only 10%; while in canned dog food, it's closer to an 8% share.

The fourth largest pet food supplier, privately-held Hubbard Milling Co., Mankato, MN, claims to be the second largest private label manufacturer of dry pet foods and the number one private label packer of semi-moist pet products. In business for 110 years, the company now provides a product line of more than 80 different items, covering dry dog and cat food, semi-moist dog and cat food, semi-moist treats, and multi-flavored dog biscuits. The firm also has interests in animal feed concentrates, specialty feeds as well as turkey products (frozen and processed).

There are branded manufacturers who can be far and away the leading player in private label within a category. A good example is Kraft Food Ingredients Corp., Memphis, TN, which commands private label cooking oils and shortening, as well as maintaining a "compelling" private label presence in non-dairy creamers and analog cheeses. In total, Kraft does nearly $300 million in private label sales. While the company does maintain a regional brand as well as a controlled label presence, most of its efforts go into private label for these items.

A company spokesman notes that this business has changed dramatically since the 1970s, when everything in private label was on an entry level price point, while the packaging looked like something out of an army   rations pack of that time. For the 1990s, the private label quality story is on a par with the brands, while packaging and graphics are upscale. Kraft, in fact, lately has innovated in private label, offering a pull-tab inner seal (like plasticized paper) that can be removed in one piece, leaving no residue inside the bottle and nothing around its cap rim. The firm also is addressing new product segments, such as canola oil and olive oil as well as new items like cooking sprays and substitute and imitation cheeses, all for private label. These efforts are being backed with promotional support monies, consumer research, and new merchandising and packaging strategies to trigger consumer interest.

This company is part of Kraft General Foods, Glenview, IL (owned by Philip Morris Companies Inc., New York), the largest food concern in the US (and third largest in Europe), its total sales reported at $29.6 billion. The parent firm's tobacco and beer revenues boost total sales to $50 billion+. Within its food operation, there also reportedly are private label interests found in its Birds Eye frozen foods division and the Maxwell House coffee division. Kraft Foodservice Group, second largest foodservice distributor in the US ($3.4 billion), however, has only its Kraft brand.

PRIVATE LABEL'S NICHE WITH THE 'GIANTS'

While the world's top manufacturers of consumer packaged food and drink products are primarily brand-name oriented, the very composition of their diversified, highly-decentralized operations allows for some private label activity. In the past, this relationship has made for strange bedfellows—brands working side-by-side with private labels—but in recent years, it has become more acceptable as private label first line quality has improved. In the process, this trend has imparted more marketing clout for private label.

Nestlé, Vevery, Switzerland, for example, ranked number one in the world in food and beverage sales—$35 billion—through its Nestle USA Company ($7 billion) alone owns one of the largest, if not the largest US private label coffee suppliers (Hills Bros.) and the largest US private label evaporated milk supplier (Carnation), both within the Nestlé Beverage Co. That entity was formed in March 1991, to capitalize on synergies within all Nestlé beverage operations (coffee, tea, juice, cocoa mixes, coffee creamers, etc.). Within Nestlé Food Company, the Culinary Division, handles Contadina brand canned tomato products, where less than 10% of its sales go to private label—sold only to large trade customers. Yet Nestlé does realize savings by shipping its branded goods along with private label. In fact, this operation has had a private label sales team active for at least six years, handling only large volume orders.

In the beverage area, (excluding its separate wine operation), Nestlé now has a specialized private label sales force of 20 people assisted by brokers. Their role has become more evident, for example, with the 1992 launch of a Private Label Retail Incentive Program, "Create a Stir," for Nestlé's powdered soft drink and tea products, which awarded points to the private label managers and the retailers, allowing them to redeem their points for prizes in a catalog or turn them into promotional dollars for more private label sales. Run January-June 1992, this program represents a first for Nestlé in giving private label this kind of marketing support. When figuring net pricing for its branded products, the firm must consider costs for: ingredients, packaging, manufacturing, sales/broker commissions, marketing, and special deals or free offers. Traditionally, the latter two areas were never considered for private label. Now they are becoming more of a factor, allowing for couponing, special end-cap store displays featuring special pricing, etc., all tied into private label. More customers are asking the company for this marketing support.

By and large, Unilever N.V., Rotterdam, The Netherlands/Unilever PLC, London (a $40.8 billion branded consumer good company) reports having no interests in private label. Its food business ($20.9 billion) is no exception. Yet the firm acknowledges that it is possible that somewhere in its worldwide operations, which also cover detergents and personal care products, there could be a situation where private label sales exist, albeit minor at best.

ConAgra, Omaha, NB, the second largest US food concern ($20 billion+) is composed of 50 independently operated companies, where private label has found niches. In its frozen foods business, about 2%+ or close to $30 million in sales go to private label. Private label also exists in its other operations; in 1991, private label became noticeably present in its acquisition of Arrow Industries, Dallas, with $100 million+ of its food business in private label, covering items like beans, rice, pepper, foil wrap, plastics, briquets, etc.

Other companies conduct similar operations: a token effort up to significant private label business, depending on the viewer's perspective. Sara Lee Corp., Chicago, IL, ($12.4 billion sales), whose mission is to become a premier global branded consumer packaged goods company—building on its Hanes hosiery megabrand initiatives for example—has private label activity in its bakery business as well as its foodservice operation, PYA/Monarch, the fourth largest foodservice distributor in the US with 55% of its total $1.3 billion volume in private label. In Europe, Sara Lee's coffee and grocery operations develop private label, too.

Sometimes, a branded firm's private label ties develop from an acquisition. The $11 billion+ Anheuser-Busch Co., St. Louis, MO, in 1982 purchased a 25-year-old refrigerated dough producer, Merico Refrigerated Products, which had been innovating in its product category with a flaky dough processing, as well as butter chip or margarine biscuits, butter-tasting biscuits, and other items. What's interesting is that Merico was basically a private label manufacturer. Today, it's total volume, estimated at $250 million, includes more than 90% devoted to private label. More interesting is the fact that Merico commands this product category in the private label sector, while taking about one-third of the total category sales, leaving the rest to Pillsbury Co., Minneapolis, MN, (owned by

Grand Metropolitan of the United Kingdom), which is a strictly branded company.

Private label can be quite attractive to the large food processor. Dean Foods Co., Franklin Park, IL, a $2.3 billion diversified concern, reports that upwards of 55% of its sales volume goes to private label because, says a company representative, "it's cheaper to sell private label." Dean Foods is primarily a dairy company, having started into business in 1925 with an evaporated milk plant. Today, it is also a major supplier of canned and frozen vegetable products, ranking itself as number three in the U.S. In its different operations, private label takes 50% of its dairy and ice cream business, 15% of its dips and prepared salads business, up to 30% of its canned and frozen vegetable products, up to 95% of its aseptically-packaged sauces and puddings for institutional markets, and that same share in powdered products, stabilizers and ingredients.

With $1.3 billion+ in private label sales, it could be argued that Dean Foods is one of the biggest private label suppliers. Yet there are bigger operations, found right in two of the largest supermarket retailing organizations in the US. Safeway Stores, Oakland, CA, now operates some 38 manufacturing and processing facilities in the US plus another 18 in Canada, producing most of the nearly 3,000 items carried under private label in its Safeway stores. Its U.S. manufacturing operation, Glencourt Inc., Walnut Creek, CA, calls itself one of the industry's largest suppliers of high quality private label products (foods, beverages, pet foods, etc.). This firm also does contract packing and customized formulations for national accounts (business outside the Safeway organization). Safeway's private label sales in manufacturing are estimated at $1.5 billion+. But the biggest private label food manufacturer has to be the Kroger Co., Cincinnati, which produces for the range of 4,000+ private label products found in Kroger's different supermarket chains. A good portion of that stock comes from its 37 food processing facilities. These plants produce well over an estimated $2 billion in sales, serving Kroger stores as well as outside national accounts, primarily as a private label supplier. Its offering covers 30-plus product categories (backed by 70-plus years manufacturing experience), including items like: coffee, tea, spices, dry prepared dinners, salad dressing, canned beans, tomato-based products, preserves and jelly, laundry and cleaning supplies, etc. Now operating as Inter-American Foods, Inc., Cincinnati, this manufacturer also is selling about 10 product categories abroad, marketing them under the Kroger label as a brand.

Both Safeway and Kroger, however, have had to cutback on their manufacturing operation in recent years to reduce their debts. For example, Safeway reported in its 1991 Annual Report that after the $4.2 billion leverage buyout by the investors Kravis, Roberts & Co., New York, the company sold off 45 manufacturing and processing facilities between 1986 and 1988, as part of a restructuring of its operations. In the past, A&P, Montvale, NJ, too, has operated an impressive manufacturing plant at its Horsehead, NY facility.

It has not been uncommon for retailers to divest their manufacturing operations entirely. When American Stores, Salt Lake City, UT, purchased Jewel Food Stores, Chicago, in late 1984, the purchaser wanted no part of manufacturing. Jewel's Park Manufacturing Division, therefore, was sold off to private investors. American Stores did the same thing after acquiring Acme Food Stores in Philadelphia. Park today is positioned as a dedicated private label supplier, selling more than 100 items (household chemicals, dry powder mixes, coffee, tea, etc.) its annual sales at about $125 million. Some 60% of its business is now centered in foodservice: Rustco, an operation started two years ago.

In 1988, Walgreen Co., Deerfield, IL, the largest US drugstore chain, decided to concentrate on being a drugstore retailer. So its production facility, Xcel Labs, doing $25 million to $35 million in sales at that time, was sold to private investors. Four years later (1992), the largest US private label vitamin and nutritional supplement manufacturer, P. Leiner Nutritional Products Corp., Torrance, CA, ($135.3 million in 1991 sales), purchased Xcel to become "big time in over-the-counter drugs," says Gale Bensussen, senior vice-president, sales and marketing. "We did it to bring in Xcel's manufacturing expertise as well as its new product development know-how."

Leiner's own OTC drug business was up by 35% in fiscal 1991—viewed as a likely growth area for the company, while its overall sales slipped by 9% for the year. Xcel, after being divested by Walgreens, continued as its dedicated private label supplier with more than 90% of its sales going to that drugstore chain. The acquisition puts Leiner, now renamed Leiner Health Products, second behind Perrigo (discussed earlier) as the market leader in private label health and beauty care products. In the US, Leiner's sales now have jumped to over $200 million.

RETAILER OR MANUFACTURER?

One can assume that a retail operation is different from a manufacturing operation, because of their respective activities—selling merchandise versus producing goods. A retailer operates stores, a manufacturer operates factories. If this is true, then what is The Sherwin-Williams Co., Cleveland, OH? This company began in 1866 as a wholesaler, dealing in paints, but four years later opened a retail store and in the following year, 1871, started manufacturing coatings. Today, the company with $2.5 billion in sales derives 58% of that volume from "external sales" out of its company-owned Sherwin-Williams Paint stores (1,981 outlets in 48 states and Canada), which exclusively distribute the Sherwin-Williams brand architectural coatings, industrial maintenance products, industrial finishes, and related items all produced by the company's coating manufacturing operation. This fact makes the company a private label retailer. But Sherwin-Williams perceives its "core business" as "the manufacture, distribution and sale of coatings and related products." In fact, 60.9% of its operating profits derive from the coatings segment of its business: primarily manufacturing, distribution and sale of brand name products under its Sherwin-Williams trademark as well as Dutch Boy, Martin-Senour, Krylon, Kem-Tone and other brands. Some of these trade names (including Sherwin-Williams) are sold as brands around the world through subsidiaries, joint ventures, and licensees. The firm's reorganized consumer division markets and sells these brands as well as handling private label business: Sears' Weatherbeater label, Kmart's own Dutch Boy medallion label, Home Depot's America's Finest, etc.), while its Coatings Division handles manufacturing, etc. So Sherwin-Williams also is a brand and private label manufacturer. Its Sherwin-Williams label on paint is sold exclusively in its own stores—a decision made in the mid-1970s. The company also labels other products (architectural finishes, industrial finishes, traffic paint, etc.), as well as motor vehicle finish and refinish products with the Sherwin-Williams identity for sale as a brand. In effect, the company is positioned basically as a manufacturer—the leading paint and architectural coatings company in the US— and the biggest supplier of private label products in that product segment. Private label's share of its total paint business by virtue of the Sherwin-Williams store sales is probably well over 50% of total volume.

Acquisitions have changed the complexion of this industry in recent years. Some brand-oriented firms have divested their private label operations, such as Chicopee, New Brunswick, NJ, selling off its private label diaper business to investors who started Arquest Inc., East Camden, AR, a private company; and Hunt Oil Co., Dallas, TX, selling Hunt Products Co., a private label manufacturer of health and beauty products to Dallas investors. Yet the reverse is true, too. Borden Co., St. Louis, MO, over the past eight years has acquired nine pasta companies, picking up 17 regional brands. This has made Borden the largest private label manufacturer of pasta. In fact, Borden Pasta also can boast to be the biggest dry pasta company in the world. It already commands 31% market share; its private label share, while not disclosed, is significant. Private label share in the dry pasta category (excluding macaroni and cheese dinners) is about 18.9% of tonnage and 14.5% of dollar sales.

There have been cases where the private label manufacturer has "matured" into a branded company—or tried that strategy. Webster Industries, Peabody, MA, a major private label supplier of household plastic bags, has promoted its environmental brand, Renew, and lately has extended that brand into paper goods to reenforce the brand image.

As mentioned earlier, this industry's "greatest unknown," J.L. Prescott, South Holland, IL, came out of the woodwork by advertising in the early issues of

Private Label magazine. Prescott was started in 1870 by James Lewis Prescott as a supplier of stove polish. Through four generations of Prescott family ownership, the company grew into a national and international distributor of branded items, expanding into shoe polish, liquid laundry bluing, house bleach, and disinfectant. With the growth of private label, Prescott became involved in this business as well, building private label sales to about $30 million in 1981. The manufacturer also innovated, introducing new packaging and product formulations to private label, such as liquid laundry detergent, fabric softener sheets, and automatic liquid dishwashing gel.

Competition in this price sensitive product category intensified over the years, while new product developments from market brand leaders like Procter & Gamble and Lever Brothers—both diametrically opposed to private label—made the going extra rough. Some major suppliers to private label, such as Purex and Armour-Dial, pulled out of the business. But Prescott survived, taken over in the recent past by Naragansett Investment Fund, as a limited partner. Its total sales for 1991 were reported at $72 million.

To strengthen its market position, Prescott lately has decided to merge with DeSoto, Inc., Des Plaines, IL, itself looking to diversify its customer base in the detergents and laundry related products business. DeSoto, as one of the top U.S. household detergent suppliers, has in the past derived nearly 90% of its sales from its private label account with Sears and its contract packing account with Lever Brothers. DeSoto also credits itself with being the first private label manufacturer to introduce ultra concentrated fabric softener. The DeSoto-Prescott merger, when completed, will result in a $175 million operation—80% or $140 million devoted to private label business.

Years ago, this author was told by one of the private label suppliers above that it was impossible to produce the quality level of Tide in a private label product. Today, Prescott reports it can now produce a laundry detergent better than P&G's Tide. Development work, in fact, is underway on introducing such a product into Loblaw's President's Choice corporate label program in Canada, where superior quality is the norm. Up until now, such an effort was nearly impossible, because of the prohibitive costs in making such a product and then pricing it competitively under the brand leader. The sales success of President's Choice make this more feasible in Loblaw stores.

Early in the 1980s, private label manufacturers were forced to sell a concept of private label as well as the products to top management at the retail and wholesale level. Lately, this 'sell' has evolved more into sales negotiations between manufacturer and buyer for the products alone, since the private label concept is now accepted as a viable method for boosting profits and building sales volume for those trade customers. It also has allowed smaller manufacturers having no advertising budget whatsoever, to join in the competition right along side the major brands.

13

A Guide To Leading Private Label Manufacturers

(50 Companies Selected By Product Category)

AID-PAK, USA (NutraMax Products, Inc.) Gloucester, MA—$26 million (55% private label) biggest private label supplier of disposable douche/enema/baby bottle liners, in North America (also in pediatric electrolyte oral maintenance solution).

AMERICAN WHITE CROSS LABORATORIES, INC., New Rochelle, NY—$35 million sales (60% in private label)—largest private label supplier of adhesive bandages/tapes.

ANDERSON BAKING CO., Lancaster, PA (owned by Stixi, AG, Saarlouis, Germany, itself owned by The Vogeley Group, Hamelin, Germany)—largest pretzel baker (private label and co-packing) in the U.S. with 35% of sales in private label. Stixi with $100 million+ sales makes crackers, cookies, pretzels, extruded snacks—40% of its business in private label.

ATALANTA CORP., Elizabeth, NJ—largest US importer of food products for private label.

AZAR NUT CO., El Paso, TX—largest private label nut supplier.

BAKE LINE PRODUCTS, INC., Des Plaines, IL—largest volume packer of private label cookies with 65% or $50 million+ sales in private label.

BORDEN PASTA GROUP (Borden Co.), Minneapolis, MN — largest dry pasta company in world and biggest in private label.

BROWN & WILLIAMSON TOBACCO CORP., Louisville, KY — largest value brand (generic) cigarette producer.

ANGEL CAMACHO S.A., Moron del la Prontera (Sevilla), Spain — largest olive supplier and largest in private label.

CARGILL, Minneapolis, a $49 billion commodities and food manufacturer—largest supplier of private label flour to US grocery trade. Also supplies: poultry products, juice concentrates, salts (table, rock, etc.), coffee, shrimp, plus numerous ingredients like sugar, corn syrups, eggs, etc.

COMPASS FOODS (A&P), Montvale, NJ — $70 million+ sales — fourth largest coffee "brand" in U.S., taking 50%+ of coffee sales in A&P-owned outlets (Eight O'Clock coffee bean program).

CONAGRA INC., Omaha, NB — $19.5 billion sales from some 50 independent operating companies, making firm second largest U.S. food manufacturer and fourth largest in world. Company has private label presence in shelf-stable foods (sauces, mixes) plus frozen foods (about 5% of that business or upwards of $30 million). ConAgra also purchased Arrow Industries, Inc., Dallas, TX, (dried beans, rice, aluminum foil, plastic can liners, charcoal products, etc.) with estimated $100 million+ in private label.

CONFAB COMPANIES, Stamford, CT — estimated $300 million+ sales — largest private label suppliers of feminine hygiene and incontinence products in the world.

DESOTO, INC. (Mt. Prospect, IL) and J.L. PRESCOTT CO. (South Holland, IL) — merger pending — $175 million (80% private label) — "The leading private label and contract manufacturer of detergents and household products in America."

DEAN FOODS CO., Franklin Park, IL — $2.3 billion sales (55% in private label — leading dairy private label supplier; also operates Green Bay Food Co., Green Bay, WI — largest private label pickle supplier.

DOANE FOOD PRODUCTS CO., Joplin, MO — $400 million+ (95% private label) — leading dry pet food supplier (dog and cat) in private label.

ELGIN-HONEY HILL CORP., Chicago, IL — largest supplier of non-dairy whipped toppings and creams in private label.

FREEDOM FOODS, INC., Odessa, FL — 75% of sales in private label — largest supplier of beef and chicken cubes and instant bouillon.

GILSTER-MARY LEE CORP., Chester, IL — Estimated $300 million+ —90% private label — dry mix food and beverages.

GLENCOURT, INC., Walnut Creek, CA (Safeway Stores) — $1.5 billion (estimated) sales, mostly in private label, from 38 U.S. and 18 Canadian manufacturing and processing facilities. Supplies many of 3,000+ private label skus in Safeway stores plus sells to national accounts.

GRIST MILL CO., Lakeville, MN — largest private label supplier of fruit snacks and granola bars, granola cereal and pre-formed graham cracker pie crust.

H.J. HEINZ CO., Pittsburgh, PA— largest private label supplier of canned soups (85% of the market) and canned pet foods.

HUISH DETERGENTS INC., Salt Lake City, UT— $170 million+ (80% + in private label) — Largest supplier of private label household chemicals/detergents.

INTER-AMERICAN FOODS (Kroger Co.), Cincinnati, OH — $2 billion+ (estimated), mostly in private label, through 37 food processing plants, supplying many of 4,000+ private label products in Kroger-owned stores plus to outside national accounts.

ITHACA INDUSTRIES, Wilkesboro, NC — largest private label women hosiery supplier.

KIDD & CO., Ligonier, IN — largest private label marshmallow and marshmallow creme supplier with 70% of sales in private label.

KRAFT FOOD INGREDIENTS CORP., (Kraft General Foods), TN — largest supplier of private label oils and shortening.

LEINER HEALTH PRODUCTS, Torrance, CA — $200 million in sales (90%+

in private label) — largest private label vitamin supplier and second largest private label health and beauty supplier.

LONDON INTERNATIONAL GROUP, London, England — LRC Products, London and Cook Bates Co., Sarasota, FL — largest private label manicure supplements producer.

McCAIN FOODS, Florencerville, New Brunswick, Canada — $2 billion+ in sales — largest U.S. private label frozen concentrate juice and frozen french fries supplier. US citrus sales equal $200 million (70% in private label).

MERICO INC. (Anheuser-Busch Co.), Carrollton, TX — $250 million+ (90%+ in private label) — biggest supplier of private label refrigerated dough products.

MI-LOR CORP./PROFESSIONAL BRUSHES, INC., Leominster, MA — $11 million+ in sales (80% in private label) — largest supplier of private label toothbrushes in the world.

THE MILNOT CO. (Engels Capital Investors Group) — $110 million (60% in private label) — only full-line supplier of private label Mexican foods and second largest private label supplier in canned milk.

NESTLE, Vevey, Switzerland — $35 billion total sales (Nestle USA taking $7 billion) — largest food company in world and largest US private label coffee supplier and evaporated milk supplier. Also largest supplier of canned tomatoes.

NICE PAK PRODUCTS, INC., Orangeburg, NY — largest private label supplier of baby wipes and second largest supplier in the US market.

ORIGINAL BRADFORD SOAP WORKS, INC., West Warwick, RI — largest private label supplier of bar soap.

L. PERRIGO CO., Allegan, MI — $280 million (90% in private label) — largest supplier of private label health and beauty care products.

POPE & TALBOT, Portland, OR — largest supplier of private label paper tissues and second largest supplier of private label disposable baby diapers with 90%+ of sales in private label.

QUALIS INC., Des Moines, IA — largest private label supplier of human pediculicide products, plus ethnic hair care and other OTC items.

RALSTON PURINA CO., St. Louis, MO — largest private label supplier of cereal breakfast.

RED WING CO., Fredonia, NY — (Ranks Hovis MacDougall, Winsor, England) — largest private label supplier of peanut butter (100% in private label).

SCHREIBER FOODS, INC., Green Bay, WI (Estimated $150 million+ total sales, 98% in private label) — largest private label cheese supplier (natural, processed, cream, etc.)

THE SHERWIN WILLIAMS CO., Cleveland, OH — largest U.S. paint company and architectural paint coatings firm — commands private label business with its 1,981 company — operated paint stores in North America exclusively distributing Sherwin-Williams branded products, while its consumer division produces those products plus branded and private label products. Of $2.5 billion net sales, net external sales in paint stores total $1.5 billion.

SOUTHERN TEA CO., Marietta, GA (owned by Tetley Inc., Shelton, CT, itself owned by Allied Lyons, London — number two tea company in the world) — largest private label tea supplier in U.S.

TRI-VALLEY GROWERS, San Francisco, CA — $825 million (35% private label) — fruit/vegetable processing and marketing co-op.

3M COMPANY, St. Paul, MN — (Estimated 70% private sales) — biggest private label photographic film supplier in world.

VENTURA COASTAL CORP., Ventura, CA — largest private label frozen lemonade producer.

WEYERHAEUSER CO., Tacoma, WA — largest private label disposable baby diaper supplier ($400 million estimated sales, some 65% in private label), planning spin off of this business into independent company, Paragon Trade Brands, in order to concentrate on forest products business.

WYANDOT INC., Marion, OH — $100 million+ (60% private label) — largest packer of private label corn-based snacks (chips, puffs, balls, popcorn, caramel corn).

WYANDOT BASF CORP., Parsippany, NJ — largest private label antifreeze supplier.

14

Europe With The Marks & Spencer Touch

There are similarities in the private label marketplace between Europe and the United Stares as far as manufacturers are concerned. That is, there are many privately-held and a growing number of branded manufacturers in Europe involved in private label. There also are century-old private label vendors, among them Drie Mollen (coffee and tea), Hertogenbosch, Holland, which started its business in 1818. There are newcomers to private label, too, including some firms that have flip-flopped from all branded production into mostly private label: For example, Seges (Societe Europeene de Glaces et Surgeles), part of the Ortiz Group, based in Saint Herblain, France, started with its ice cream brand Frigecreme in 1981, sold in supermarkets; then in 1989 entered the private label business becoming the largest private label ice cream and sherbert supplier in France; it began phasing out its brand business except in catering and home delivery service (about 40% of its sales). Additionally, there are manufacturers who have created specialized companies within their structure, such a Goupe Bonduelle (canned and frozen vegetable products), Vegchel, The Netherlands, which started the Prineurop Company early in 1990 just for its private label sales.

As in the US, private label throughout Europe, has had to compete against the brands that dominate in some markets — in Europe, referred to as so-called A brands. At the 1991 PLMA World of Private Labels trade show in Amsterdam, speaker Robert Heyning, a senior consultant at GloBrands Consultancy Group, also Amsterdam, described the Dutch foodstuff market as being divided into A labels, representing strong national and international brands primarily; B labels covering smaller national and regional brands plus many private labels, and C labels known as the price-fighters. About a dozen years ago, generics were fitted into the C label category, selling at up to 50% less than A brands, 25% less than B brands, and even 5 to 10% under C brands. More recently, retailers in that country have upgraded their private label quality image and packaging, moving from the B quality level into the A brand category as well. In fact, private labels now are represented on all three category levels.

But there are important marketing differences between Europe and the US as well. One important distinction is found in products, where consumer taste

Expensive pouch packaging, featuring outstanding graphics, carries a line of St Michael brand fruit drinks

preferences or indigenous likes and dislikes can vary greatly from country to country in Europe, while the US has regional consumer differences, which are not as sharply drawn. One of the biggest differences is the more direct influence in export/import trading by the own brands market in England on the rest of Europe. In England, private label market share is the strongest in the world, estimated at close to 30% of the food market. This phenomenon can be traced to the decades-old influence of 100% own label retailer Marks & Spenser (£5 billion revenues in 1991), one of the leading retailers in the United Kingdom. Over the years its progress and strong customer following are attributed in part to its cooperative relationship with manufacturers and the raw material suppliers to its products. Back in the 1930s, when its St Michael brand was first established, this retailer began working closely with manufacturers, getting them to make goods especially

In this specialty line of low-fat yogurts, Marks & Spencer uses Looney Tunes characters to attract young customer interest.

for Mark and Spencer — sometimes 100% dedicated to this effort, while the retailer, in turn, worked to improve the product quality, acting as production engineers, industrial chemists, and laboratory technicians.

Marks & Spencer continues to source "high quality, well-designed, and attractive merchandise representing good value to the customer." It encourages its suppliers to use the most modern and efficient techniques of production, based on the latest scientific and technological developments, then follows up by enforcing its own high standards of quality control. It is a one-on-one relationship — no brokers or wholesalers involved—where Marks & Spencer guarantees large orders for the goods it purchases on the basis of its own specialized information, which the manufacturer would not ordinarily have, while diligently working to improve the quality. This strategy, formed more than 60 years ago, has convinced some of the finest quality brand manufacturers for the first time to relinquish their own brand identity, allowing Mark & Spencer to claim the products as its own, under the St Michael's brand—companies like Sara Lee (United States), United Biscuits (United Kingdom), and others. Even today, the retailer scrupulously protects the identity of its manufacturers, many who wish not to be known as private label vendors.

Marcus Sieff, who wrote about these strategies in his book, "Don't Ask the Price, Memoirs of the President of Marks & Spencer" (1986, Weidenfeld & Nicolson), also reports that "usually we are our supplier's largest customer; we have been doing business continuously with 127 of them for over 25 years, 41 for more than 40 years, and with Dewirst LTD. [clothing] we have done uninterrupted business for more than a century. These companies are the backbone of our business and are our friends." This attitude today is beginning to catch fire around Europe, as private label grows in importance and as more A-brand manufacturers begin for accommodate the demands of their trade customers, who are asking for more of higher quality private label products.

Top brand manufacturers, in fact, will supply cheaper quality. More of them are willing to work jointly with their customers in developing new products, new packaging, while addressing different market segments. Says Rien Voormolen, manager marketing-sales for Douwe Egbetts Coffee & Tea International B.V., (a subsidiary of Sara Lee/DE), Utrecht, The Netherlands: In private label, "we deal with the winners in the retail scene." These winners, of course, are the major retailers and wholesalers, especially those in the UK, Holland, Belgium, Spain (now being influenced more by French retailers moving into that market), and Denmark. Some 15 years ago, Mr. Voormolen recalls, the relationship between manufacturer and customer was a straight-forward, follow-the-brand-leader procedure, where private label was priced 15% lower than the brand. Now his firm takes a more customized approach, emphasizing quality products, targeting niche markets for private label, and providing the retailers and wholesalers with program market support, especially in the strong own brand UK market. His company is no longer simply a supplier, but an add-on marketing contributor. Still, less than 5% of Douwe Egbert's branded coffee sales go to private label because, afterall, Sara Lee is a branded company first and foremost.

Another Sara Lee/DE subsidiary, however, Grada B.V., Amersfoort, a producer of household care products, personal care items, and liquid/powder detergents, produces only private label and B-brand products. It competitors are three major branded manufacturers — Procter & Gamble (US), Lever (UK/The Netherlands) and Henkel (Germany) — who do not make private label at all. Up against these giants, Grada has a better chance for market share outside the A-brand sphere, selling private label of comparable quality, but 25% cheaper, as well as B brands (50% cheaper), white label, or lower-quality products. The B brands work better in France as "premier prix" items, but not in the UK or Germany—both stronger private label markets for its product range. But in Germany, a price differential between private label and A brands is more important than in England. The company started producing private label products some 50 years ago and has cornered some 60% of the private label market for house care products in Holland.

Another important and growing influence on retailing across Europe has been Aldi in Germany. Operating out of two head offices, Essen and Mulheim, this limited assortment retailer, which also does some manufacturing as well (coffee, for example) stocks about 1,000 high-velocity items (80% in private label). Its strength has come from discount pricing.

Overall, market leaders in each country have been influenced directly or indirectly by these two private label retailers—Marks & Spencer in quality standards and by Aldi in discount pricing. Their competitors, in turn, have been pressured to follow suit. Lately, these influences are being felt more in the US market.

It could be stated that in recent years, there has been a general awakening to private label's potential in Europe as more manufacturers address this business within the European Community, which is now easing its trade barrier restrictions, thus encouraging more export activity from the manufacturers. It is beyond the scope of this book to present a country-by-country analysis of private label market conditions by virtue of the required length for such a discussion. It is more practical here to present a sampling of major private label manufacturers, who have literally come out of the woodwork in recent years, thanks to these changing market conditions. Many of them also have begun exhibiting at the European and US private label trade shows, sponsored by the Private Label Manufacturers Association, New York/Amsterdam, and/or by advertising in *Private Label International* magazine. In fact, that publication can take credit for helping to launch the world's second largest razor blade producer, Malhotras of India into the private label business. This manufacturer, through M/S Alliance Industries (UK) Limited, London, first advertised is capability some five years ago in the magazine. In 1991, the firm made its PLMA show debut in Amsterdam. It is now building private label business in the US, the Middle East, Africa, as well as in Europe and expects to have 60% of its sales in private label within the next three to four years. The company has sales of approximately $500 million with 25% of its European trade in private label.

Officially, the now 140-year-old C. Hahne Mills, Bad Oeyhausen, Germany, started into private label some seven years ago—right about the time of the start-up of the PLMA European trade shows. Hahne became one of the early supporters of this organization. Today, its private label cold cereal sales in Germany amount to about 20% of total sales; while in export throughout Europe, the US, and Far East, 50% of its sales derive from private label accounts.

EXPORTING WITH PRIVATE LABEL

This, in fact, has been the general tendency for private label manufacturers: Stick to branded business in their home country primarily, while opening up export markets with private label, that share often exceeding 50% of sales. In the UK, where own label has significant market share, manufacturers, of course, are more receptive to private label, while also seeking similar business abroad.

A case in point is F.E. Barber Ltd., Manchester, England, a subsidiary of the Co-operative Wholesale Society, which has 85% of its £650 million turnover concentrated in the domestic market, mostly within the CWS operations. This company is now targeting mainland Europe for expansion, already supplying a range of 1,000+ food products from its 12 manufacturing plants, exporting private label and exclusive brands to 32 nations overall. Barber ranks itself as one of Europe's top 50 food processors. Up to 90% of its total sales are now in own label.

Another top European food company, Hazlewood Foods plc, Derby, England/Amsterdam, its sales volume at £600 million+, has close to 60% of that volume in own label, featuring a full range of products—non-foods, frozen and fresh foods. This firm also is moving aggressively into the export area with private label.

Through acquisitions and international growth and expansion, some multi-billion dollar companies have had to regroup. In fact, there has been a general trend toward grouping of companies under similar products to better structure the size of the operation. Hazlewood Foods operates under this "European model," consisting of a supervisory board (corporate affairs and strategic policy) in the UK and a trading board (financing and trouble-shooting at the company level) in the Netherlands. Its different companies are grouped into three divisions: Frozen, Fresh, and Grocery. They, in turn, form sub-groups: ready meals/fish/shellfish; convenience foods/meat/produce; and bottling/bakery/non-food, coordinated by a specialist board or a strategy group.

This product-oriented structure has been adopted by other manufacturers/processors as well. For example, Molnlycke AB (part of the SCA Group) Boteborg, Sweden, operates in at least 22 countries through its subsidiaries and joint venture companies. In 1991, the company reorganized from a divisionalized organization into the group structure for greater strength in its different businesses and for

While it's not certain that Union Kaffee supplies Edah Supermarketen, Helmond, The Netherlands—most private label trade customers do not advertise their suppliers—this retailer markets its Cafe Cruz brand of coffee aggressively. Here a special display offers a bonus: a baked "sweet" attached to each coffee package, free to customers. Cafe Cruz is a sub-brand appearing under the Edah identity.

control on a global basis plus to better defined decision-making. So now the firm has seven business divisions (three of them involved in private label—baby products, tissue products, and toiletry items) and three marketing divisions (consumer products, health care, and new markets development).

One of Europe's largest private label coffee producers, Union Kaffee GmbH & Co., Hamburg, Germany—owned by commodity investors DWD of Paris—has rallied around its new Kaffee logo for its coffee subsidiaries in seven countries, each addressing different consumer tastes and practices. For 30 years, this firm has served private label accounts. Its private label business today is estimated at 80% of total sales—some 550 million DM. The company overall produces upwards of 400 private label products, targeted to niche markets, special blends, and the like.

IV
Market Research

15

Private Label as Proteus

"The fact is, private label goods take on an almost unlimited number of different, even contradictory, forms and images in consumers' minds at different times and in different countries. As a result, it's hard to pin down the common core, the universal meaning of private label across all these variations.

"In that sense, private labels might be compared to the ancient Greek sea god, Proteus. As you remember, Proteus had the confusing habit of taking on a wide variety of different forms and shapes in different circumstances. Often, even contradictory forms. The one shape that Proteus was most reluctant to assume was his own true form—his real identity." —Carolyn Huey, manager of marketing and sales, Global Information Services, Nielsen Marketing Research, Chicago. (Private Label International Magazine, March 1990).

How can anyone take measure of something so protean...something like private label that has so many different identities, so many different owners? It is nearly impossible, yet some yardsticks must be established. In fact, a number of them have been introduced. The reader should decide which measure best describes the "true" picture. One fact is certain: Private label sales and market share are growing. Most market research people agree on this point.

Two major business publications recently acknowledged the emergence of private label or more precisely the decline of brand loyalty. *Forbes* Magazine (Sept. 16, 1991) ran a cover story, "Hell no—we won't pay!", telling how "the jewels of the 1980s," the packaged consumer goods companies, are beginning to lose market share as "consumers are starting to balk at the prices on some of their favorite packaged goods and are starting to switch to house brands. The trend so far is only a trickle. But it shows signs of growing fairly rapidly." Market share of the top three brands in 11 product categories were shown to have dropped between 1985 and 1990: Disposable diapers from 81.2% to 53.8%, salad dressings from 48.5% to 35.5%, baking mixes from 68.9% to 43.1%, household cleaners from 36% to 22.9%, heavy-duty hand cleaners from 91.3% to 64.1%, breakfast snack/nutritional bar from 61.8% to 33.9%, popcorn from 45.5% to 37.9%, prepared dishes/dinner mixes from 80.1% to 64.2%, barbecue sauces from 44.3% to 36.8%, dishwashing detergent from 76.8% to 65.7%, and canned cat food from 64.9% to 49.6%. *Forbes* was quoting from a trade magazine, *Supermarket Business* (March 1991), which analyzed 350 product categories over a five-year period, showing that "Brand Power" has weakened in 47% of the cases for the top three brands. That publication drew its data from Mediamark Research Inc., New York, which derives its database from annual national probability surveys of 20,000 individuals, tracking statistics on 3,500 product categories and services and on 5,700 individual brands.

In bold headline print in its Dec. 2, 1991 issue, *Advertising Age*, a respected business newspaper on marketing, announced: "Brands in trouble...Marketers say they want to return to brand-building in the package-goods industry. But consumers are tuning out ad messages and flocking to discount stores." Again the focus was on brand loyalty crumbling. *Ad Age* quoted The Roper Organization, which has measured brand loyalty for a decade: "Three years ago, 56% of those polled by Roper said they know what brand they want to buy when they enter a store. That figure fell to 53% in April 1990 and plunged to 46% by mid-1991." Various factors are cited as possible reasons: the recession, the proliferation of new products, the onslaught of couponing, even compromised quality. The article mentions: "With pressure on to increase sales and profits in a country with flat population growth, package-goods marketers are cutting product costs—usually under the 'productivity' banner. But by shaving a little here and a little there off product quality, marketers are at least partly responsible for the gap in consumer trust."

Tod Johnson, president of NPD Group, New York, which uses focus groups to test product reformulations, is quoted in the article: "When we tested products in the 1960s and 1970s, I'd say 75% of the changes were product improvements. Today two-thirds or even three-quarters of the testing we do is asking for consumer opinion on cost reductions. Product quality is being ignored."

Then *Ad Age* addressed store brands: "Unlike their generic ancestors of the 1970s, these brand alternatives make quality a priority, a critical ingredient to bargain-hunting shoppers. Private label sales in supermarkets are at $24.7 billion, up 13% since 1989, Nielsen Marketing Research says, and are making serious inroads into classic marketing categories like ready-to-eat cereal, pet food and beverages."

More recently, *Ad Age* (July 20, 1992) ran its first "Brand Scorecard" of the top 10 brands in 10 of the fastest growing supermarket categories. Private label placed in the top 10 for six of those categories: #1 in ready-to-eat cereal with a 4.8% share ($340.2 million), #3 in peanut butter with an 18.1% share ($176.4 million), #3 in canned soup with a 5.8% share ($120.9 million), #4 in disposable diapers with a 12.6% share ($269.8 million), #5 in shelf stable drinks with a 6.6% share ($115.7 million), and #6 in frozen pizza with a 6.4% share ($82.2 million).

THE SAMI SAGA

Probably the first "reputable" tracking of private label sales in the US began in 1969, when the then three-year-old Selling Areas-Marketing, Inc. (SAMI), formed by Time Inc., New York, started issuing biannual reports of national projected share trends of private label brands in food stores. (In its first 20 years, SAMI grew into "the world's third largest market research company," tracking movement in food stores of all brands and items in 475 different product categories in 54 major markets, accounting for 88.42% of U.S. food store sales. SAMI worked primarily for national packaged goods companies—its clientele. Its focus was on major US markets including the major supermarket chains, tracking warehouse withdrawals of product for their stores.)

It should be stated here that SAMI had an attitude toward private label. In the July 1980 issue of *Chain Store Age/Supermarkets*, Allen B. Miller, vice-president of SAMI, wrote: "As a 25-year veteran in this business of marketing, I don't like private label brands very much. In fact, I don't like them at all. I'm afraid of them. I like the excitement of new products too much. When was the last time you saw an innovative new product from A&P? I know the answer to that. Never! Private label brands are like leeches, living off the products which were developed as a result of vision, investment and the marketing skills of our fine packaged goods companies." (In all fairness to SAMI, Mr. Miller eventually began writing data reports in *Private Label* later in the 1980s.)

When private label market share began "eroding" in 1983, according to SAMI, its explanation, as discussed in a *Private Label* editorial (January-February 1984), was that inflation rates were not so bad, so consumers were looking again for the best value for their dollar; brands also had increased their new product introductions within an improving economy; and there was an increase in the use of couponing and other promotional activities, which cut the price disparity between brands and private label. At the time also, the country's leading supermarket chains, which SAMI covered in its major markets, had begun deemphasizing private label and making a commitment to reemphasize national brands in order to strike a proper balance between the brands and private label.

The brands, they felt, drew customers into their stores along with advertising and trade promotions. Private label merely gave the customers an alternative product choice in the stores.

Responding to this analysis, one food broker, quoted in the editorial, said that SAMI's projected national trends from its sampled food chains were "one-sided" and did not represent total private label activity in the marketplace. What SAMI was missing was both direct store delivery of products from the manufacturer (bypassing the warehouse) and the growth of private label business by food wholesalers for their independent grocer customers, many of them located outside those major markets tracked in the data research. Also, co-op programs were maturing with strong growth for private label again with both independent and smaller chain store operators.

The overall result was that SAMI first reported private label market share at 13.65% in 1971; 10 years later that share crept upward by only 0.84% to 14.19%. With generics added in, SAMI restated the 1981 market share at 16.26%. But then SAMI thereafter continued to track a gradual slippage back below the 1970s average to 12.3% total private label share (Dec. 29, 1989), as generics weakened in the marketplace (See Chart 1). This data suggests that regular private label market share declined. Perhaps it did when averaged out in those major markets measured by SAMI. But across the country, private label was experiencing phenomenal growth—attracting retailers to start-up programs, encouraging other retailers with dormant programs to revitalize them, and extending and expanding sku counts into new product areas. This latter activity was picked up somewhat by SAMI in its breakout reports for health and beauty aids in particular.

In 1986, SAMI acquired Burke Marketing Services, which with Control Data Corporation operated an Arbitron cable tracking network. Additionally, SAMI had been expanding its methodology from only warehouse withdrawals to more scanning data. In looking at is Arbitron/SAMI data in those later years, private label still performed poorly.

For the 1980s, SAMI tracked total private label sales (including generics) in the dry grocery food category, climbing from 14.2% in 1980 to 15.3% in 1982, then slipping back to 11.2% by the end of 1989. In dry grocery non-foods, SAMI plotted growth from 1980 of a 10.8% market share to 13% in 1982, then back to about 10.9% at the close of the decade. Frozen foods, a stronger private label category, began the decade at a 20.7% share, then quickly climbed to 22.9%, the next year and thereafter slid back to 14.9% in 1989. Another strong category, refrigerated foods, tracked from 1981, showed a steady decline from a 28.3% share to a 19.2% share by 1989. The only upward trend was registered in health and beauty aids, which SAMI saw climbing from a 3.3% share in 1980 up to 4.7% share by 1989. In all categories, generics, a fraction of the total, dropped—after peaking about 1982-83. (Full details appear in the Glossary, Charts 1A-1E.)

CHART 1

FOOD STORES
PRIVATE LABEL & GENERIC DOLLAR SHARES
ALL DEPARTMENTS COMBINED

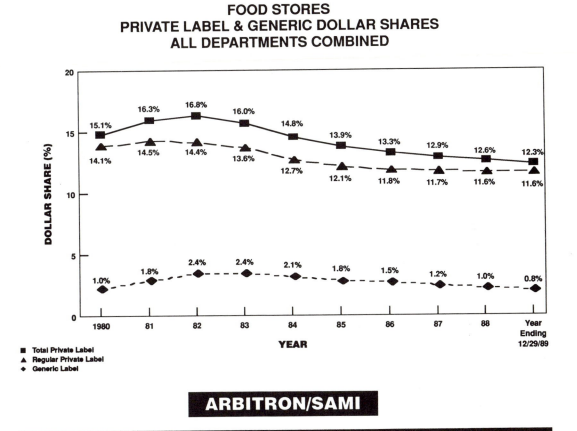

■ Total Private Label
▲ Regular Private Label
◆ Generic Label

ARBITRON/SAMI

SAMI chart, taken from PLMA Special Report, July 1990, tracks only warehouse product withdrawals; direct store, product deliveries not included. Copyright owned by Information Resources Inc., Chicago, IL.

16

The Era of Scanning

Market research evolves pretty much like everything else. When SAMI failed to modernize or did not muster the support to change accurately into scanning data, its future turned gloomy. In October 1990, SAMI ceased to exist, signing over rights to its clientele plus its tie-in with Arbitron data to Information Resources Inc., Chicago. IRI itself had evolved with its expertise in building a database from scanning data. Its InfoScan reports began in January 1987 and have since improved with sophistication. IRI learned to identify brands from private labels, the former sold by any retailer, the latter being exclusive to a retailer. *Private Label* published its first InfoScan private label report for calendar 1990, showing a dollar volume of $22.7 billion for private label in 165 product categories—109 of them gaining and 54 losing over the previous year. Overall, private label sales were up by 4.9% for the year.

For 1991, IRI's database was expanded to 195 categories, showing private label sales at $25.8 billion, up 2.2% over the previous year. IRI says that it tracks only 2,700 supermarkets (each with sales of $2 million+) in 64 major US markets, because it's too expensive to report on all 32,000+ US supermarkets. Its coverage, however, does extend to regions in less densely populated areas to allow for geographic coverage nationally.

IRI remains confident about its data, especially since it has been "validated" by major package goods companies which compare sales and market share with their own internal reporting systems.

Information Resources, Inc., founded in 1979, has built its reputation around standardizing the industry to the use of scanner data, thus changing the methods that the packaged goods industry collects and uses for consumer purchase information. In 1986, IRI introduced its InfoScan syndicated service, measuring the performance of products sold through supermarkets, drugstores, and mass merchandisers. Its weekly sales and price data, collected from 2,700 supermarkets, picked up the advantage of Arbitron in 1990. Today, IRI also reports on about 500 drugstores and some 250 mass merchandisers in 10 cities.

In InfoScan's 1991 Vendor Multi-Category Report for Private Label (the year ending Dec. 29, 1991), out of 195 product categories, collectively representing $25.8 billion—up 2.2% over calendar 1990—the top five categories commanded 39.1% of those sales, the top 10 claimed just over half (50.6%), while the top 20 categories exceeded more than two-thirds of total private label sales (63.9%). Of those 20 product categories, eight slipped, each by no more than 5% from 1990, while the balance showed strong gains: cold cereal up 33.4%, diapers up 16.9%, cookies up 12.1%, shelf-stable juices up 8.1%, carbonated beverages up 6.9%, cheese (the #3 category) up 5.4%, ice cream (#4) up 5.3%, chips and snacks up 5%, etc.

InfoScan showed the biggest private label dollar gains at the bottom of its listing for items like refrigerated lunches up 871.9% to $336,112, frozen cookies up 427.6% to $118,562, oral hygiene products up 116.2% to $432,346, meat pies up 139.1% to $745,516, etc. But there also were impressive gains near the top of the chart—the larger volume categories, such as cigarettes up 39.8% to $74.1 million plus those categories mentioned above in the top 20.

CHART 2

INFOSCAN'S TOP 10 PRIVATE LABEL CATEGORIES

—SALES DOLLARS—

Categories	1991 Dollar Sales	
	($ Millions)	(Change from 1990)
Total Private Label Sales	$24,774	—
1. Milk	5,432	-2.8%
2. Fresh Bread & Rolls	1,556	2.1
3. Cheese	1,370	5.4
4. Ice Cream	911.9	5.3
5. Frozen Plain Vegetables	815.9	-4.2
6. Carbonated Beverages	620.3	6.9
7. Shelf-stable Vegetables	604.7	-1.1
8. Sugar	603.9	-2.1
9. Frozen Juices	540.9	-4.8
10. Shelf-stable Juices	518.1	3.9

SOURCE: Information Resources, Inc. 1992.

The IRI data shows three categories each with more than a 50% category share of sales, the biggest private label category of all, milk taking the largest share at 64.1%, followed by cheesecake at a 56.5% share, and frozen fruit at 50.9% share. Five other categories claim a 40-to-50% share, the biggest taken by frozen plain vegetables (the #5 category) at 46.5%, followed by dry beans/vegetables at a 43.6% share, then refrigerated bread/baked goods at 42% share, the #8 category of sugar next at 41.6% share, and butter at a 40.3% share. Ten other categories are in the 30-to-40% share range, while 20 fall into the 20-to-30% share range. That totals 38 categories in all at 30%+ market share, leaving a balance of 157 categories at under 20% share each—43 of them in the double-digit range. (See Chart 2A in the Glossary for a complete reading of all 195 categories.)

When InfoScan tracks unit sales in 1991 for these categories, private label shows a stronger gain overall—up 3.4% to 22.9 billion units. The unit sales tally again puts milk on top at 3.2 billion units, followed by the #2 category, fresh bread and rolls at 2.1 billion units. After that, shifts occur in the descending order, showing carbonated beverages next at 1.4 billion units, then shelf-stable vegetables at 1.2 billion units. Cheese, #3 in dollar sales, slips to fifth spot at 840 million units and other shifts in 'the pecking order' follow after that.

Of the 195 categories traced, only 45 are off from 1990 in unit sales. The size of these losses are in small increments, all under the biggest loss of 33.6%, suffered by hair spray (except for the smallest unit category listing, non-shelf-stable non-fruit drinks off 99.2%). Unit sales gains, however, produce 10 categories each with in excess of 33% unit share gains—some at an astonishing rate, such as refrigerated lunches up 939.1% and frozen cookies up 712.9%, both near the bottom of the listing. IRI also found 31 categories each with a 30%+ unit share gain, while five of them claimed more than a 50% share: first aid treatment at 64.9%, milk (the #1 category) at 62%, frozen fruit at 55.3%, pest control at 54.3%, and frozen plain vegetables (the #5 category) at 52.5%. Outside of the egg substitute category, which was established in 1991 with a 32.8% unit share, there were no other additions for 1991. (See Chart 3A in the Glossary for a complete reading of unit share data in these 195 categories.)

CHART 3

INFOSCAN'S TOP 10 PRIVATE LABEL CATEGORIES

—UNIT SALES—

Categories	1991 Unit Sales	
	(Millions)	(Change from 1990)
Total Private Label Unit Sales	22,884	3.4
Milk	3,171	1.5
Fresh Bread & Rolls	2,095	0.3
Carbonated Beverage	1,388	3.8
Shelf-stable Vegetables	1,182	2.9
Cheese	840.7	9.9
Frozen Plain Vegetables	809.7	-4.0
Frozen Juices	627.1	6.5
Shelf-stable Fruit	523.2	-0.3
Tomato Products	498.9	6.5
Ice Cream	467.8	6.8

SOURCE: Information Resource, Inc. 1992.

Nielsen Marketing Research, Northbrook, IL, which calls itself the world's leading marketing and media information services company, operating in 28 countries, began its first full-year report on private label ("controlled brand") and generic market share in 1987, showing that total market share at 14%, but then slipping to 13.6% in 1988 and 13.3% in 1989 for supermarkets at $4 million+ in sales. Then Nielson changed its reported methods, offering private label data on a full-year basis, up through the first quarter of the year. The recent data (now available) so far covers only edibles, that is, dry grocery, frozen, dairy and deli products (excluding fresh meat, produce and any deli products not prepacked). Nielson covers supermarkets with $2 million+ in sales for this report.

Interestingly, Nielsen's tracking of private label in the 1990s so far shows weaknesses in each department, except the biggest, dry groceries—its dollar and unit shares climbing upward steadily. Frozen, dairy and deli show a decline, particularly in the latest figures, the year that ends in the first quarter of 1992.

While recent data for non-food private label is not available from Nielsen at this writing, another market researcher, Towne-Oller and Associates, Inc., New York, has been tracking data on health and beauty care volume in food stores for years. Unfortunately, the private label breakout is not shared outside of its clientele. T-O did publicize private label market share up until 1988, at which time, private label share was outpacing the total Health-and-Beauty-Care (HBC) category sales in both dollar and unit volume. The researcher showed private label share for 1986 in food stores up by 13% versus the total category's 3.5% climb. For 1987, similar results were recorded for dollar volumes: up 14.5% in private label versus 7.3% for the total category. In unit volume, private label advanced by 8.3% versus the total category climb of 4.8%. These results, in fact, embarrassed the national brand manufacturers, who pay T-O for its research. The firm, therefore, stopped publicizing the private label sales gains thereafter.

Towne-Oller, however, has been kind enough to share some of its recent data for both food stores and drugstores, covering the 12-month period, ending May 1992 versus a year earlier. Ranking the top 10 HBC categories by dollar volume, T-O again finds private label gains outpacing the total categories in the food stores; while in drugstores, private label is ahead in most categories. The food stores show private label registering gains of from 6% in shampoos up to 460% in menstrual tampons. The biggest private label category share is found in vitamins and tonics at 31% (up 8%); second is mouthwashes at 11.4% (up 16%) next is analgesics (the #1 category) at 10.8% (up 10%), followed by cold remedies at 9.8% (up 30%). (T-O's overall focus is on a $12.6 billion HBC market in food stores). In unit sales volume, private label shows strong gains as well, except for shampoos, up only 1%.

The top 10 HBC categories in drugstores repeat six categories from food stores; ranking them 1 through 6: analgesics, cold remedies, vitamins, tonics, antacids, deodorants and shampoos. Six of the top 10 categories show gains in private label share in both dollar and unit volume. In this market segment, vitamins and tonics again claim the biggest dollar market share for private label at 37.6% (up 6%), followed by laxatives at 20% (up 7%), then cold remedies at 19.3% (up 12%), and so on. Only two HBC categories overall show declines, shampoos and contact lens preparations, which also declined in private label. On a unit share basis, the pattern is similar, where vitamins/tonics take the biggest private label share at 48.9% (up 6%), followed by laxatives at 31.7% (level with previous year), cold remedies at 27% (up 5%), and analgesics (#1 category) at 25.5% (up 7%).

GUIDE TO CHARTS
(PAGES 124 – 134)

CHART 4

TOP 10 HBC CATEGORIES
(12 MONTHS THROUGH MAY 1992 VS. 1991)
FOOD STORE AUDIT DOLLAR SHARES

Category	Total $ Volume (Millions)	% Change	Private Label Share (%)	Private Label % Change
1. Analgesics	$1,302.4	-2	10.8	+10
2. Dentrifices	816.4	+3	1.0	+56
3. Deodorants	778.1	—	1.0	+22
4. Shampoos	760.4	-6	2.3	+6
5. Cold Capsules/Tablet-Powder & Liquid	739.3	+6	9.8	+30
6. Razor Rack	434.8	+2	5.3	+17
7. Antacids	387.6	+4	4.4	+30
8. Vitamins & Tonics	376.8	+3	31.0	+8
9. Menstrual Tampons	347.0	+6	0.4	+460
10. Mouthwashes	333.7	-12	11.4	+16

SOURCE: Towne-Oller 1992.

CHART 5

TOP 10 HBC CATEGORIES
(12 MONTHS THROUGH MAY 1992 VS. 1991)
FOOD STORE AUDIT UNIT SHARES

Category	% Change	Private Label Share (%)	Private Label % Change
1. Analgesics	+2	15.9	+14
2. Dentrifices	-1	1.7	+58
3. Deodorants	+1	1.3	+25
4. Shampoos	-3	2.7	+1
5. Cold Capsules/Tablet-Powder & Liquid	+4	16.3	+21
6. Razor Rack	-6	8.8	+7
7. Antacids	-1	5.3	+26
8. Vitamins & Tonics	+1	41.3	+8
9. Menstrual Tampons	+8	0.4	+507
10. Mouthwashes	-12	17.3	+16

SOURCE: Towne-Oller 1992.

CHART 6

TOP 10 HBC CATEGORIES
(12 MONTHS THROUGH MAY 1992 VS. 1991)
DRUGSTORE AUDIT DOLLAR SHARES

Category	Total $ Volume (Millions)	% Change	Private Label Share (%)	Private Label % Change
1. Analgesics	$983.7	+11	19.1	+15
2. Cold Capsule/Tablet Powder & Liquid	711.9	+10	19.3	+12
3. Vitamins & Tonics	555.3	+4	37.6	+6
4. Antacids	369.1	+6	9.7	+10
5. Deodorants	362.5	+2	2.6	-1
6. Shampoos	363.5	-6	3.8	-2
7. Diagnostic Kits	363.9	+25	2.5	+11
8. Contact Lens Preps	346.7	-4	4.7	-6
9. Laxatives	341.3	+3	20.0	+7
10. Face Makeups	346.0	+5	0.0	—

SOURCE: Towne-Oller 1992.

CHART 7

TOP 10 HBC CATEGORIES
(12 MONTHS THROUGH MAY 1992 VS. 1991)
DRUGSTORE AUDIT UNIT SHARES

Category	% Change	Private Label Share (%)	Private Label % Change
1. Analgesics	+2	15.9	+14
2. Cold Capsule/Tablet Powder & Liquid	+6	27.0	+5
3. Vitamins & Tonics	+2	48.9	+6
4. Antacids	+2	12.4	+4
5. Deodorants	+1	3.5	-4
6. Shampoos	-6	4.1	-6
7. Diagnostic Kits	+13	1.7	+10
8. Contact Lens Preps	-26	10.5	-8
9. Laxatives	0	31.7	0
10. Face Makeups	+2	0.0	—

SOURCE: Towne-Oller 1992.

CHART 8

FULL-YEAR DOLLAR/UNIT CONTROLLED
LABEL SHARES (1989-92)
PERIOD ENDING 1ST QUARTER OF EACH YEAR
(BILLIONS/% OF DEPARTMENT SHARE)

DEPARTMENT	1989	1990	1991	1992
Dry Grocery				
Dollar Share	$8.6	$9.2	$9.8	$10.1
	(10.6%)	(10.5%)	(10.6%)	(10.8%)
Unit Share	14.5	14.9	15.5	15.8
	(18.3%)	(18.2%)	(18.6%)	(18.9%)
Frozen				
Dollar Share	$2.6	$2.7	$2.8	$2.7
	(16.0%)	(15.3%)	(15.2%)	(14.6%)
Unit Share	4.7	4.5	4.6	4.6
	(29.5%)	(28.2%)	(28.4%)	(27.7%)
Dairy				
Dollar Share	$7.9	$7.8	$8.4	$8.3
	(34.1%)	(34.2%)	(34.5%)	(34%)
Unit Share	18.8	19.4	19.9	20.0
	(46.1%)	(45.9%)	(46.2%)	(45.7%)
Deli				
Dollar Share	$0.048	$0.068	$0.073	$0.068
	(9.2%)	(8.4%)	(7.1%)	(6.3%)
Unit Share	0.037	0.044	0.045	0,040
	(15.1%)	(14.0%)	(12.4%)	(10.5%)
Total Dollar Share	**$19.1**	**$19.8**	**$21.1**	**$21.2**
Total Unit Share	**38.0**	**38.8**	**40.0**	**40.4**

SOURCE: Nielsen 1992.

CHART 9

TOP 20 CONTROLLED LABEL CATEGORIES
DOLLAR VOLUME-1990

Product Category	Volume Millions	(%Gain/ Loss)	Product Category	Volume Millions	(%Gain/ Loss)
1. Dairy-milk refrigerated	$7,222,054	(+14.8%)	11. Lunchmeat sliced-refrig.	$355,034	(+1.3%)
2. Bakery bread- fresh	1,468,331	(+5.4%)	12. Butter	347,422	(-7.1%)
3. Eggs-fresh	1,368,768	(+4.3%)	13. Cheese- cottage	297,521	(+7.1%)
4. Soft drinks- carbonated	764,495	(+12.6%)	14. Cereal ready-to-eat	280,946	(+35.8%)
5. Ice cream- bulk	690,753	(+2.2%)	15. Bacon- refrigerated	277,160	(+18.0%)
6. Sugar granulated	707,524	(+7.0)	16. Cheese- shredded	274,471	(+22.6%)
7. Fruit Juice orange-frozen	428,267	(+5.3%)	17. Cookies	263,188	(+8.2%)
8. Bakery-buns- fresh	442,211	(+5.7%)	18. Disposable diapers	253,700	(-10.7%)
9. Fruit Juice - orange other containers	403,390	(+2.7%)	19. Snacks- potato chips	234,770	(+4.0%)
10. Cheese- processed slices American	393,046	(+17.2%)	20. Vegetables mixed-frozen	229,456	(-1.0%)

Source: Nielsen Marketing Research 1991.

CHART 10

TOP 20 CONTROLLED LABEL CATEGORIES
DOLLAR VOLUME SHARE (AT 50%+ OF THEIR CATEGORIES)

Product Category	1990 Category Share (%)	Change Vs. 1989	Dollar Volume (000)	%Change Vs. 1989 (Points)
Cheese-natural-brick	69.1	+10.5	$1,154	-2.8%
Eggs-fresh	66.7	-0.5	1,368,768	+4.3
Vegetables-lima beans-frozen	66.2	-1.5	58,961	+10
Vegetables-carrots-frozen	65.3	+1.2	24,059	-4.1
Vegetables green beans-frozen	62.6	-0.9	93,745	-2.8
Vegetables-broccoli-frozen	60.6	+1.6	145,319	-0.8
Fruit juice-grapefruit-frozen	60.5	+4.8	20,116	+3.9
Bakery biscuits-fresh	60.0	-5.9	8,001	-14.8
Dairy-milk-refrigerated	58.9	+0.6	7,222,054	+14.8
Vegetables-remaining frozen	57.3	-0.1	167,754	-3.5
Sugar-granulated	56.4	-0.6	707,524	+7.0
Fruit juice-grapefruit-canned	56.1	+0.1	45,498	-7.8
Milk-powdered	54.2	+3.3	69,089	+21.6
Canned fruit-grapefruit	53.9	+3.9	10,360	+2.7
Vegetables-beans-wax canned	53.8	-4.1	6,586	-5.6
Cherries-maraschino	52.3	-2.7	136,527	-4.9
Vegetables-corn-frozen	51.6	-3.2	111,434	-3.3
Vegetables-potato canned	50.9	-2.6	27,676	+0.7
Fruit juice-orange-canned	49.9	+1.0	28,051	+3.5

Source: Nielsen Marketing Research 1991.

CHART 11

CONTROLLED LABEL/GENERIC SALES*
(MARKET SHARE PERCENTAGES IN PARENTHESES)

Year ending mid-December	1988*	1989*	1990**
Controlled Label Brands Total Measured Packaged Goods			
($ Millions)	$19,831.8	$20,999.5	$31,737.7
Market Share	(13.6%)	(13.3%)	(8.7%)
% Change vs. year ago	+3%	+6%	NA
Generic Brands Total Measured Packaged Goods			
($ Millions)	$938.0	$828.5	$895.5
Market Share	(0.6%)	(0.5%)	(0.3%)
% Change vs. year ago	+8%	-12%	NA
Total Controlled Label/ Generic Brands			
($ Millions)	$20,769.8	$21,828.0	$32,633.2
Market Share	(14.2%)	(13.8%)	(9.0%)
% Change vs. year ago	+2.7%	+5.1%	NA

*Sales importance in US Supermarkets $4 million+

**Sales projected for all US food stores. Market share is based on Nielsen's estimate of food store sales of $363,207 million, or 20.1% of total US retail sales of $1,807,000 million for 1990—based on data from the US Dept. of Commerce; Bureau of Census.

Source: Nielsen Marketing Research 1991.

CHART 12

1990 CONTROLLED LABEL/GENERIC UNIT VOLUMES (MILLIONS)
(BY CATEGORY)

	Controlled Label	Generic
Dry Groceries	15,684.1	492.2
Frozen	2,756.3	34.5
Refrigerated	8,648.2	74.8
Non foods/ general merch.	2,141.2	280.6
Health & Beauty Aids	273.6	4.6
Total of all categories	**29,503.4**	**886.7**

Unit volumes projected for all US food stores.

Source: Nielsen Marketing Research 1991.

CHART 13

CONTROLLED LABEL SALES TRENDS*
(BY CATEGORY)

Year ending mid-December	1988*	1989*	1990**
Controlled Label Brands Total Measured Packaged Goods			
($ Millions)	$19,831.8	$20,999.5	$31,737.7
% Change vs. year ago	+3%	+6%	NA
Dry Grocery			
($ Millions)	$7,938.9	$8,373.3	$11,921.2
% Change vs. year ago	+4%	+5%	NA
Frozen			
($ Millions)	$2,491.0	$2,497.7	$3,450.2
% Change vs. year ago	+4	0%	NA
Refrigerated			
($ Millions)	$6,962.1	$7,490.6	$13,389.7
% Change vs. year ago	-1%	+8%	NA
Non-foods/general merchandise			
($ Millions)	$2,063.2	$2,220.4	$2,247.9
% Change vs. year ago	+4%	+8%	NA
Health & Beauty Aids			
($ Millions)	$376.7	$417.5	$728.7
% Change vs. year ago	+18%	+11%	NA

*Sales importance in US Supermarkets $4 million+
**Sales projected for all US food stores.

Source: Nielsen Marketing Research 1991.

CHART 14

GENERIC BRAND SALES TRENDS*
(BY CATEGORY)

Year ending mid-December	1988*	1989*	1990**
Generic Brands Total Measured Packaged Goods			
($ Millions)	$938.0	$828.5	$895.5
% Change vs. year ago	+8%	-12%	NA
Dry Grocery			
($ Millions)	$450.3	$394.4	$450.0
% Change vs. year ago	+9%	-12%	NA
Frozen			
($ Millions)	$37.6	$31.8	$33.9
% Change vs. year ago	+28%	-16%	NA
Refrigerated			
($ Millions)	$95.9	$82.6	$109.9
% Change vs. year ago	-8%	-14%	NA
Non-foods/general merchandise			
($ Millions)	$336.7	$306.3	$292.7
% Change vs. year ago	+11%	-9%	NA
Health & Beauty Aids			
($ Millions)	$17.4	$13.5	$9.0
% Change vs. year ago	-2%	-23%	NA

*Sales importance in US Supermarkets $4 million+
**Sales projected for all US food stores.
Source: Nielsen Marketing Research 1991.

17

Segmentation Equals Maturity

"One thing Nielsen data suggests is a positive correlation between retail concentration and private labels. That is, where retail turnover in a given country is controlled by a relatively small number of players, that country is fertile ground for the growth of private label goods," according to Carolyn Huey, manager of marketing and sales for the Global Information Services Division of Nielsen Marketing Research, speaking in Sao Paulo, Brazil in October 1989 at an industry trade conference. Ms. Huey cited concentrated markets like Australia and Canada, where the "top 10" retailers control 97% of the trade buying versus Japan with only 14% or Italy with 35% such concentrations.

Nielsen, which started its first European office in the United Kingdom in 1939, has steadily built up its coverage of the European market: 10 countries in the 1960s up to 17 countries in 1991. In the first major effort at "harmonizing" its data, this division issued a 1990 study, called "Nielsen European Passport, A Strategic Assessment of the New European Grocery Marketplace." Thomas Ottinger, European manager of Nielsen Europe's Global Information Services, Lucerne, Switzerland, addressing the 1991 Private Label Manufacturers Association's trade show in Amsterdam, pointed to one significant development: The emergence of supermarkets. Nielsen projects in its European Passport that hypermarket and large and small supermarkets will control 58% of European turnover in fast-moving consumer goods by 1993. The top grocer retailers, Mr. Ottinger indicated, are growing at a tremendous rate. From 1983-88, the top seven grocers grew at a 3.5% annual rate in number of stores and a 5.5% rate in trading space. Recent developments have been more dramatic; for example, Tesco in the UK is expected to increase its total selling space by almost 25% within three years; while in Spain, 5,400 clerk shops closed in the past year, as 23 new hypermarkets opened, making them the market leaders in that country for the first time with a 26% market share in grocery retailing. The speaker added that these major retailers also are diversifying into non-food activities, such as health and beauty care, clothing, textiles, fashions, etc.

These developments bode well for private labels, which, Mr. Ottinger observed, are "getting bigger and improving in quality." He indicated that there now is a segmentation in the private label marketplace. Segmentation, he added, is a sure sign of "a fully mature private label marketplace, where marketers are commited to branding their products." This has come in evolutionary stages, from

CHART 15

13.5 Market share and growth of own label products

Annual growth rate (1983–88)

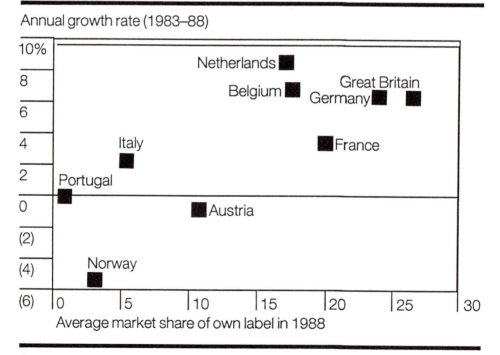

Source: Nielsen European Passport Survey

CHART 16

13.6 Own label market share: all stores vs. own label stores

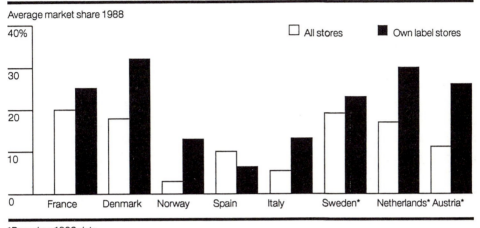

Average market share 1988

Based on 1986 data
Source: Nielsen European Passport Survey

inexpensive generics, to special private label lines at chain stores, to own labels carrying a retailer's name, to "private brands" of high quality. One example: Monoprix in France, which has high-quality Monoprix Gourmet, low-calorie Monoprix La Forme, ecological Monoprix Vert, and ready-to-eat Monoprix Vite Pret brands.

DISTRIBUTION PATTERNS

Beginning with a limited perspective in a 1987 study of 11 major European countries, Nielsen Marketing Research International Division, Paris, averaged private label market share at 15.9%, based on its weight sampling of common product categories, averaging 27 per country. This study found that except for those countries with overall market share distributed among many retailers, such as in Norway, Sweden, and Spain, "a consumer niche" was developing in private label between a 20 to 30% market share. (Interestingly, those retailers with private label programs in Norway or Sweden, for example, were found to give private label strong support.) At that time, Nielsen also found private label distribution in

CHART 17

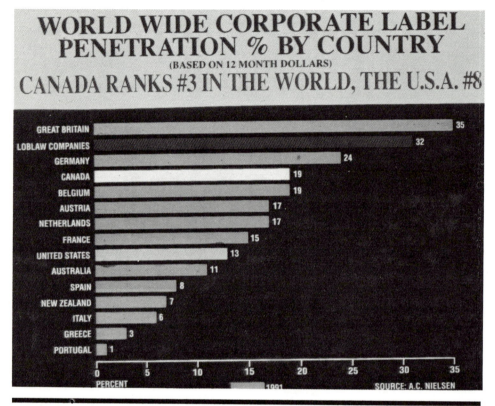

**WORLD WIDE CORPORATE LABEL
PENETRATION % BY COUNTRY**
(BASED ON 12 MONTH DOLLARS)
CANADA RANKS #3 IN THE WORLD, THE U.S.A. #8

GREAT BRITAIN	35
LOBLAW COMPANIES	32
GERMANY	24
CANADA	19
BELGIUM	19
AUSTRIA	17
NETHERLANDS	17
FRANCE	15
UNITED STATES	13
AUSTRALIA	11
SPAIN	8
NEW ZEALAND	7
ITALY	6
GREECE	3
PORTUGAL	1

PERCENT   1991   SOURCE: A.C. NIELSEN

This perspective of 'corporate label' market penetration in selected countries was presented by Loblaw Company at the June 1992 PLMA Consumerama meeting in Toronto. The Nielson data for 1991 shows Loblaw ranked second behind Great Britain, while Canada's overall private label penetration is third in country ranking. Germany is listed second perhaps because Aldi stores are factored into the total market.

retail outlets was greatest in Great Britain at 74.8%, then France at 72.7%, the Netherlands at 71.9%, and West Germany at 64.5%. Those countries, in fact, are the leaders in Europe for private label. Nielsen estimated private label volume share at: 24.8% for Great Britain, 17.3% for France, 21.3% for the Netherlands, and 16% for West Germany.

In its more recent data, Nielsen's European Passport Survey (1989), 12 countries are tracked, where the private label market share is averaged out to 15.6% in 1988. In eight of those countries, Nielsen shows private label growth rate at 4.9% average per year from 1983 through 1988. The private label share for those eight countries averages out to 12.5%. When Nielsen focuses only on those retailers stocking private label, that average shoots up to 21.6% share.

The price discount on private label versus brands varies from country to country, from a low of 8.2% in both Denmark and Sweden up to a high of 36% in Switzerland. These variances in price differential have indicated to Nielsen that price alone does not move private labels. Consumers look for value or a "unique selling point" in each product.

The latest Nielsen data, unveiled at a 1992 PLMA Consumerama meeting in Toronto shows private label shares more on an international scale.

Another market research organization, Frost & Sullivan, Inc., New York, reporting in "The European Market for Private Label Food and Drink," published in 1990, takes measure of seven countries, showing the total retail market for food and beverages in 1989 at $447 billion. Some 18% or $81 billion goes to private label, according to F&S. The researcher expects that share to climb to 20.4% or $190 billion by 1994, as the total market increases to $535 billion.

EUROMONITOR'S OWN BRAND REPORTS

Perhaps the most market research efforts have been focused on the United Kingdom's own label phenomenon. This is understandable since England in particular leads the world in private label commitment.

Euromonitor, London, a leading market analyst in the UK, through the 1980s has issued three "Own Brands Reports," the most recent for 1989, which indicated that own brand sales growth still significantly outpaces that of total retail sales and total sales of packaged foods. Its study found that own brands for 1988 were worth £26 billion or 23% of all retail sales in the UK. While the report also indicated a "slowing" of own brands growth in some sectors and a "ceiling of own brands market penetration in the grocery trade soon to be reached," it also predicted that own labels will account for 27% of total retail sales by 1992. The report also showed own brands with major shares in cooking oils, paper products, bleaches and disinfectants, and canned and frozen vegetables.

Euromonitor noted that Marks & Spencer was the largest own brand retailer, Sainsbury was the largest own brand retailer selling other own brands, and the Burton Group was the largest non-food own brand retailer, the latter with 75% of its sales in own brand. Burton, which started in men's tailoring shops along with its own manufacturing, has diversified over the years into womens wear, children's wear, and even department stores. The report indicated that "the Burton Group is a supreme example of market segmentation, with its various subsidiary chains under different fascias, targeted at defined sectors of each market. There is no one own brand—far from it, for the multiplicity of fascias results in a multiplicity of own brands. These are not necessarily exclusive to the particular fascias from which they take their name, but are also to be found in other Group stores: for example, Principles for Men is to be found in Debenhams and so is Top Shop. There are usually several exclusive brands to be found in each store group..."

Euromonitor provided a "short requiem" for generics, reporting their emergence in the UK in 1977, subsequently achieving a share of only 1 to 2% of the grocery market. The ranges were limited, consisting mostly of staple high-volume products like tea, instant coffee, washing-up liquid, toilet tissues and pet food; while prices were on average 20 to 25% below own brands and up to 50% below manufacturers' brands. The trend now is toward "value products rather than basics," according to the report.

Since the own label market in England is truly the most outstanding in the world, a more recent look from another indigenous market research source is in order. Mintel International Group Ltd., London, has issued a "Special Report, Own Label in Packaged Grocery Retailing 1991," which shows own label accounting for one-third of all packaged grocery sales through grocer retailers—up by 4% since 1985. Retail sales in England are concentrated in the hands of the multiples, most specifically the top five grocery multiples. They account for 47% of sales, while the large multiples overall account for 63% of sales, as reported by Mintel for the period 1989-90. Mintel further observes: "Leading multiples have developed their own marketing skills to improve operating performance. This had involved developing a unique identity around the retail store offer, which consumers perceive as being a brand in its own right." This retail brand strategy involves development of "an accurately targeted retail offer, which includes creating an identity and values for that brand to give it a unique position in the market and exploitable competitive advantage to rival other retailers." Their strategy, in effect, centers around "the concept of strategic branding to the extent that they feel own label products are often more appropriate to the needs of target consumers than branded products. During the 1980s, this was manifested in 'healthier' products, and in the late 1980s and early 1990s the emphasis moved towards environmental friendliness.

"Own label is, therefore, no longer seen solely as a cut-price alternative but as encompassing the whole ethos and is crucial to the retail brand offer."

Their strategies vary. Mintel cites Marks & Spencer as setting exacting standards for its suppliers plus seeking innovation in its own label ranges. Sainsbury follows the same strategy, Mintel continues, but with a focus on ranges for everyday usage; Waitrose focuses on the more affluent consumer in the South East, offering own label quality products at a price, while collecting around 40% of its packaged grocery sales in own label; Tesco stresses added value to its own label products, improving their quality with emphasis on change to constantly upgrade and improve products from its "rigorous product testing," Safeway with a long own-label track record offers a diversity of selection; and ASDA, which in 1985 switched from a brands-only policy, establishes own label as a key element in its sales mix. The exception is Kwik Save which has no own label products, maintaining its distinction in the market as a discounter of major brands.

ASDA Stores Ltd., Leeds, positions itself as England's market leader in superstores. Its ASDA brand products debuted in 1986 first in stable foods like baked beans, sliced carrots and marrowfat processed peas. Within the first year, this retailer, which today carries some 30,000 food, clothing, home and leisure lines, built its own label range to 1,000+ products. The next year that range multiplied to 2,500 products. Today, there are more than 8,000 ASDA brand products in both food and non-food lines. The firm's strategy for own brands basically is:

- to improve customer choice,

- to allow for innovation,

- to control its product offer, and

- to strengthen its company identity and image.

Mintel measures an average unweighed market growth of 40% for 30 packaged grocery categories in current price value terms since 1987 versus a 30% actual growth in all spending on food for in-home consumption for the same period. In volume terms, the average market growth was 21%, while just under one-third of the categories studied experienced a decrease in volume sales. "This suggests," the researcher notes, "a shift across all the categories towards more value-added products, largely prepared and part-prepared foods, reflecting the trend towards convenience." For the categories studied, own label penetration in constant price terms is 25%. The categories with the highest level of own label penetration are: wine (61%), dry pasta (51%), jam (47%), and potato crisps (41%). Lowest own label penetration levels are: low-fat spreads (6%), colas (8%), detergents (8%), and canned steak (8%).

In those 30 categories, Mintel finds 13 static in the past four years, 10 increasing, and seven with the brands gaining share. Mintel also notes that: "Research indicates a high degree of disloyalty to brands and suggests regular switching between over time. Thus, choice, variety and interest are likely to influence consumer buying decisions and promotional activity—as well as new product development—all having a role to play in keeping consumers interested in what is going on in-store."

GUIDE TO CHARTS
(PAGES 143 – 146)

EUROMONITOR DATA

CHART 18

TRENDS IN TOTAL RETAIL SALES AND OWN BRAND SALES IN THE UK (1980-1988)

£ million	Total retail	% annual growth	Own brands	% annual growth
1980	£58,377	–	£10,010	–
1981	63,164	8.2	11,065	10.5
1982	69,784	10.5	12,600	13.9
1983	76,168	9.1	14,450	14.7
1984	82,790	8.7	16,500	14.2
1985	89,240	7.8	18,500	12.1
1986	96,425	8.1	21,000	12.3
1987	104,415	8.3	23,600	12.4
1988	114,500	9.7	26,600	12.7

Source: Business Statistics Office/Euromonitor estimates.
Copyright 1989 - Euromonitor's UK Own Brands Report, London 1989.

CHART 19

OWN BRANDS TOTAL MARKET SHARE IN THE UK (1980-1988)

% total retail sales

1980	17.1%
1981	17.5
1982	18.1
1983	19.0
1984	19.9
1985	20.7
1986	21.8
1987	22.6
1988	23.2

Source: Euromonitor estimates.
Copyright 1989 - Euromonitor's UK Own Brands Report, London 1989.

CHART 20

ESTIMATED OWN BRAND SALES BY MAJOR UK RETAILERS
1987

	£ million	% of total sales
Marks & Spencer	4,175	100
Sainsbury (including Homebase)	2,000	55
Tesco	1,650	40
Co-op	1,250	24
Burton Group (including Debenhams)	1,000	75
Argyll Foods (including Presto & Safeway)	800	25
Boots	750	34
BhS (subsidiary of Storehouse Group)	600	92
Gateway	600	12
Next	400	50
MFI	400	90
Littlewoods	375	75
C&A	375	75
Bejam	350	64
Waitrose (subsidiary of John Lewis)	350	55
Woolworth Group (including B&Q, Comet, Superdrug)	350	17
Asda	300	11
British Shoe Corporation (subsidiary of Sears – including Freeman, Hardy & Willis, Saxone, Dolcis)	300	60
Mothercare (subsidiary of Storehouse Group)	250	100
John Lewis	250	26
Dixons (including Currys)	325	20
House of Fraser	200	15
Spar	150	20-25
WH Smith (including Do-it-All)	120	12
Electricity Boards	90	10
Other retailers	6,190	8
TOTAL	**23,600**	**23**

Source: Euromonitor estimates.
Copyright 1989 - Euromonitor's UK Own Brands Report, London 1989.

CHART 21

UK OWN BRAND SALES BY PRODUCT SECTOR
1987

	Consumer retail spending £ million	% share own brand	Own brand sales £ million	% total own brand sales
Food (in home)	33,643	27	9,000	38.1
Alcoholic drinks (off-trade; est)	5,200	20	1,000	4.2
Tobacco	7,653	8	600	2.5
Menswear	4,974	48	2,400	10.2
Womenswear (including girls & infants)	9,634	35	3,400	14.4
Footwear	3,180	52	1,650	7.0
DIY goods	3,715	24	900	3.8
Furniture and floor coverings	4,707	21	1,000	4.2
Major appliances	3,832	7	250	1.1
Soft furnishings	1,864	24	450	1.9
Hardware	2,479	10	250	1.1
Household cleaning products	1,379	25	350	1.5
Radio, television durable goods	3,158	14	450	1.9
Sports goods, toys, camping goods	2,819	14	400	1.7
Other leisure goods	4,253	8	350	1.5
Books, newspapers magazines	3,529	3	100	0.4
Pharmaceutical products (est)	600	17	100	0.4
Cosmetics and toiletries (est)	3,300	20	650	2.8
Jewellery, silverware, watches, clocks	1,886	8	150	0.6
Other goods (est)	2,611	6	150	0.6
TOTAL	**104,415**	**23**	**23,600**	**100.0**

Source: Euromonitor estimates/Central Statistical Office.

Copyright 1989 - Euromonitor's UK Own Brands Report, London 1989.

CHART 22

OWN BRAND PACKAGED GROCERIES IN RELATION TO
WHOLE UK GROCERY SECTOR
1980 - 1988

£ million	Turnover all grocers	Sales of packaged groceries	Sales of own label packaged groceries	% packages groceries
1980	£17,371	£5,800	£1,280	22.0
1981	19,296	6,300	1,470	23.5
1982	21,071	6,900	1,720	25.0
1983	22,571	7,300	1,900	26.0
1984	24,015	7,900	2,130	27.0
1985	25,895	8.600	2,410	28.0
1986	27,775	9,500	2,750	28.9
1987	29,980	10,500	3,150	30.0
1988	32,240	12,000	3,700	30.8

Source: Euromonitor estimates based on various sources.
Copyright 1989 - Euromonitor's UK Own Brands Report, London 1989.

18

Today's Value-Driven Consumers

Recession, unemployment, mounting credit card debts, job insecurity, these recent economic problems are making consumers today much more value-conscious about what they buy. They want the price of goods lowered, but they are not willing to compromise on quality. In effect, consumers, knowing better economic times, have become smarter shoppers, particularly when it comes to buying private labels, which they recognize now as delivering quality comparable to national brands, but at a lower price.

Brand manufacturers are not standing by idly. Some of them have adopted the practice of Every Day Low Pricing, which grocery retailers have used for some time in different competitive situations. The EDLP concept for brands may create more price parity between brands and private label, as the branded manufacturer cuts out promotional monies, special deals and the like to offer his products at the lowest price possible. That EDLP brand, however, can be sold by a competitor the same way—competitively priced in the market. The retailer with private label has something extra: an exclusive quality range, which has added appeal when it's an upscale line, still offering value with the very best quality at or below the national brand pricing.

Consumer attitudes about store brands were documented in May 1984 by The Gallup Organization, Princeton, NJ in a special report, "Gallup: Store Brands Vs. National Brands, The American Consumer Speaks Out," commissioned by the Private Label Manufacturers Association, New York. This survey was subsequently updated and issued in May 1991 by the same parties as "Gallup: Store Brands in the 1990s."

One of the most striking differences between the two studies was the consumer's change in perception about store brands versus national brands. The first report showed a pretty much divided concensus, 42% of consumers agreeing that store brands "are equal or better quality than nationally-advertised brands," while 44% disagreed, and 14% were unsure. In the more recent Gallup report, a strong 67% of consumers felt "store brands items usually perform as well or taste as good as nationally-advertised brands." In fact, the quality issue has become

CHART 23

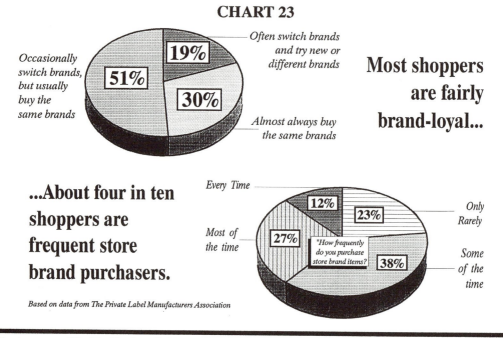

Often switch brands and try new or different brands

Occasionally switch brands, but usually buy the same brands

Almost always buy the same brands

Most shoppers are fairly brand-loyal...

...About four in ten shoppers are frequent store brand purchasers.

Based on data from *The Private Label Manufacturers Association*

Every Time

Most of the time

"How frequently do you purchase store brand items?"

Only Rarely

Some of the time

Chart courtesy of The Food Institute, Fairlawn, NJ

more of a priority in their shopping habits. The second study also showed 83% of consumers citing quality as the most important factor in repurchasing a store brand, while 73% quoted price. The earlier Gallup report revealed 80% listing quality as "very important," and 74% indicating price.

The 1991 Gallup study identified 51% of consumers as occasionally switching brands, and 19% often switching brands. In 1984, most consumers, 56%, said they always buy the same national brands, while 35% noted they switch between different national brands. More brand switching now, of course, indicates less brand loyalty.

Other key findings from the 1991 Gallup survey of 1,215 primary grocery shoppers (18 years or older) via telephone were:

- About 86% of shoppers have purchased a store brand, those most likely to do so being the brand switchers, middle income consumers ($25,000 to $45,000), and males.

- Versus a year ago, about 33% of shoppers are buying more store brands, while 11% are buying less; additionally, 20% anticipate buying more store brands next year and 5% plan to buy less. Increased store brand purchases are motivated uppermost by price savings (50% of consumers), while 12% name improved quality of store brands as the chief factor.

- On average, 25% of shopper's grocery purchases are store brand items.

In the world of private labels, the label owners are not always the 'usurpers,' so to speak. In 1980, Topco Associates, Skokie, IL, a buying co-op of retailers, placed its Valu Time private label cigarettes on a second-tier pricing level. Many of the major retailers followed suit with their generic private label brands, Kroger's Cost Cutter, Safeway's Scotch Buy, etc. By 1983-84, this new price-value segment—quality as good as the brands but at a lower price—convinced R.J. Reynolds to price its Doral brand down into this price segment; other brand competitors copied with their brands, such as Alpine, Viceroy, Cambridge, Raleigh, Montclair, etc. Since 1985, Brown & Williamson Tobacco Corp., under a licensing agreement with Marketing Management, Inc., Ft. Worth, an account specific private label broker, has produced and distributed GPC Approved plain/private label cigarettes. Five years later, that brand was repositioned at an extra low-price and now sells below extra low price. Packaging also has been produced in 11 styles to distinguish this brand from other plain/private label offerings. All this manuveuring has made this B&W generic entry the 10th largest selling brand in the US during 1991, according to the Maxwell Consumer Report (Feb. 10, 1992). In fact, Maxwell says that for 1991 "the price-value category continued its momentum, increasing to 25% of the market. Branded generics grew to 10.7% of the market from 10.4% in the previous year. Black & Whites were up 2.9% points (almost double) for the year in share of the market. Sub generics increased, up 3.3 points in share of the market.

Interestingly, in Maxwell's top 10 brands, every premium brand, including kingpin Marlboro fell in points for the fourth quarter of 1991, except the RJR Value brand, Doral (#6) up 5.7%, and B&W's generics brand (#10) up 80%.

19

The European Single Market & Private Label

"Nearly all of the European retailers think that own-labels will play a more important role in their marketing strategy in the future and that their market share ought to advance still further ... The total opening of frontiers (post 1993 in the European Single Market) will enable an enlargement of the range offered in private labels and bargain products. Some manufacturers, whose margins are weak or in decline will be able to clutch at this as at a straw."

This prediction by SECODIP (Société d'études de la consommation distribution et publicité) Chambourcy, France, is contained in its 1992 study, "Manufacturers, Retailers and Consumers in Europe, Prospects for After 1993," published by the Institute of Grocery Distribution — Europanel Database in three volumes. This comprehensive, "truly European (market research) venture," brings together the efforts of SECODIP, the European member in France; its partners Openers Euro Socio-Styles, AECOC, AFT-IFTIM, and INA (Institute National Agronomique); and the Europanel members AGB UK, Dympanel (Spain), and G&I (Germany), plus the expertise of Eric Maillard, Etienne Thil, and Gerard Mermet, editor of the report. Olivier Geradon de Vera, managing director of SECODIP, conducted this research project. The report offers some interesting data about private label, especially in five countries, where overall awareness of private label is 70%, the rate of awareness at 85% in both Spain and Italy, 81% in Britain, 75% in France, and 65% in Germany. Consumers in Germany and Great Britain, especially feel that their "ideal store" of the future would contain more private label, registering response rates of 47% and 48%, respectively. Enthusiasm for private label diminishes in other countries: Spain at 40%, France at 39%, Belgium at 37% and Italy at 20%.

In the five countries under study, consumers perceive private label products as less expensive and of comparable quality to major labels. Price differentials are especially "clear" to shoppers in Great Britain, Germany and Spain. The German consumers are "most enthusiastic" about private label quality (a 90% rate), while the other countries show a weaker rate between 80 to 90%.

Retailers in each country, SECODIP's study indicates, project a different image about private label. In Germany, Edeka private label products are perceived as being as expensive as other products; in Spain, Alcampo and Mercadona private labels have a slightly less favorable image than that of products from other chains in terms of quality and level of confidence; in France, Carrefour carries the "best image" for private label, while Leclerc and Continent obtain scores of confidence below the average for all French chains; in Italy, Esselunga's own labels score the highest in quality and confidence; while in Great Britain, Gateway's own label are regarded as "very inexpensive," carrying a lower level of confidence. (Marks & Spencer was not factored into this analysis.)

SECODIP also finds that basic foods are preferred as private labels over national brands; while the most sophisticated products (frozen vegetables, fresh pasta, cereals or powdered soups) are purchased infrequently as private labels. The exception is in Great Britain, where own label has a strong following in these categories, according to the report.

When consumers were asked if they would buy a product if it existed under private label, the positive response rate often exceeded 30%. Italians were most receptive to this idea, especially for expensive products. This is understandable, SECODIP says, since private labels are not widespread in that country; but the study also contradicts the opinion of Italian retailers who do not believe in the growth of private labels or in the Aldi discount store concept.

The report indicates that private label over the past 10 years has registered "very strong growth," but within a great diversity of products and strategies covered by that term. In Germany, for example, all the large retail groups sell own labels products; but together, excluding Aldi, their private label market share is estimated at 5%. Aldi by contrast sells on price—30 to 40% lower than its competitors—stocking only 700 lines with no known brands. National brands, in fact, take less than 5% of its stock. Its 700 m2 stores are Spartan in appearance, displaying goods in their shipping cartons or on pallets.

In quizzing 50 European retail distribution management sources, SECODIP discovered that the Germans are the least interested in own labels: "They do not play a major role in their marketing strategy and this role will barely increase in the future."

For Great Britain, the report tracks own label market share from 22% in 1980 to 30.5% in 1990. It's expected to continue growing in this highly-concentrated market, where four chains take more than half the total grocery turnover. Retailers there view the new high value-added products as providing high margins.

France, too, has witnessed private label growth, up from 11.2% in 1980 to 19.6% in 1990. But within this market, private label share varies from 30% at Monoprix to 5.5% at Euromarche. Actually, four chains carry between 20 to 30% private label share of sales (Monoprix, Casino, Intermarche, and Carrefour) while operations like Systeme U, Leclerc and Mamouth keep the share around 10%.

SECODIP traces rapid private label market share growth in Spain, up from 1.7% in 1984 to 8.7% in 1990. This market, however, remains very fragmented, where the top nine chains carry 29% of the groceries, 17% of perfumes, and 32% of household products. While Simago (neighborhood stores) and El Corte Ingles (department stores) have carried private label for decades, it is really the top four chains, all of French origin, that have been in the forefront of private label development. Continente (19 hypermarkets from the Promodes group), starting with six products in 1981, now stocks more than 500 private label items, representing 13% of its sales. That share is expected to climb to 20% in 1992. Of its 60 best-selling lines, the study adds, 30 are under the Continente label.

Alcampo (Auchan group's 17 hypermarkets) started with private label in 1985 with private label, now has some 350 mass-consumption products under the Pryca label plus another 700 non-grocery products under its Diseno identity. In the markets where private label is stocked, the chain claims 38% private label share in groceries, 27% in fresh produce, 10% in textiles, and 17% in bargain items, and 8% in small household electrical goods.

Like the Aldi concept from Germany, DIA (359 grocery discount stores of the Promodes group) has some 500 private label lines, claiming 50% of turnover. Promodes' acquisition of Dirsa with 989 outlets is expected to expand this operation in Spain.

Also in this country, the cooperative chains command 50% of the market, all of them relying on private label: Spar with 600 own labels, representing 11% of its turnover; Una Vivo with 314 own label lines, taking 4% of its turnover; and IFA Espanola with 10% of its sales in private labels like IFA, Cibon, Suki, and Bajel.

Other players in Spain are the Makro cash-and-carry operation which has 4% of its turnover in private label and the Eroski co-op with 807 lines, taking 25% of its sales, under different identities, carried in its supermarkets, hypermarkets, cash and carry outlets and other stores.

For Italy, dominated by "old-style stores, markets and small self-service stores," the retail structure is fragmented, where hypermarkets take only 6% and supermarkets just 37% of the market. Private label's presence has existed the longest in the Coops, Standa (neighborhood stores) and Rinascente (large stores);

but more recently (since the 1970s) private label also has emerged in Despar, A&O, Selex, Vege, Conad, and Crai. The overall private label share does not exceed 6%, yet retailers in Italy do plan to develop their lines in the future, according to SECODIP. Most retailers do not want to expand beyond the basic big-volume ranges. Only the co-ops are looking into more sophisticated private label products.

The growth of Aldi in Germany (2,300 outlets there generating DM 23 billion of its total DM 33 billion volume) has over the past 15 years spread to Austria (130 stores), Belgium (249 stores), Great Britain (30 stores) and France (32 stores). Aldi also has spun imitators like Dia in Spain with 391 stores, Carrefour's Ed or Europa Discount (300 stores), Norma (33 stores), Lidl (49 stores) all in France, etc. Retailers like GB Inno and Delhaize in Belgium, for example, have reacted by developing "bargain brands," like *produit economic* (a white product range with a piggy bank-and-coin motif) and Derby, respectively. These ranges, SECODIP notes, allow retailers to keep their private label image, offering the "bargain" items at prices lower than private label and in some cases cannibalizing private label sales. The report continues: "The growth in the number of products sold under label names and the presence of 'bargain' products in the high-volume markets will reduce the shelving space available for national brands. The (market) leader has nothing to fear, the challenger will keep its guard up, but the third, fourth and lower-placed labels will have difficulty in finding space on the shelves."

SECODIP also indicates that in all European countries, the areas most often cited as difficult for private label entry are: detergents, chocolates, baby foods, soft drinks and cosmetics—all protected by powerful brands and manufacturers' know-how.

The report generally notes that despite the economic convergence of countries in Europe, along with the less developed countries catching up, "widely differing patterns of consumer dynamics can be observed in countries of comparable economic performance ... Fewer British (9% in 1990) than French or German (more than 30%) own a dishwasher; the Spanish are at the same level as the British. On the other hand, more British people (52% in 1990) than Germans (27%) or French (22%) own a microwave oven; the same applies to tumble-dryers and video recorders." Religious practices, while in decline, still play a role on attitudes toward money, the body and material life, for example, the study adds: "Protestant Europe uses twice as much soap as Catholic Europe. Fish is still eaten on Fridays and lamb at Easter in the countries of the south of the Community."

Demographic differences in the population, regarding age, unemployment, life-styles, etc., also come into play by regions of Europe. All this means that "Europe will remain a multiple market for a considerable time."

Consumption trends are heading toward dietary and low-calorie products, as the "heavy" products (potatoes, pasta, sugar) decline. Additionally, soft drink consumption has increased, while fruit juices particularly in France and Spain are gaining market share and mineral water growth has been "spectacular." Frozen product consumption, between 1980 and 1988, doubled in most countries, the report adds.

The Coop program in Germany has hit a responsive chord with consumers, who favor more private label stock in stores. Coop's product range varies widely over a number of categories as seen here.

V

Today's Trends

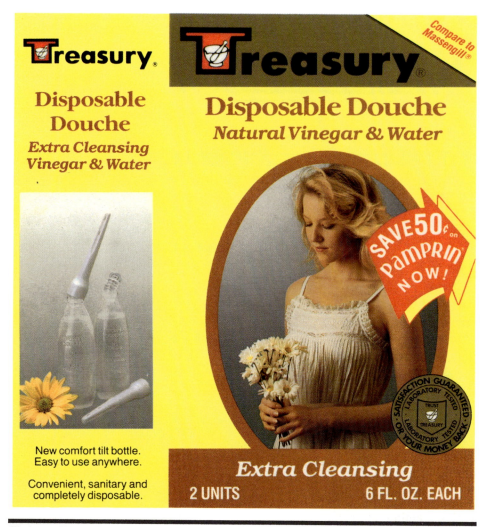

The largest US supplier of private label douches, Aid-Pak USA, Glouster, MA, provides this product to Thrift Drug, Pittsburgh, PA. Its product is positioned against a brand, "Compare to Massengill," it carries a "Satisfaction Guaranteed or Your Money Back" seal along with a Laboratory Tested emblem, plus it offers a 50-cent coupon on another brand, Pamprin diarrhoetic pills, made by Chattem, Inc. The packaging graphics are beautiful for such a personal product.

20

What's Happening to 'Me Too'?

"Private label is a win-win business. Our customers enjoy consistently fine quality at exceptional savings. We enjoy higher margins and brand loyalty that can be satisfied only at Safeway." — 1991 Annual Report, Safeway, Inc., Oakland, CA.

"The Company promotes a branded marketing philosophy for all its store brand and national value brand products, working as a partner with its customers to design account-specific, sales-building programs. These include innovative promotions such as cross-merchandising with national brands, couponing, displays, and trial sizes, as well as consumer market research, utilizing both direct to consumer mailings and professionally moderated focus groups." — 1991 Annual Report, Nutramax Products Inc., (Aid-Pak), Gloucester, MA.

This support for private label from Safeway, a major US supermarket chain (estimated 15%+ of its total sales or $2.3 billion in private label), and Aid-Pak, a major category manufacturer (estimated 55% of its sales or $14.3 million in private label) coupled with a growing consumer acceptance of top-quality private label products in attractive, modern packaging, priced lower than leading name brands (especially important during recessionary time) and supported with "brand-like" marketing, altogether is slowly helping this industry to shed its 'me too' image—an image that once relied only on price as the most important selling point. Built-in value is what sells today's sophisticated consumer.

While the days for private label copycat packaging are not quite over, they are becoming more passé, Around the world, retailers are now setting higher quality standards, creating new, sometimes unique product and/or packaging ideas for their private brands...

In the highly-fragmented market of Japan, for example, the food-oriented ryohanten retailer Seiyu has established a strong private label grocery presence with its Majirushi Shohin line plus its Seiyu program. Mujirushi Shohin is based on three principles to realize exceptional value: unique raw materials sourced abroad, sophisticated and thorough inspection procedures, and simple packages. In October 1990, Seiyu launched the S'Ribbons private label line—priced like national brands, but offering superior quality through process control and raw material sourcing. This new program replaced its Seiyu line, which promoted both price and quality. The retailer, part of the Seibu-Saison Group, admits that its move was inspired by own label retailers like Marks & Spencer, Sainsburys and others in the United Kingdom. Seiyu now calls S'Ribbons a 'retailer brand' or 'the national brand from Seiyu."

Discounter Aldi with its low-priced Amica label helped establish shelf-stable ready meals in Germany. This technology was first developed in 1983 by canned goods producer Robert Klein, who invented a three-section PET tray with separate hot-sealing of the sections, thus allowing a great variety of food products of high quality to be packed shelf-stable for months without chilling or freezing. Mr. Klein, who supplied Aldi, also developed his own Benedict brand and did contract work for Unilever (its Du darfst brand) and Nestle (its Maggi brand). But lacking capital, he had to eventually sell out to Nestle Germany. Meantime, Aldi's Amica brand at its lower price became a market leader in this category. Interestingly, Aldi was on the ground floor of this pioneering effort with a private label.

In Switzerland, Migros is now doggedly pursuing effective environment practices, such as:

- REQUIRING that 90%+ of its Migros brand batteries no longer contain mercury or cadmium,

- SELLING stringless, unbleached tea bags without the paper tab or aluminum staple,

- PROMOTING its M Plus cleaning household agents as more biodegradable and featuring refill bags (refill bags also available for its private label coffee, spices and cosmetics),

- PACKAGING its own refrigerated milk in special light-inhibiting plastic bags, and

- GROWING cereal grains for whole wheat bread in fields that ban the use of pytoregulators, insecticides, and fungicides, etc.

Britain's most profitable and largest food retailer, J. Sainsbury is rolling out new Sainsbury's brand products at a clip that any name brand manufacturer would envy: 1,500 new items in 1991 alone. Its latest selection includes creative new taste sensations, such as Sorbet & Cream (a combination of sorbet and ice cream), Pak Choi Chinese cabbage, 'loose' bacon strips (not packaged), Boboli pizza (its base enriched with olive oil, parmesan and mozzarella cheese), 36 vintage selections of wine out of 106 new wines added, etc. This new product development covers many proprietary products.

MARKS & SPENCER'S 'ARTISTIC' TOUCH

There's no question that Marks & Spencer has pioneered in the marketing of high-quality chilled ready meals—as good as those made at home. Its St Michael exclusive brand has come to be recognized as the number one best-seller in different product categories, i.e., take-out sandwiches, ladies knickers (underwear), fish products, and so forth. Its new product introductions—everything under the St Michael label—constitute a marketing study by itself. The strategy is simple: Develop new products, working as a partner with manufacturers, using the latest technologies; put the new item into some test stores, highlighted only with a small "NEW" shelf talker, then track sales. If the items proves to be a sales success, it is then rolled out into other stores. St Michael packaging is kept simple and straightforward. M&S in partnership with its manufacturers produces the highest quality products. In fact, this retailer approaches its work almost like an artist.

In the summer 1992 issue of its "The M&S Magazine," the "art of fruit juice tasting" is outlined, showing how M&S sets quality and freshness as its top priorities. "Every day at the company's head office in London's Baker Street, there are tastings to judge whether a juice is suitable for sale. The M&S team tastes to see if a juice is too pithy, unripe, over-ripe or just right..." Its team "scours the world, following the seasons to such far away places as South America, Florida, Israel, Egypt, the Mediterranean countries and the Caribbean." It taps into "a wealth of tantalizing flavors—from traditional orange, grapefruit, ruby orange, and pink grapefruit to such blends as orange with raspberry puree. For that traditional taste, there's even a good old-fashioned still lemonade made with freshly squeezed lemon juice. In the pipeline for the freshly squeezed treatment are orange and apricot and a traditional still ginger beer made from freshly squeezed lemon juice and fresh root ginger."

In the article, M&S soft drink technologist Phillip Kent says: "We bring the whole fruit to this country, and once it has been washed, squeezed and chilled, it's in our stores within 24 hours." Packed in bottles, M&S experts combine one, two or even three types of fruit into a product, because "different climates give different flavors...the fresh and sharp Mediterranean oranges, and the sweeter flavors from Florida and the Caribbean and this specialist fruit knowledge goes into creating each blend which is tasted at least twice a week." This slick, four-color magazine, sold in its stores, also informs consumers about new products at the M&S stores.

Through the years, Marks & Spencer has established a foothold in a number of European countries, Hong Kong, and Canada with its own store concept. But in the United States, M&S has chosen acquisitions—Brooks Brothers clothing stores and Kings Super Markets. In the latter case, M&S is working its own label ideas into the format, in dry groceries as well as the toiletries area with the St Michael brand, but in the prepared food section, using a combination label: Kings of Marks & Spencer. The priorities of quality and freshness are at work here in a wide selection of refrigerated desserts, salads, vegetable, side dishes, sandwiches, and entrees. Items include kabobs, fusilli salad, quiches, chicken pot pie, chili with beans, etc.

In France, Monoprix, a variety store retailer, has just unveiled a new generation of natural cosmetics with no perfumes added. Its 'naturellement Monoprix' line of nine items includes milk to remove makeup, a night cream using egg yolk oily extracts for nourishment of the skin and plants like camomile and lime in a vegetable complex to calm the user, or a day cream made of onager oil for nutrients, rose oil and a vegetable oligoproteins (including pine and lemon) to protect the skin and a sun screen. For the past couple of years, Monoprix has addressed natural products in its private label program covering foods, household items and chemical cleaners, plus bath products like shampoos and conditioners. Its tradition has been to provide luxury, high-quality products to the average shopper. The new naturellement Monoprix line is no exception. Even its packaging is natural, using fine ribbed corrugated brown cardboard boxes with beige paper labels and unpolished glass or white tube cylinders inside, sealed with white caps. The graphics are elegantly executed with a plain but sophisticated line drawing on each container, suggesting the part of a woman's body that the product treats.

Also in France, Carrefour, which just acquired Euromarche, has long been an innovator with an attitude asset (not problem). Its thinking is aptly summed up by Amédée Chome, executive director in charge of the mission (a special section of Carrefour): "When you are a leader, everybody follows you. And when you are followed, you must be different to always be out in front of the competition." Carrefour jumped out front in 1976 with its *produits libre* line of products that are "brand free (and) as good as the best, but less expensive." This move helped inspire a revolution in food distribution around the world with the debut of generic products. Then in 1986, Carrefour distinguished itself further with the establishment of a "Cellule d'Innovation" at the University of Anger, under the direction of Prof. Bernard Taravel, director of the university's Science and

Simplicity of design from France. (Above) Monoprix's 1992 line of natural cosmetics (naturellement Monoprix) with only a suggestion of the parts of a woman to be 'treated.' (Right) Carrefour 1976 introduction of "produits libre," that is, brand-free products. Only the Carrefour logo is carried on the bottom band.

Petit-déjeuner

Poids net : 1 kg e

Technologies in Innovation program. With his students, Prof. Taravel worked with Carrefour to develop new products, new services and new technologies. Carrefour called these products—such as a dentrifice to whiten teeth, a caramel-type spread for bread made from milk, a sponge for dusting that "breathes in" and holds the dust, etc. — Innovation on the label.

In Canada, Loblaw calls many of its private label products unique. Influenced by European private label trends, Loblaw kicked off its move toward unique corporate brands with the No Name yellow label generic program in the late 1970s—organized like a first-line private label program just the way Carrefour had programmed its 'brand-free' program (carrying a tiny Carrefour logo). In 1983, Loblaw launched its upscale President's Choice program with the Decadent chocolate chip cookie made with butter and containing 39% chocolate chips versus the brand leader Nabisco's Chips Ahoy!, containing 24% chips. The Decadent cookie's smashing success led to other "superior quality" products in the program, eventually extending into environmentally-friendly G.R.E.E.N products—the first such private label line in North America—and "Body Friendly" G.R.E.E.N food products, with controlled fat and cholesterol content. The latter line evolved into the new Too Good To Be True range of healthy foods. This overall strategy has centered around Loblaw's belief that "'marketing is the art of meaningful, sustainable differentiation.' The ultimate marketing strategy is found in the President's Choice program of unique families of unique products," as stated in a recent Loblaw advertisement.

While most of Loblaw's efforts have centered in the food area, the firm lately is developing more unique non-foods items as well: One recent example: President's Choice's Out of Africa 2-Minute Botanical Shampoo/Conditioner for dry scalp and dandruff. This product contains unique botanical extracts, such as stinging nettle, horsetail, coltsfood, and aloe vera. It also has shea butter, "a vegetable emollient derived from a tree in the West African savanna to promote shiny manageable hair."

It is not uncommon for both Loblaw and Carrefour to often work with talented individuals, inventors, chefs, etc. in creating new private label products. Loblaw, for example, now works with the Lipid Clinic in Toronto General Hospital in an effort to produce "nutritionally superior products," within its Too Good To Be True line, items like no-oil salad dressing, low-fat yogurts, bread slices containing under 50 calories etc. Carrefour discovered a cook in a small village in France who had developed a special fish mousse recipe. Carrefour made it into its *mousee de brouchette* which in 1990 sold one million boxes—amounting to close to $3 million in sales.

While Loblaw admits to being influenced by the Europeans, it also pays tribute to a regional food chain, Trader Joe's, So. Pasadena, CA. This 36-store chain is cued right into its customer's health, pocketbook, and gourmet fancies, offering numerous exotic or unique items—branded and private label. With a penchant for punning and/or dubbing products with interesting or humorous names, Trader Joe's puts its own name on items like Habeus Crispus; Big Hawaiian Style Vinegar Potato Chips, which are naturally flavored and cooked in safflower oil—made to order for the chain; and Aristocats entrees for cats, featuring no preservatives, artificial colors or flavors. Sometimes the chain dubs a product Trader Darwin vitamins or Trader Giotto's Italian bread. This presentation was originally made to consumers in a highly readable newsletter, *Trader Joe's Insider Report*, which impressed Loblaw so much that it purchased the rights to the name, *Insider's Report*, which it now publishes four time a year, each edition reaching 100 million circulation as a newspaper insert in Canada. Its *Dave Nichol's Insider's Report*, which was voted the best newspaper insert of 1989 in Canada, reaches nearly 60% of the households in Ontario province. Readers are said to spend no less than four hours reading it! Meantime, Trader Joe's continues issuing its newsletter under the new identity, *Fearless Flyer.*

21

Toward "Brand Essence"

At the 1989 Private Label Manufacturers Association's (PLMA) trade show in Rosemont, IL, Colin Porter, a founder and head of design for Coley Porter Bell, a London-based package design consultant, described "brand essence," which European retailers have harnessed in their private labels, as being "equal and beyond the brands." This phenomenon practiced foremost in the United Kingdom, has spread across Europe and into Canada.

"What started as a way of improving margins and undercutting the prices of branded goods has now become a battle to improve the quality of private label and hence create a strong corporate image." Mr. Porter continued: "Retailers have certainly developed a new responsibility towards their consumers via private label, addressing green environment problems, innovations in new product development; and the manufacturers have a huge role to play in this new scenario. Flexibility and innovation are key, but the rewards are to be found in margin and profitability." He further noted that the US grocers' margins are "pitifully low at approximately 1.5%" versus the UK average of around 5.7%. "Manufacturers in this scenario seem on the whole to be locked into high-volume/low-margin mainstream products, which is a vicious spiral. With the domination of manufacturers brands and the control of retailers, private label suppliers need to break out of emulating branded competition and generics and seek opportunities to add value."

Mr. Porter's firm has been doing just that through its work for A&P "...looking to move its private label range away from a generic price platform to one which

The back panel of A&P's Master Choice frozen pizza box tells the quality story – real cheeses, handmade crust, whole tomato sauce, Italian spices, etc., all part of a Chicago pizzeria recipe: Truly "Gourmet Pizza."

still offers honest value for money, but which creates product promise. Not necessarily a brand leader 'me too' either, but simply bringing the emotion of the product to the fore through its packaging..." His firm also is working to maximize private label through the Master Choice retail format. That identity, he noted, "sums up the personality and statement of the brand: Using the best ingredients, supplied by the best manufacturers, presented in the best possible way and with every attention to detail that Master Choice suggests. Manufacturers are sourced internationally and must be recognized as leaders in their own field. Pricing, interestingly enough, considering the normal psychology of buying private label, is also pitched at a 'premium' level. Master Choice products' price points are level with the brand leader equivalent or even more expensive, but less than the imports."

The Master Choice program, now with more than 130 items, and positioned as an alternative upscale choice to A&P's first-quality labels, has not "outdone" all the national brands it competes against. In fact, A&P reportedly is contemplating a strategy change, following the lead of Loblaw's President's Choice and Wal-Mart's Sam's American Choice with an America's Best program.

It is support from the manufacturer and the retailer that counts most. A&P apparently has not given Master Choice all the support it deserves, especially with products that represent such outstanding quality and packaging. A consultant can put together strategies for the client, but the retailers in this case must execute these strategies along with tactical support.

A 'pro' in this area, Zal Venet, president of Venet Advertising, NY, speaking at a PLMA Leadership Conference in Ft. Lauderdale, FL in March 1991, put it best: "The national brand is every bit as good as our brand...(and) remember, anything they (national brands) can do, you (private label) can do cheaper." Mr. Venet, whose agency for decades has supported effective advertising for the Pathmark label, owned by Supermarket General Holding Corp., Woodbridge, NJ, offered 10 strategic rules to follow:

1. COMMITMENT to value and savings identified in the private label program via a broad array and availability of merchandising; offers of substantial price savings, value comparisons in signage, rotos, circulars and advertising; contemporary packaging; effective displays; a meaningful balance of stock between national and private brands; and store personnel indoctrinated as to the value of private label.

2. CONTINUITY in the year-long business plan, sticking with the game plan to develop awareness and sales and penetrating all the basic merchandising activities in the store.

3. COMPARISON of pricing side-by-side with the national brand.

4. SAVINGS emphasized and reemphasized in dollars and cents terms: "'Save 29 cents on the 8-ounce can' is one of your most powerful selling messages."

5. GUARANTEES on the product with the store name on the package signalling a commitment of satisfaction: A money-back guarantee without question.

6. COMFORT, that is, addressing the psychology of consumers who once thought that private labels purchases meant a loss of status, because at a cheaper price they were considered inferior. The image of value comes into play here.

7. ADVERTISING private labels to make them look important, again zeroing in on the value-and-savings comparisons, but with appeal: "It's the best awareness-builder you can employ."

8. SALES PROMOTIONS, using what the national brands use—coupons, large-size pack savings, on-pack offers, illustrated displays, end-aisle displays, in-store demonstrations. Also punch up store signage, hand out colorful rotos on circulars, use ROP, radio-TV, in-store broadcasting, whatever promotes the program.

9. OPTIONS — keep them open, but always give the customer an option of choice: private label at a savings versus the national brand.

10. BALANCE stock by not going overboard into too much private label or too much into brands, keeping enough penetration in both by product category to make private label look important throughout the store.

Mr. Venet also offered a dozen tactical tips:

1. PACKAGING—upgrade it to four-color and foil presentations or glass containers—and ensure that the label information is up to date and easy to read.

2. PRODUCT QUALITY should never vary—always kept at the very best.

3. PRICE ADVANTAGE by always keeping that advantage over the brand and never allowing for parity pricing.

4. NEW PRODUCTS flowing onto your shelves, featured and handled the way new brand products are introduced.

5. STORE TRAFFIC—built up with coupons.

6. THE ADVERTISING MIX, experimenting until the right combination is found between national versus private brand, which can vary from week to week.

7. SIZING private label to include trial sizes to stimulate new users , a value buy or even spark indirect interest to the product (from the recipient of a trial-size gift).

8. NATIONAL BRAND COPYCATTING — of formulations, packaging innovations, convenience or product features that target customers (health or diet conscious), etc.

9. IN-STORE ACTIVITIES, including demonstrations to convince customers of the quality or a good taste of a product.

10. LARGE-SIZE packaging to compete with the club membership packs.

11. SPECIAL MARKETS addressed, such as ethnic market needs or attention to minority groups with easy-to-understand packaging.

12. PRICING—frequently pre-price the item to broadcast its value.

Mr. Venet's advice—perhaps one of the meatiest "how-to" sessions at a PLMA meeting—can be summarized in one word: SUPPORT.

A "SENSATIONAL" REPORT

Other sound advice came more recently from another PLMA speaker, Herbert Meyers, managing partner of Gerstman & Meyers, Inc., New York, a design firm, at a Tuscon, AZ, Leadership Conference in March 1992. Mr. Meyers suggested when introducing a new private label brand or repositioning an existing store brand, "the first rule is to be unique and to create an image that will generate curiosity and interest from customers. Private label packaging that either copies or tries to look like the leading national brands will only breed confusion and fail to build equity for the store brand..." Equal attention should also be paid "to the overall brand identification in packaging, advertising, merchandising, retail store design, signage, and various types of promotions, the character of all these should be developed as a whole in order to build the brand's franchise. It is not enough to simply rubber-stamp a logo on all packages or using stock vignettes, available at little or no cost from your label supplier. The only way to compete head-to-head with national brands is to look just as good or better and to communicate product quality. Only then can your private label brand be marketed as an alternative to the national brands, rather than just as a cheaper product. Offering the alternative of purchasing products at a better price that are of equal quality, will build store and brand loyalty. It is critical that the label program communicates this clearly to the consumer."

Mr. Meyer has applied this rationale to the relatively new Sensational brand introduced by First National Supermarkets, Cleveland, OH, owned by Ahold N.V. Zaandam, The Netherlands. The client's stores already carried a generic brand, Guaranteed Value, and a "budget brand," Finast. Sensational brand offered them premium (not luxury) quality products at a lower price than national brands. The target customer for this new line is the quality-oriented, somewhat higher-income and educated consumers.

He explained: "Entirely produced on computers, our package design program started by developing a unique, eye-catching brandmark that is the cornerstone of the program and that unifies the entire brand line. The post-modern brandmark with its geometric shapes is easy to spot and conveys a contemporary, somewhat European image. The geometric shapes create many additionally opportunities for various uses: as pointers to draw attention to the product, as bullets to highlight product attributes or emphasize features on a package, as window shapes to allow consumers to see the product they are buying, or as decorative details and borders. The shapes are also lifted from the packages and used for shelf hangers, in-store displays and other promotional needs. The brandmark communicates quality, is easily recognizable in the supermarket, conveys an upscale image and, applied to packaging, provides strong shelf impact—boldly standing out among the national brands."

It is not surprising that parent Ahold is now moving the Sensational program into its other US properties, including Bi-Lo, Mauldin, SC; Giant Food Stores, Harrisburg, PA; and Tops Markets, Inc., Buffalo, NY.

A brand's trade name and trade dress are among the few elements left that can be owned and legally protected in today's marketplace, according to Elinor Selame, president of Selame Design, Newton, MA. "Whether it's a house brand (private label) or national brand, the elements are the same. These include its name, positioning (reason for being), trademark/trade dress (symbols, colors, typestyle, package configuration) and brand communications. These brand elements, when successfully developed and managed, create a strong identity for a company or retail store. Over time, this creates strong brand authority."

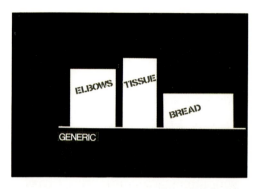

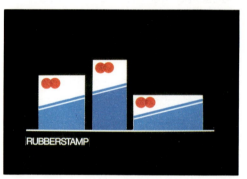

Private labels pick up "brand authority" through these four major routes: generic or no identity, identical 'rubber stamping', retailer's identity highlighted, and individual proprietary brands per category. Photos courtesy of Selame Design.

That "brand authority" has been established in the private label world via four major routes, says Ms. Selame. They are:

1. The GENERIC BRAND, which carries no store or brand identity, makes minimal use of color, utilizes cheaper packaging materials, and works best in the product categories of household cleaners, paper products and condiments.

2. The RUBBER STAMP BRAND, which is the most cost-effective strategy, using the identical corporate name, symbol, typestyle and color on all products.

3. The RETAIL BRAND ENDORSEMENT, highlighting the retailer's name and identity but with the packaging design, color and graphics varied depending on product categories.

4. The PROPRIETARY BRAND, where products take on their own identity with little or no indication of their true ownership in order to project a national brand image to a retailer's products. This branding strategy, in fact, appears to gaining the most momentum in the marketplace today.

22

Exporting Exclusivity/ Adopting A Personality

"If there is a world consumer emerging, then there is a world market. Harvard's Ted Levitt forecast it already in his ground-breaking 1983 article, 'Globalization of Markets.'* But recently, companies are reacting to it more and more ... Consumers everywhere want good quality products at a fair price." Prof. Fred W.I. Lachotzki, vice-chairman, ASKO Deutsche-Kaufhaus AG, speaking at the PLMA 1991 Private Label Trade Show. (*Harvard Business Review*, May-June 1983, pp. 92-102.)

In the past, when private labels have been exported, they usually have been adopted as just another brand without any exclusivity attached. Efforts lately, however, have been directed more toward exporting not only products, but the private brand equity and image built into them. For decades, branded manufacturers have been building their "brand trust" on a global basis. What happens when a private brand owner decides to market that brand in another country via an acquisition, a licensing agreement, or a subsidiary operation?

Quoted above, Prof. Fred Lachotzki represents a giant German retailing operation, a market leader in four retail formats: out-of-town hypermarkets, DIY building marts, furniture, and discount clothing outlets in out-of-town locations. ASKO Group's 1992 projected sales are DM 22 billion, while an additional DM 8 billion sales come from a hypermarket joint venture with Metro (Metro and Massa concepts combined), called MHB. Half of its total consolidated sales derive from food sold in classic discount supermarkets, out-of-town hypermarkets, and a wholesaling operation.

ASKO also is the driving force behind the O'Lacy's international private brand in Europe—an A-brand quality range, priced competitively against the brands. It's a 500-plus item range that Prof. Lachotzki has described as one "with personality, with added value, with an umbrella label; a product range that took into account the environment; and a product range that was internationally usable and a defense against possible strategic alliances without ASKO." This international private brand is based on a fictitious consumer, Isabelle O'Lacy, the first part of that identity coming from one of ASKO's operations, Isabelle, and the last part, a common name, O'Lacy's, which can be protected worldwide. In May 1990, the line was launched with 300 basic food and non-food items, carrying the O'Lacy's brand. ASKO now holds the exclusive license in Germany; while the program is promoted internationally through O'Lacy AG, Biel, Switzerland.

In part, the O'Lacy's program works where suppliers pay O'Lacy's a small royalty, while licensees pay for their own sales promotion and advertising material. The language on the packaging and in the sales material and photography varies from country to country, while the brand itself receives point-of-sale support plus TV commercial backing. The line is positioned 10 to 15% under the price of comparable top brands. Within four months of the launch, three non-competing chains, Vomar, Konmar, and Nieuwe Weme in the Netherlands formed a buying union to pick up the program; and in June 1991, O'Lacy's also was licensed in Sweden.

Despite this support and following, reports indicate that O'Lacy's has not necessarily spread like wildfire across Europe. In fact, there are indications of weaknesses in its product mix within different countries and a strategy change underway in its image. Still in the early stages of development, the O'Lacy's repositioning efforts have not yet been spelled out.

While Europeans work toward opening their trade barriers for free commerce, they are learning something that wars and strained relations have taught them in the past: The English, the French, the Dutch, the Germans, the Italians, the Swiss, the Scandinavians, the Danes, etc., are different. They have different tastes, different likes and dislikes, different preferences, or whatever. When marketing alliances form among a number of retailers and wholesalers from different countries, each has its own private label program in place. The group then introduces economies in sourcing products, marketing them as so-called eurobrands. While group member can pick up these products exclusively in their own trading areas, the question remains: Do consumers perceive them as being the store's own label or just another brand?

As long ago as May 1988, the GIB Group, Brussels, formed the SODEI Group with a French retailer, Paridoc. By year end, another joint venture group was established, including Paridoc and GIB along with the Rewe Central Organization

GB Inno of Brussels puts its logo on a eurobrand, calling it an import.

in Germany, the Vendex Food Group in the Netherlands, and (joining later) Coop Switzerland, together called Eurogroup S.A., Cologne, Germany. This marketing alliance since has been promoting international private brands, such as Jufri fruit juices and nectars; four brands of pet foods (Colt, James, Persa, and Star Cat); Solane sherry; EuroCuisine household products, etc. for its members.

As this idea has developed, group members have selectively picked up the brands they needed in their product mix. There is a feeling that the brand name by itself does not offer an exclusive presence in the store—these products just get mixed in the shuffle with other brands. GIB-Inno in Brussels has taken steps to rectify this by now putting its own GIB logo on a line of ready-to-eat cereals under the brands Rizzy's, Choco Rizzy's, Puppies, and Blizzy's, being marketed as international private labels. The dual label is now identified on a side panel of the boxes as being imported by GB-Inno-BM and made in France. GIB wants to identify these products as exclusive to its stores rather than just display them as another brand. Other members in this group as well as in other alliances are beginning to feel the same way: Label exclusivity gives a special presence to the product in any store.

While competitors in a given market can carry the same brands that are supplied by manufacturers, they cannot stock an exclusive label owned or licensed by another retailer. If that exclusive label gets support from the retailer, it can serve as an effective marketing tool. When that exclusive label offers top quality products that are unique or special in a marketing area, the retailer can capitalize on drawing customers into the stores that offer the line. The clincher comes when the retailer can sell these products competitively against the brands, thus giving consumers value for their money.

PRESIDENT'S CHOICE IN NORTH AMERICA

In North America, Loblaw Companies, Toronto, over a period of eight years has built its President's Choice corporate brand program into a smashing success in Canada, while it's taken more than five years to market that same upscale brand in the United States, mostly under licensing arrangements with major retailers and wholesalers. President's Choice has been most successful on Loblaw's home turf because Dave Nichol, president of Loblaw International Merchants, has been on television, promoting it over its entire life span. President's Choice, in fact, is now becoming a success in the US, because of greater consumer understanding about private labels, an erosion of brand loyalty in the marketplace, more upscale private label market penetration—viewed as the first "real threat" to national brands, and a build up of the President's Choice product selection coupled with more marketing and sales support, according to Tom Stephens, vice-president of Unique Product Developments at Loblaw International Merchants.

Additionally, Mr. Stephens notes, the program "stateside" has picked up steam recently because of bigger, "more respectable" retailers and wholesalers coming on as licensees: Harris Teeter in Matthews, NC; Smitty's Super Valu in Phoenix, AZ; and most recently, American Store's Jewel operation in Chicago and Fred Meyer Co. in Portland, OR. Loblaw's consulting relationship with Wal-Mart, Bentonville, AR, helping to develop its new Sam's American Choice upscale private label program, has served as another major step toward encouraging US retailers and wholesalers to adopt their own programs. The crowning achievement for Loblaw has been the return of Tom Thumb Supermarkets in Dallas, TX, to the President's Choice program. That chain, in fact, was the first to adopt the program in 1986, but then decided to drop out in 1988. Tom Thumb returned to the fold in 1992. (Full details appear in the Strategies Chapter later.)

The key to President's Choice's success in the US—now adopted by a dozen retailers/ wholesalers and carried in more than 2,000 stores—is the commitment by its licensees. "The program," says Mr. Stephens, "delivers when it gets this commitment from the top down—chairman of the board to the guy stocking store shelves. The program also requires media and operations support, that is, advertising backup and the proper shelf sets and facings in the store."

Smitty's presidents and CEO Dave Schwartz has literally stepped into Dave Nichol's shoes as the 'president' making the 'choice,' by appearing in TV commercials tasting the President's Choice products. Mr. Schwartz also is planning an *Insider's Report* newsletter, just like Mr. Nichol's, but using his own words. Jewel Stores also reportedly is considering a similar newsletter. Jewel already has provided broadcast and print support for its program.

President's Choice started in the US with less than 100 items. In 1992, it's expected to top 650 items. More licensees are expected to sign on to the program, which itself may be transplanted to other continents as well.

Dr. Anthony J.R. O'Reilly, chairman, president and CEO of H.J. Heinz Co. USA (a $5.8 billion global enterprise that generated 40% of its sales in 1989 outside the US), speaking at a June 1990 Executive Congress held by the International Association of Chain Stores in Berlin, said that the true power for global brands "lies not just in their ethos. It lies in their ability to pioneer new market opportunities in response to changing consumer tastes. This is the case with many major brands. The discerning retailers must realize that while local or private labels may help settle occupied territory, the big brands make the initial assault. They use their power to inspire consumer interest and demand, often whether the related products are available or not."

President's Choice has embarked on a similar 'assault,' becoming a global brand in its own right. The program succeeds in the US, because the licensee can adopt whatever fits their own personality. Their marketing efforts allow them to express their own personal style. So this type of program has to be flexible. When it's rigid, it can falter...

OK FOR THE UK, BUT...

More than 20 years ago, Marks & Spencer Canada was launched, fashioned after the successful M&S operation in the United Kingdom. Its St Michael brand, too, has assaulted its marketplace, inspiring interest and demand. Today, Canada is

The wholesale export of this UK format, including the sizes and ranges of clothing under Marks & Spencers St Michael brand, does not necessarily work in Canada, says one former employee.

the company's strongest "foreign" base for the M&S store concept—in terms of number of stores (74 at the close of fiscal 1991 versus 291 M&S stores in the UK and Republic of Ireland). Yet in sales terms, Canada is close to becoming a disaster today. M&S in its 1991 annual report points to the "depressed conditions in Canada" plus the GST (Goods and Services Tax) imposed on clothing in January 1991 as the reasons for this failure: M&S Canada reported its M&S store sales dipped from £79.7 million to £73.3 million in 1991. A former employee, however, sees a deeper rooted problem in this operation.

Marks & Spencer in part states its principles as follows: "Selling clothing for the family, fashion for the home, and a range of fine foods—all representing high standards of quality and value." The firm further states: "Supporting British industry and buying abroad only when new ideas, technology, quality and value are not available in the UK." In fiscal 1991, 81% of M&S goods purchased were sourced from British suppliers.

The M&S formula is nearly perfect: Unique, top-quality products offered to consumers at a value within an inviting retail environment. This strategy has made the St Michael brand the best-selling own label brand in the UK. Why not in Canada, too, after a 20-year track record?

Charlene Rausch, a principal with Russell Design of Toronto, feels that more than the economy is to blame. Ms. Rausch, who worked early in the 1980s for M&S Canada some 3 1/2 years, dealing with merchandise managers in both the

food and textile areas, sees one problem in management's attitude about sourcing product. In the UK, the strategy works, elevating the standards of the manufacturer, "encouraging them to use modern and efficient production techniques," (as described by M&S), and supporting these suppliers with strong orders for goods as a result of thriving retail sales in the M&S outlets. That attitude really translates into: "Make it our way or forfeit our business." The policy works in the UK; but in Canada, where the sales volume is smaller, the payback to manufacturers is limited. Still the same attitude prevails.

The next miscalculation, Ms. Rausch feels, is M&S' perceptions about the Canadian consumer. Canadians—Ms. Rausch being one of them—are different from shoppers in the UK. During her M&S tenure, she recalls one M&S executive, recruited from the UK to Canada, remarking: "One of these days, these Canadians will smarten up and start shopping at Marks & Spencer." It still hasn't happened the way he envisioned it. The potential for ex-Brits shopping M&S stores is small: Those residing permanently in Canada represent less than 5% of the total population.

Canadian consumers, Ms. Rausch believes, really do not identify with the M&S message: "They don't get it—its form of store design, its corporate identity, its product mix, its advertising, its word-of-mouth strength, etc." In fact, she suggests that it's difficult to shop in an M&S store: "M&S has, for example, merchandised shoes in UK sizes rather than clearly communicating sizing information in a way that is easily understood—an example of an arrogant and stubborn attitude toward customers. Also, rather than develop product names that would communicate positive and meaningful food product benefits, products that are actually quite delicious are denigrated with names like Melton Mowbray, Bangers & Mash, Bubble and Squeak, Scotch Eggs and, one that always elicits a lot of giggling, Spotted Dick."

Rather than just criticize, Ms. Rausch does offer some suggestions for improvement. M&S faces a serious problem, having recently announced plans to close 25 Canadian stores, thus leaving 42 outlets in operation. The M&S formula in the UK can be adapted to Canada by allowing the Canadian operation "to develop their own distinct personality," This will be difficult, she maintains, but it will entail redefining the M&S retail image and store design to better communicate with customers and entice them into the stores. Mixing textiles and food products in one environment is OK, but it must be merchandised properly: "Socks right next to tea bags still leaves me uncomfortable."

M&S also has not yet developed a strong corporate brand identity, for example, like market leaders Loblaw and Shoppers Drug Mart in Canada. Instead, M&S makes "all products look as different from one another as possible. This weakens its overall communication of the store brand and also results in an inconsistent communication of quality, value, etc."

Lastly, M&S may be a leader in Canada with its policy for accepting returned merchandise with no questions asked, but its store personnel do not make customers feel welcome: "Shopping is an emotional experience," says Ms. Rausch. M&S apparently doesn't get too emotional in its marketing and merchandising efforts.

Then again, how can anyone criticize a company that reports group profits up by 6% to £670.4 million on a turnover of £5.8 billion in 1991, while its European sales alone rose 30% with profits ahead by 26%? In fact, M&S is now developing franchised M&S stores through its export business to 22 countries, combining the experience of local partners with M&S retail skills. M&S also has adopted a different strategy in the U.S. within its Kings Super Markets division, putting the Kings name as well as its own identity, Marks & Spencer, on a growing line of prepared foods. Additionally, M&S in the UK is taking a new creative tact with its "take-away food and food stores," sectionalized into specially developed lines—deli, wines, produce, etc. Some 40% of M&S turnover now comes from the food trade.

23

Trading Partnerships

While major grocer alliances have been formed throughout Europe, not to mention more takeovers by European retailers/wholesalers of a number of large US supermarket chains and wholesaling operations, there also has been similar or joint venture alliances formed by US wholesalers, retailers, and co-ops looking to expand internationally. Private label has been integral to the success of these efforts. This activity also is producing more of a global marketplace for private label, as a cross-pollination of strategies develops.

For IGA, Inc., Chicago, IL—one of the first US grocer alliances formed back in 1926—the move outside the US started in earnest in February 1988, when C. Itoh, Tokyo, Japan, through its subsidiary, C. Itoh Food Systems, sought and secured membership in IGA as its first international wholesaler-owning company. Three months later, Davids Holdings PTY., LTD., Sydney, Australia, became the second IGA international partner, followed by Foodland Associated Ltd. (FAL), Perth, Australia, and most recently a Korean member.

Started by 25 independent grocers, IGA was formed as the Independent Grocers Alliance around a wholesaler, W.T. Reynolds & Co., Poughkeepsie, NY. IGA grew along with its wholesalers—many of them owing their formative growth to the IGA business. By the close of 1930, IGA had grown to some 10,000 stores in 37 states. The concept really was ahead of its times in the US—a partnership among the mom-and-pop retailers, their wholesalers, and manufacturers-suppliers. One of its founders, J. Frank Grimes, who became IGA's first president, was a true visionary, who started a franchise in Canada in 1951, then set his sights on Europe and the Pacific Rim countries. Slow transportation at the time, however, curbed his progress, while his successors failed to understand how IGA could work on an international scale. The Canadian franchise, in fact, 13 years later was sold to Canadian wholesalers, who have since maintained only a "paternal relationship" with the US group.

This IGA Super Ogawa store in Japan is typical of the units there, ranging from 3,000 square feet in downtown Tokyo up to 10,000 square feet in the suburbs. Stores average $18 per square foot versus about $8 per square foot in the U.S.

Today, IGA has some 3,750 affiliated supermarkets in 49 states, as well as in five countries; Japan, Australia, New Guinea, Canada, and Korea. There are a total of 21 owning wholesaler companies, including four of the top five US food wholesalers, servicing this voluntary retail group. Together, the retailers account for worldwide gross sales of $16.2 billion. ($11.5 billion in the US alone).

Now back on track, IGA recognizes that its concept can work anywhere in the world. As Jeff David, former IGA senior vice-president and chief administrative officer, once described the alliance: "It's a piece of clay ... (that) we wish to further develop and enhance so that it suits the particular marketplace it's in. That same philosophy applies in the US, where you cannot take a program that works, say in Billings, MT, and put it in Miami, FL." (Mr. David has since rejoined his father's wholesaling business, Davids Holdings, in Australia.)

This yellow label import from Thailand, under the Black & Gold identity, is packed for Amalgamated Australian Wholesalers Proprietary Ltd., Burwood, Australia.

Market conditions vary significantly by country. For example, generics in the US are considered by many observers as "dead." But in Australia, which is trying to pull out of an almost two-year recession, generics are evolving from low-grade, down-market products into upmarket products in terms of both quality and packaging, according to *Foodweek* (March 24, 1992), a trade publication serving that market. In 1991, *Foodweek* reports, retailer Bi-Lo expanded its generic range from 230 to 800 items, while Woolworths boosted its range from 170 in 1987 to 780 in 1990. Coles Supermarkets, too, increased its Savings range to 450 items by June 1990, which when added to its Farmland and Embassy private label ranges, brings its total house brand count to 1,200 items. The publication notes elsewhere that generics are now becoming more like private labels, moving closer to becoming the number three or four branded product in their category.

When Davids Holdings reached 90 IGA products in its program, *Foodweek* reported that six of those products within six months became category leaders.

This wholesaler, which commands about 40% share of the food and general merchandise wholesale distribution in Australia, serves stores along its East Coast, where 50% of the population lives. Large towns in that market can include up to 2,700 people, but most towns contain no more than 500 to 600 people, while there is one case of a town with four people, who shop their local pub, which serves as a supermarket. (FAL covers the West Coast for IGA.)

Within the US, IGA also experiences dramatic market differences. For example, in Miami, FL, the company is now working through Malone & Hyde division of Fleming Companies (one of the IGA owning wholesalers) and with local brokers to source "superior products" under the IGA brand for the large Cuban/Hispanic population there. IGA plans to introduce bi-lingual labels.

Its initial line includes: Cuban-style barbecue sauce, Naranja Agria bitter orange, cooking wine, dry beans and rices, various canned dry pack beans and canned fruit nectars, a six-pack malt beverage, seasoning and spices, Spanish olive oil, and guava paste.

Another US alliance, the wholesaler-owned cooperative, Shurfine-Central, Northlake, IL, representing 36 shareholders (medium-size wholesalers) serves more than 10,000 independent retailers in 46 states, their retail volume exceeding $25 billion. Shurfine supplies private label not only to supermarkets, but also to convenience stores, cash-and-carry outlets, nursing homes and hospitals, the military, and gas stations. This diverse customer base has encouraged the co-op to expand its private label business into these other markets, customizing product to fit the market, i.e., smaller diaper packs or a sandwich program for C-stores.

Recently, Shurfine teamed up with C. Itoh of Japan, the huge trading conglomerate, through its US office, to develop export business with Shurfine range of products, starting in Sweden, Japan, Malaysia, and Singapore. Shurfine also has recently signed a deal with a trading group in Russia to develop Shurfine brand sales in Russia. Acting through its US wholesalers, the co-op via Western Empire Distribution Inc., Hemet, CA, has developed private label business with Calimax Stores in Tijuana, Mexico; and through Associated Grocer of Florida, Inc., Miami, FL, exports private label product to the Caribbean, Central America, and at least six South American countries. Its different private brands, such as Saver's Choice, Price Saver, and Shurfine, are now distributed internationally into Central and South America, as well as into Europe and the Middle East.

WETTERAU'S INTERNATIONAL JOINT VENTURES

Wetterau Inc., Hazelwood, MO, one of the largest US food wholesalers (managing one of the country's largest IGA wholesaler-owned programs throughout its 15 divisions as well as owning the country's second largest grocers voluntary group, The Foodland International Corp.) has lately embarked on joint wholesaling ventures with entrepreneurs and entrepreneurial companies around the world—using its own controlled label programs. Greg White, vice-president, assistant director of sales and procurement for Wetterau's Food Distribution Group, boasts: "We feel that our quality and the overall private label program is as good, if not better than anything else that's out there. Our graphics on the Nature's Best, Foodland, Homebest, Foodland, and Topmost labels plus the recent redesign of our Bi-Rite line lend themselves very well to the international sales efforts with vignettes and the image that they project now."

As a result, Wetterau is now working on five tentative agreements:

• A JOINT VENTURE internationally with RALSTON PURINA

INTERNATIONAL, St. Louis, MO, which operates offices in 164 countries, each typically staffed with a full sales force and marketing everything from batteries to dog food to baby food. This program initially targets Puerto Rice and the Caribbean, branching out into Mexico and other countries later.

- INTERMARKET SERVICES, Ligonier, PA, has agreed to work with Wetterau in developing Central America, particularly Chile, as well as Taiwan.

- In EASTERN EUROPE, specifically Romania, Yugoslavia, and Hungary, Wetterau has appointed MICA International, Berkley Springs, W. VA as its representative.

- TECHNI MARKETING INTERNATIONAL, Los Angeles, owned by Masaki Murakami, tentatively is scheduled to venture into Japan with Wetterau.

- PACIFIC BUSINESS DEVELOPMENT, INC., Beijing, China, is earmarked to handle exclusive distribution to China, Korea, Hong Kong and Singapore.

Wetterau's director of international sales, Mack Forsyth, who recently returned from a trip to Russia, describes food distribution systems in most Eastern European countries as highly inefficient: no organization, where orders are frequently accepted at the back door of an operation. For a former communist country, the problem he explains, is that "the people need technical training in how to run food distribution efficiently, because now they're entering into the requirements of amortization of debt, retirement of equipment, appreciation expense, scheduling labor, motivating labor, quality controls, and so forth. These were disciplines that were dictated before; now some entrepreneur must be responsible for them."

Wetterau is looking southward into Central and South America as well, where its greatest immediate opportunities exist in terms of sheer logistics, dealing with lower freight shipping costs. Its partner, Sam Hayden of Intermarket Services, indicates there is now strong interest expressed in canned private label goods and other non-perishable products. Customers in Chile, already a sophisticated market, are asking for Wetterau's controlled brands, as long as the labels are in Spanish. Argentina is another potential growth market for private label. A wholesaler based in that country and also operating in Brazil, already has its own private label program in place, including imports that carry its label as well. In other South American countries, Mr. Hayden says, the mom-and-pop operators dominate.

French retailer Carrefour (Paris) operates its hypermarkets in both Argentina and Brazil. The latter, its biggest operation in South America, has 28 units, which stock private label. Actually, Carrefour launched its first hypermarket in Rio de Janeiro in 1988 and then introduced Brazilians to the private label concept with its Bonjour label on bed and bath sheets. Consumers recognized that they could only buy that "brand" at Carrefour. Success with the program led Carrefour to develop a line of 96 grocery items, all under its Carrefour label, including both dry groceries and refrigerated foods.

Carina Betts, president of Corporate Brands Inc., Ft. Lauderdale, FL, who researched this market, indicates that now Brazil's largest chain of stores, Pão de Acúcar, as well as others, have followed suit ... but sticking mainly to grains and dry staples such as coffee and seasonings (for their private label programs). Ms. Betts adds: "As the Brazilian economy grows stronger, the average consumer's discretionary income will rise. One can suppose then that non-staple items will begin to emerge under private label in Brazilian chain stores. After all, this country holds title to the world's seventh largest economy with a population of over 130 million people.

Further north, private label has existed in Mexico for decades, started in government-run stores. But the quality left much to be desired. In fact, it wasn't until Jewel Food Stores, Chicago, formed a partnership with Mexican retailer Aurrera in the mid-1970s that a true quality private label program was established. Other retailers like Gigante and Comercial Mexicana followed suit with their own private label programs.

Today's market in Mexico has completely changed. Aurrera is now part of the $2 billion diversified retailer, Cifra, N.A., which has lately joined with Wal-Mart Stores, Bentonville, AR, to build Club Aurreras, membership wholesale stores, in Mexico City. Competitor Comercial Mexicana is looking to form a similar partnership with Price Club Co., San Diego, CA.

Mexicans, of course, are no strangers to private label. Shurfine-Central has been supplying Comercial Mexicana with its Shurfine Price Saver and Saver's Choice labels for some time. Shurfine also has been supplying Calimax Stores in Tijuana for a couple of years with phenomenal success—private label sales up by 425% from a substantial beginning volume, thanks to the support Calimax gives to the program through advertising and merchandising efforts. This retailer is now planning to expand the program southward via its grocery wholesaling operation into Central Mexico.

On a limited basis, two other wholesalers, Fleming Companies, Oklahoma City, OK, and Certified Grocers of Ca., Los Angeles, have been shipping their own brands, Rainbow and Springfield, respectively, into Mexico. Fleming has just signed a joint venture deal with Groupo Gigante to develop "price impact" stores in Mexico. This interest from 'the States' relates to the free-trade agreement now signed between the US and Mexico. With private label already firmly established there, its potential for growth is limited only by the size of Mexico.

24

Quality –
'The Great Equalizer'

"Quality has become the great equalizer. As house brand quality has become more and more comparable to that of national brands, house brand pricing will fall into an ever-narrowing range, and the quality issue will no longer be an issue. This has led to the introduction of premium house brands, not only as its relates to product quality but more especially to packaging and presentation in its broadest form. These are the elements that will improve both consumer perception and consumer satisfaction with house brands."—Dr. Herbert V. Shuster, chairman, Herbert V. Shuster, Inc., Quincy, MA. (*Private Label*, March/April 1992).

More than 30 years ago, a food technology faculty member from Massachusetts Institute of Technology set up a quality assurance testing facility in Boston. Since then, Dr. Herbert Shuster has been dedicated to—as *Forbes* Magazine (Sept. 17, 1990) phrased it—"reverse engineering (of) big-name consumer products for supermarket and drugstore chains that wanted house brands." More than helping those retailers to match national brand quality in their private label products, Dr. Shuster also has served as an industry guru, offering advice on the best ways to stay "comparable to the leading or target national brand in appearance attributes such as color, opacity, pourability, particle size, odor, flavor, nutritional quality, etc." and to stay right in step with the latest government regulations on nutritional labeling, environmental requirements, and so forth. As a broad-based consultancy operation today, his company serves clients not only in the US but lately in Europe as well.

Dr. Shuster, in fact, has participated in this industry's maturation process initially orienting *Private Label* Magazine to the industry players. Most of them were buried in the woodwork about 12 years ago. He also participated in the organizational meeting of the Private Label Manufacturers Association, often speaking at its trade shows. In reviewing industry developments over a decade in the 10th Anniversary issue of *Private Label* Magazine (March/April 1989), Dr. Shuster wrote: "Many (private label) retailers not only want identical ingredient statements to the national brand reference, but also the identical order of these ingredients. This may not be practical in every case, particularly with chemical specialties where it is more practical and more economical to use existing bulk ingredients which are regularly used by the manufacturer. In all cases, comparability of performance is the most significant criterion."

Throughout the 1980s, the private label industry has taken 10 "key criteria ... national brand comparability; specifications; product consistency; informative labeling for the consumer; open date coding; facility audits; quality assurance; fill and weight control; physical, chemical, micro biological, sensory stability; and claims validation—and made them industry standards," according to Dr. Shuster. He continued: This has not been easy, especially since for manufactured products, "there are no universally acceptable product specs as in canned and frozen fruits and vegetables ... Most retailers find that the cost of preparing their own specifications across the board is not only impractical but prohibitively expensive. Further, and most important, the drafting of intelligent specifications requires a tremendous amount of product knowledge and great integrity on the part of the manufacturer. Standard testing protocols are sorely lacking with most manufactured products and even though standard methods of evaluation exist under the auspices of the United States Government or trade or other associations, there is no universal set of criteria. This presents serious problems in preparing intelligent specifications and in carrying out testing protocols to evaluate conformance with these 'specifications.'"

To maintain strict standards of product consistency, purity, and stability, for example, private label manufacturers must comply with all Federal Food and Drug Administration regulations and follow Good Manufacturing Practices to ensure that product quality.

Dr. Shuster argues further that "one of the biggest consumer selling points for the national brands is that these brands are dedicated to consistency. In fact, whenever a national brand makes a product change which, even if it is made for the purpose of cost reduction, it is communicated to the consumer, usually in the form of stressing an improvement, not only on the packaging but through media advertising ... When the national brand promotes such changes as producing a more acceptable product to the consumer, the private label manufacturer is pressured by the retailer to make the same changes in the private label product so

In the lab at Certified Grocers of California, Ltd., Los Angeles, Terry Lack (second from left), quality assurance manager of the Private Label Division, checks specifications on the Springfield brand, while president and CEO, Everett Dingwell (third from left), and two other lab personnel discuss the quality. Photo: Courtesy of Certified Grocers of California.

as to avoid losing market share. Once again, this moving target philosophy is the greatest defense mechanism for the national brand ... Another protective device used by the national brands is to systematically make changes in products in accordance with the moving target principle. This is particularly effective where EPA (Environmental Protection Agency) approval is required, as in the case of certain chemical specialties. EPA registration could become a lengthy procedure— up to as much as two year—thus providing the national brand manufacturer a significant lead time advantage."

The question is: What are private label manufacturers and retailers really targeting? Answer: Branded specs that consumers think are the very best available.

Private label players, in fact, are now changing those rules, while consumers, too, are beginning to change their minds. The national brand reference is no longer the final word on quality.

In today's marketplace, there is more confusion about private label versus brand standards. Private label's multi-tier quality structure compounds this problem. Even on the upper end of the quality spectrum, for example, there are variations in so-called upscale products, a term that needs clarification. There can be gourmet products that are truly the best quality available anywhere, but these higher-priced items often are relatively slow sellers. Then there are the upscale products, such as President's Choice chocolate chip cookies, containing 39% chocolate chips, which are high-velocity, best sellers. Wal-Mart has targeted products like this in its Sam's American Choice private label line. These products often present value-enhanced differences when compared to the brands, in terms of their product quality or any packaging, health or environmental features.

Traditionally, the term first-quality private label has suggested products that match the so-called brand standard. Just what that "standard" means remains questionable. Some brands fluctuate in their quality standards. They are not always the best product available. The market leader can command market share in numerous markets across the United States, but not always be the number one seller: Heinz ketchup may be the favorite in metro New York, but in markets in North Carolina, for example, it could trial behind Hunts ketchup. More than from taste preferences, a product can be the standard in a given market because of its positive environmental features or other factors. It becomes an illusive issue. In fruits and vegetables today, private label quality, in fact, is considered better than the brand versions.

On the extra standard grade quality level, private label products are set a notch below the 'brand quality standards,' again at a quality level that can vary by geographic area, by supply-and-demand marketing conditions, and by the definitions applied to describe a product function.

Except for naturally-grown products, like fruits and vegetables, there really are no manuals written that delineate the quality standards for manufactured products. Since many different private label players prescribe their own standards, it's expected that this confusion will continue into the foreseeable future.

Perhaps this can all be related to the psychology of consumer buying habits. When someone totes around a shopping bag that carries the Harrods logo, the idea is that the person purchased the goods inside at "the Rolls-Royce of stores," Harrods of London. If that bag contains Harrods label stationery, whisky, chocolates, butter, bacon, Aberdeen Angus steak, or whatever, those items have got to be the very best quality, because they come from a "superior" retailer, really a "store legend." There's nothing to compare that merchandise to, because it

Jewel Food Stores, Chicago, recently shed it original drab generic label look (top right) for the Econo Buy identity with color graphics from its parent firm, American Stores. Consumers were informed in a brochure (left) that talked about the addition of nutritional information, kosher symbol, recycled symbol, and upgraded packaging where color photographs and the bold red Econo Buy name are added. These new "generics" come with a satisfaction guaranteed or your money back – for whatever reason.

comes from Harrods. Of course, there also could be branded merchandise in that bag. Still the perception is that whatever was purchased at Harrods is the very best product that money can buy.

Today, a retailer's reputation alone can be the best guarantee for quality merchandise. Retailers are gaining more consumer confidence and trust in their private labels, because they are doing something about private label quality, assuring that it is "as good as or better than national brands." For example, the buying-merchandising co-op Shurfine-Central Corp., Northlake, IL, often goes beyond national brand quality for its Shurfine brand products. In some product categories, Shurfine offers consumers a choice of different brand quality standards set by leading competitors within the category.

Not too long ago, *Consumer Reports* rated Shurfine brand peanut butter at the bottom of its listing. John Stafford, vice-president of quality control, relates how his department then went to work, visiting all the vendors of that product around the US, seeing first-hand how they produced the product: its quality grade, its roast time, its standing time, and so forth. Shurfine searched for someone to produce formulae to match both market leaders, Jif (with a touch of molasses added and a clean consistency) and Skippy (with more peanut taste). The co-op then marketed both under its first line Shurfine label, according to customer taste preferences by region of the country.

Even though the national brands use reconstituted juice made from tomato paste, Shurfine demands only fresh-squeezed tomato juice for its private label line, according to Michael Zadny, director of quality assurance. Double-cooked tomato juice, he says, betrays itself by its inferior "cooked flavor." Shurfine's "fresh" strategy has expanded its sales in an otherwise declining product category.

When the branded quality "slipped badly" in the tuna category, Shurfine switched to tuna packed above brand quality. Also, its first label canned pineapple is 100% Hawaiian, while the brands use Thai and Philippine pineapples, Mr. Zadny indicates. Even Shurfine brand jams exceed the brand standards for whole fruit, while the Shurfine label crackers aren't over baked like the brands. (*Private Label*, March/April 1992).

Acting as host, Marketing Management Inc., Fort Worth, TX, generously invited representatives from leading retail and wholesale organizations to a meeting, Oct. 31-Nov. 1, 1989, at its headquarters to explore the need for the private label industry to share information in order to improve private label product quality across the board. MMI, a program-services-and-procurement broker, opened its doors to a number of trade people including some who were not clients. Those attending the meeting included quality assurance people from Kroger, Safeway, Super Valu, Shurfine-Central Corp., Fleming Companies, White Swan (foodservice), Spartan Stores, and Cullum Companies, plus a manufacturer, Clements Foods Co., and a lab technician from the Oklahoma Food Labs. The result of this meeting was the formal launch of The Quality Assurance Association on Nov. 13, 1990, at the Private Label Manufacturers Trade Show that year in Chicago. The group voted on and passed its by-laws, which included five objectives:

1. TO PROMOTE the interest in the field of quality assurance in all aspects of private label brand products.

2. TO ENCOURAGE and provide means of discussing and disseminating technology and other information relating to the quality of products through sensory evaluation and processes of technical testing.

3. TO ADVANCE the profession of quality assurance by promoting the maintenance of high professional standards among its members.

4. TO PROVIDE cooperative relations with government, manufacturers, testing facilities, and educational institutions that will be instrumental in providing good science, technology and related courses.

5. TO PROMOTE cordial and helpful relations among the private label industry participants (i.e., manufacturers, government, associations, wholesalers, retailers, brokers, testing laboratories etc.).

QAA president Gail Drew (quality assurance supervisor at Spartan Stores, Inc., Grand Rapids, MI, a retailer-owned co-op) reports the group now consists of 38 members, including active members (retailers, wholesalers, foodservice distributors, co-ops and brokers) and associate members (laboratories, government agencies, manufacturers). It's a small group that up until now has concentrated on networking, that is helping members develop new product areas, recommend plant improvements after visiting manufacturers' plants, personnel placement, conducting educational seminars, and the like. QAA has yet to decide on whether it will maintain its present low-profile or move into a more national posture.

The private label quality issue received notable coverage in a recent article in *The Wall Street Journal* (March 6, 1992), reporting on "more fizz" for store brands. The *Journal* quoted *Beverage Digest*, an industry newsletter, which showed that Pepsi-Cola's market share over the past three years had dropped by 0.2%, while Coca-Cola has gained only 0.7%. The newsletter said that private label soft drinks had enjoyed their biggest three-year jump in market share in at least two decades: up nearly a full percentage point to 8% market share. (Soft drinks represent one of the largest dollar category in supermarkets at more than $9 billion.)

The *Journal* also quoted David Litwak, senior editor at *Supermarket Business* magazine, who said both market leaders, Coke and Pepsi, fetch only about 21% profit versus the average store brand (selling at about a 35% discount to regular-priced national beverages) generating up to 30% gross profit margin. The brands argue that their higher volume and turnover really produce more profit for the retailers. Then the *Journal* referred to Loblaw's success with President's Choice cola in 135 of its scanning stores in Ontario, Canada last June, where its cola market share soared from 10% to 50%. David Nichol, president of Loblaw's product-development division was quoted as saying, "when there is no difference from a product performance point of view, people aren't willing to pay the premium for Coke and Pepsi.

To test the performance theory, the *Journal* conducted "The Great Atlanta (GA) Taste Test," putting eight staff members in its Atlanta Bureau to "The Private Label Challenge." They sipped different colas from unmarked white cups: Coke or Pepsi in one cup challenged by other drinks in the other two cups. Like professionals, they cleaned their palates with unsalted crackers between tasting the samples. The "winner": Nobody! Actually, two people put Pepsi in first place, one picked Coke, another chose Kroger's Big K, someone else selected Wal-Mart's Sam's American Choice, one taster liked both Coke and Sam's, and two people thought every cola tasted the same. Most surprising, said the *Journal* was that Coke and Pepsi did not rank "superior."

Comparative performance counts the most, according to Dr. Shuster. These consumers proved it.

VI

The Strategies

25

The Dawning of Corporate Brands

"In my opinion, the ultimate retailing model and threat for North America is going to be a club store stocking nothing but President' Choice products. When you take superior products and put 8 or 10% gross markup on them, and you offer a better quality than the national brands, and you're a good communicator, I think that this combination will result in the ultimate retailing model. And I don't see any reason why you couldn't move from that product mix (food and nonfood grocery products) into tires, or TV sets, or VCRs. Maybe that's how the true Marks & Spencer model will come to North America." — David Nichol, president, Loblaw International Merchants, Toronto (Ontario) Canada.

This opinion deserves more than passing attention, especially when one reflects on what Loblaw Companies (Canada's largest food distributor) has accomplished over the past 15 years with its own corporate brands—'no name' generics and President's Choice upscale foods—as well as the role played by Dave Nichol, president of the Loblaw division charged with developing and managing those brands. Mr. Nichol has become a catalyst for reworking dominant European private label strategies into food distribution systems across North America, where national brands rule market share. His influence now touches even the world's largest retailer, Wal-Mart, Bentonville, AR, which commissioned Loblaw in 1991 to assist in developing its Sam's American Choice private label program, modelled after President's Choice.

In Canada, Mr. Nichol has delivered on a 1981 observation: "Generic is the most powerful weapon that retailers have developed since the introduction of the self-service supermarket." His 'no name' generics program today, comprised of some 2,000 skus, is the most successful of its kind in the world. 'No name' captures up to 75% of Loblaw's $1.4 billion (Canadian dollars) in corporate brands sales. Lately, it has become even more popular in an economy suffering from severe recessionary problems. This program together with President's Choice (some 1,000 skus) takes 32% of Loblaw total sales of $4.3 billion in Eastern Canada—still not as high as the private label share experienced at many European retailers, but far ahead of the US food retailers, who have private label sales penetration averaging somewhere in the teens. Loblaw readily admits that its profits, while not breaking any records, are maintaining their momentum, thanks in part to its corporate brands. Meantime, its competition in Canada has suffered dramatically from the recession of the early 1990s.

'No name' is generic only because it does not identify itself under a brand or label logo, but relies on yellow packaging for recognition. The 'no name' reference, together with the yellow, is picked up on store signage and print advertising. This program has evolved as "a totally integrated marketing approach, from the signage, to radio-TV, to the product quality, to the packaging, which is radically different from anything else in generics in North America," according to Mr. Nichol.

Loblaw's style of generics has been marketed more like the generic concept first developed in 1976 by the French hypermarket retailer, Carrefour, Paris—that is, a top-quality private label program and nothing like the versions of other generic programs developed in the United States, which mostly offered standard grade or acceptable quality products. Those programs, in fact, today are mostly dormant, kept very limited in scope, or have since been reprogrammed into secondary quality private label programs. Carrefour, too, has since dropped its generic look, adopting the Carrefour identity on its private label line. (Because of the stigma now attached to generics in the US, Mr. Nichol refuses to market his 'no name' program there today.) The Loblaw 'no name' quality continues to be positioned as not necessarily below national brand standards, but "in some cases, it's better, in some cases, it's the same, and in some cases it's different, but always offering a better value." Also, 'no name' packaging has been upgraded over the years with design refinements and colorful graphics, but still keeping its dominant yellow appearance.

(Right): Dave Nichol, the man behind Loblaw's President's Choice and No Name corporate brands, shows off one of the latest products in the PC line: hamburgers basted with Memories of Kobe sauce. Outstanding packaging reinforces the quality message of this product.

Back in 1981, Mr. Nichol recognized three mistakes that North American retailers were guilty of committing:

1. A.C. Nielsen data showed that 50%+ of the items carried in food stores sold less than six times per week. SAMI data showed that in seven year, out of 38,000 new product introductions, only 138 of them reached $5 million or more in sales. Yet the retailers were sticking with their dominant national brands product mix.

2. US retailers were destroying their newest and most effective marketing weapon—generics—by producing "horrible packaging, bad quality," while marketing that concept like "garbage," that is, generics versus good food.

3. Those retailers also were completely ignoring unique products, adopting instead existing national brands, their "improved" formulas, and their line extensions.

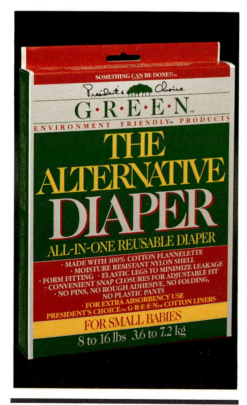

This G.R.E.E.N. concept failed to attract a big following perhaps because washable or flushable liner pads are too inconvenient versus disposable diapers.

Under the President's Choice G.R.E.E.N. program, Loblaw has had phenomenal success with this energy-efficient light bulb. Products in this range often carry messages right on the packaging.

With 'no name' established, Mr. Nichol is 1985 embarked on another corporate brand program—President's Choice products, offering better quality than the national brands, but at a lower price. He made that program work first in Canada, then eventually started marketing it in the US. In Canada, President's Choice is now perceived by consumers to be a national brand, but available only in Loblaw stores. In the US, Loblaw has placed this program into its St. Louis, MO, and New Orleans, LA, divisions, and licensed others outside those markets to carry President's Choice on an exclusive basis: At least six major retailers and wholesalers have signed on as of this writing. The executive also is now talking with parties in Australia for the possible development of a spin-off on this program, called Aussie's Choice. Additionally, on a consulting basis, his division, working through Loblaw's Intersave Buying and Marketing Services, has helped Wal-Mart develop the Sam's American Choice program, modelled after President's Choice and launched late in 1991.

Mr. Nichol believes that the revolution of corporate brands in North America will be triggered by two trends. One is the new Wal-Mart program, because "in my opinion, it's going to be the biggest thing that's ever happened to private label in North America, especially with the incredible success that Wal-Mart has had with those products. They must have 20 or 30 products right now in major product categories like cola, cookies, snack, etc. What's interesting about this development is that Wal-Mart has skipped over the entire grocery industry and gone right to the ultimate solution."

The ultimate solution, of course, is adoption of a corporate brand program just like President's Choice, which, in turn, is modelled after the St Michael program at Marks & Spencer in England. In fact, Mr. Nichol adds, "the majority of people now developing products on our staff at one time or another worked for Marks & Spencer in South Africa, England, or Canada. Marks & Spencer, they're the people we admire; and yet I don't anticipate they're going to have any success in North America. They have to have things their way. They can't adapt to other markets. They're not chameleon-like. But in terms of developing new products, they're the best."

A second trend—the emergence of non-U.S. retailer involvement in the United States food distribution industry—is also helping to revolutionize this industry in North America, according to Mr. Nichol. He points to the English "looking with eager eyes toward North America." Marks & Spencer already has a foothold through its ownership of King's Super Markets, West Caldwell, NJ. London-based J Sainsbury, the largest supermarket multiple in the United Kingdom, now owns Shaws Supermarkets, East Bridgewater, MA. Sainsbury's itself generates more than two-thirds of its sales of £8.2 billion in the UK in own label (7,000+ products) and now has 169 product developers working on new products for those lines: 1,500 own label products introduced in 1991, including many new proprietary products. At Shaws ($1.8 billion in sales), private label now takes some 5% of sales under the Shaw's brand (800+ skus). Plans call for pushing that penetration to 30% within two years. In fact, Shaw's has increased its product developers from two to 20.

Mr. Nichol indicates that Tesco, another leading UK supermarket multiple, is now shopping around for a US supermarket. Meantime, some 25% of the supermarket chains in the US are controlled by non-US companies, many of them Europeans, who have built their business on unique private label products. What all of this suggests to him is that the US food distribution industry is caught in between a sort of "pincer movement," squeezed on one side by Wal-Mart, moving toward becoming the fourth largest food distributor in the US, and on the other by outsiders, invading the US market. The obvious solution, he believes, is to "go to premium quality, signature private labels, offering better quality than the national brands, but at a lower price and with more cents profits."

This very strategy was adopted by Loblaw some 15 years ago, at first subtly but lately having more of a snowballing effect. In 1992 alone, Loblaw has licensed President's Choice to major retailers like Jewel Stores and Acme Markets (pending), both owned by American Stores, Salt Lake City, UT, as well as Smitty's Super Valu of Phoenix, AZ, Tom Thumb, Dallas, and Fred Meyer, Portland, OR, while talks now continue with others, such as Lucky Stores, Dublin, CA (another American Stores operation).

Loblaw developed its own corporate brands "revolution" first with the 'no name' program, started in 1978, designed at the time to rescue the company from a tarnished price image, picked up in the 1970s during some "horrific price wars" in Ontario Province. That was followed by the launching of President's Choice in 1985, consisting of a line of "luxurious foodstuffs (that) indulge sophisticated palates." More recently, niche segments have been created within the President's Choice program: "G.R.E.E.N." imaginative products that address important environmental concerns, introduced in June 1989; "Club Pack" larger-size packs (less packaging material but more product) to offer consumers savings, launched in May 1991; and the "Too Good To Be True!" line of nutritionally-superior products, established in late 1991.

Corporate brand strategies in the US have been underway for several years, too. Most of the them, however, are positioned as first-line private labels. Another important difference from the Loblaw strategy is that they are not supported as aggressively with TV advertising. The Kroger Co., Cincinnati, for example, sells Big K soft drinks throughout its operations as a corporate brand. American Stores, owner of Osco Drug, markets Osco brand health and beauty care products as a corporate brand in its different supermarket operations. Fleming Companies, Oklahoma City, OK, a wholesaler, positioned its Marquee brand of health and beauty care products, plus its Rainbow food products line as corporate brands available to any one of its retailer customers. More on the upscale side, A&P, Montvale, NJ, 52.5% owned by Tengelmann, a major retailer in Germany, has Master Choice, marketed as a corporate brand—not to mention its Eight O'Clock coffee bean program, which is sold to non-competitors as a brand, while marketed throughout the A&P divisions in different store concepts. The Ahold supermarket chain, Zaandam, The Netherlands, owns four US regional supermarket chains, which could eventually all stock the new Sensational brand upscale food line as a corporate brand.

Nevertheless, corporate brands in North America are the most successful at Loblaw. Its president, Richard Currie, reported in the firm's 1991 Annual Report: "Corporate brands offer high quality and low price—real value—and these products, when linked to our computerized merchandising systems ensure the preservation of retail margins, which would be greatly diminished if we engaged solely in national brand discounting practices. At the same time, such a computerized connection allows our overall pricing levels to be sharply competitive."

Speaking at the PLMA Consumerama meeting, held in Toronto in June 1992, Tom Stephens, vice-president of unique product development at Loblaw International Merchants, noted that the company now has an annual $22 million commitment to development of unique products under its corporate label program—$12 million allocated to sourcing these products and another $10 million spent on TV advertising. The payout—despite the recession in Canada—is that President's Choice sales alone grew by 35% in 1990, then repeated that gain again in 1991. This is based upon the so-called Haagen-Daz syndrome, said Mr. Stephens, because people still feel they can afford the "luxury" of Haagen Daz ice cream, while things like a BMW, new VCR or TV are out of the question.

Mr. Stevens then outlined four key factors that have made corporate labels a success at Loblaw:

1. THE COMPANY CAN DIFFERENTIATE ITSELF FROM ITS COMPETITORS as well as from the manufacturers' brands with corporate brands it controls and which are recognized by consumers as coming only from Loblaws.

2. THE COMPANY HAS BECOME A PRODUCT KNOWLEDGE LEADER IN THE MARKET, talking about its corporate brand products (not about price) with consumers. For years, Dave Nichol has appeared on TV for both 'no name' and President's Choice. Also the company's entertaining *Insider's Report*, a quarterly corporate brands newspaper insert, reaches nearly 60% of Ontario households. Both Mr. Nichol and the *Insider's Report* are merchandised

and/or referenced in Loblaw stores via signage, "devastating displays," TV monitor information tapes, etc.

3. LOBLAW ALSO HAS DEVELOPED NEW CORPORATE BRAND PRODUCTS TO MEET "FRAGMENTED GROUPS OF CONSUMERS," i.e., the G.R.E.E.N. program of environmentally-responsible products, for example, a compact fluorescent light bulb said to equal nine conventional bulbs, thus saving the consumer $27.30 in energy cost over a three-year period; or the Too Good To Be True! line of healthy, nutritious products that "taste delicious." Some of the latter were transferred from a President's Choice G.R.E.E.N. G.O.U.R.M.E.T. line. The range includes: no-oil salad dressings, 11 varieties of low-fat yogurts, breads with less than 50 calories per slice, vegetarian items, etc. Loblaw has co-developed some of these products with the Lipid Clinic at Toronto General Hospital and continues to sponsor research at the University of Toronto and St. Michael's Hospital into development of soluble fibers in foods to allow drug-free reduction in cholesterol levels. (Loblaw took a leadership role in the G.R.E.E.N. program in North America, while other retailers and wholesalers have followed that lead with their own private label programs).

4. THE FIRM OVERALL HAS ESTABLISHED A MULTI-TIER MIX OF PRODUCTS, including corporate brand and national brands, all controlled with a data system used to look for ways to change the profitability of that mix, while showing the "incredible value" of President's Choice and 'no name' products. In fact, the company now has data showing that "when you start from no penetration of corporate brands, you lose $150,000 a year in our 135 scanning stores. With only 10% penetration of corporate brands, you reverse that to a $160,000 profit per year. With a 40% penetration it's a $640,000 profit per year."

It's no wonder that Mr. Nichol expects to reach a 40% penetration with corporate brands within the next five years. But he isn't working toward the Marks & Spencer 100% own label penetration: "We're not going in that direction. We definitely need the national brands so the consumer can see how much money is saved...Do I see us hitting the 58% own label penetration that Sainsbury has? Down the line, it is a possibility."

Mr. Stephens explained how the corporate brands can be effectively priced against brands. In one Loblaw store in Ontario, 'no name' peanut butter is the leading product in that category, taking a 15% sales share, while Kraft is the leading national brand: "We pay $3.16 for Kraft and $1.82 for 'no name' in the same size. Then we retail Kraft for $2.99 and 'no name' at $2.89. So we lose 17 cents on Kraft and make $1.07 on 'no name.' That happens when you have a good product that the customers are happy with. Any retailer who hasn't got the same quality mix cannot do what we do. Our President's Choice in that category sells for $3.99, while we pay $2.11, making a $1.88 profit. Since we make more profit overall on the corporate brands, we can afford to sell the national brands below cost—and beat any retailer who wants to position themselves as a national brand retailer."

Loblaw has now made about 450 President's Choice skus available in more than 1,000 stores in the US, with more products and more licensees on the way. The retailers and wholesalers there like this program, because it gives them something "exciting" to talk about with their customers, especially, when Every Day Low Pricing is the hot topic of the day. The experience with Tom Thumb supermarkets (The Cullum Companies, Inc., Dallas) illustrates this point. In 1988, Loblaw was selling the President's Choice program to Tom Thumb in Dallas; but because of a better economic environment then, the program was dropped for lack of interest and/or support. In 1992, when competitor Food Lion, (Salisbury, NC) decided to open up to 50 stores in that market, Tom Thumb had to lower its prices to stay competitive. The chain realized that President's Choice could give it something to talk about in its advertising, other than low price. So Tom Thumb has since reintroduced 250 skus of President's Choice, as something unique to that market. In markets where there is heavy EDLP (Every Day Low Price) competition or where competition is strong, retailers have little to differentiate themselves other than something like President's Choice or a similar program.

Mr. Nichol's commitment to corporate brands solidified early in the 1980s, when he joined Mr. Currie and Galen Weston, chairman of Loblaw, on a trip to Europe to visit market leaders in four countries, each with its own distinctive retailing style. One stop was at Paris-based Carrefour, the leading hypermarket retailer (huge 2,500+ square meter stores) in France. Carrefour traditionally has been an innovator in its market, having opened the first hypermarket in France in 1963 and having inspired the generics phenomenon with its debut of "produits libres" (free products, that is, free from the costs of name brand marketing, advertising, and packaging) in April 1976. The trio also visited Aldi stores in Germany, that country's leading discount chain. Started by the brothers Karl and Theo Albrecht, Aldi's turnover in 1981 was estimated at $7 billion, covering stores in six other countries besides Germany. The brothers took over their mother's 1,000-square-foot shop in 1946, right after WWII, when people faced shortages of food, while goods were rationed. A no frills setting was perfect, carrying only the bare essentials, but producing fast turnover, a small product selection, and the lowest prices. This concept grew to a range of 1,000 items—all fast movers, mostly products under their own brands (80%+ of the mix). "It's a private label store disguised as a branded store," interjects Mr. Nichol. Aldi built its success on a simple premise, voiced long ago by Karl Albrecht: "Poor people have to buy cheaply, rich people like to."

The trio then traveled to Zurich, where Migros bases it organization of 12 regional cooperatives operating in Switzerland and commanding the biggest market share. The 'M' brand in Switzerland, in fact, stands for Migros, perceived as a national brand. Migros' central headquarters acts like a wholesaler, buying product plus handling packaging, advertising, market research, administration, and distribution coordination. The firm also manufactures up to 30% of the goods stocked in its stores. Private label presence in its stores is inescapable: More than 95% of the merchandise falls under the M umbrella identity.

Finally, the executives toured Marks & Spencer's Marble Arch store in London to view what Mr. Weston called the "ultimate retail model"—nothing but corporate brand merchandise, but also highly innovative products, unique products.

All four retailing concepts have had a lasting impact on Loblaw's strategies. It has tested the no frills concept with 'No Name' stores. The Carrefour generic look was adopted with 'no name.' Migros' self-sufficient operation has been adopted in a number of disciplines: in-house packaging, advertising, product development, etc. The Marks & Spencer approach to innovative and unique products has spear-headed most of Loblaw's corporate brand strategy.

This European trip resulted in one of Loblaw's first big successes in the President's Choice program: Decadent chocolate chip cookies, featuring 39% chocolate chip content versus brand leader Nabisco's Chips Ahoy! with 20% chocolate chips. Mr. Nichol observes: "I attacked the chocolate chip cookies, because that's the biggest cookie category we have in terms of A.C. Nielsen numbers—the fourth largest category they monitor. You don't have to be too smart to make a better product than the national brand. We have a large test kitchen and a laboratory, plus we work very closely with our manufacturers. Since we control approximately 27% of the Canadian food market, they were very anxious to work with us. The Decadent chocolate chip cookie, available in only 22% of the stores in Ontario, has become the best-selling cookie in the province. In our stores, Chips Ahoy!, Nabisco's top-selling items in the chocolate chip area, has less than 2% of the sales."

Loblaw's strategy basically is to introduce signature products with unique added value, i.e., raisin cookies, where raisins are the biggest ingredient on the ingredients listing—nearly double that of the leading brand; a unique 20-bean soup (now being developed), unique sauces (Schechewan peanut sauce and the like), carrot juice mixed with passion fruit to make it tasty (and healthy), free and clear soft drinks (no coloring, natural flavoring), etc.

The company realizes a number of cost efficiencies in spite of the fact that it becomes involved in product development and TV advertising just like national brands. Loblaw, as part of George Weston Limited, can tap into Weston's full-service lab facilities, Diversified Research Laboratories; a satellite lab at

Loblaw's main warehouse, the Erin Mills Quality Assurance Division; and a group of specialists at headquarters with their own test kitchen. While the company did work with celebrity Bill Shatner for TV commercials in the early 1970s, its strategy today focuses on Dave Nichol, as spokesman on TV and radio, as well as in print advertising. He notes: "I think it's a terrible waste of time and money, using celebrities. We have our own TV commercials here. I do my own, including writing the script, for $10,000 each, whereas the average cost for TV commercials in Toronto is $150,000 and in New York City, it's $250,000.

"When you look at Pepsi-Cola paying Michael Jackson $20 million to advertise Pepsi, that's almost ante-diliuvian. That's the past. People don't fall for that anymore. (Consider that) versus the guy whose job is on the line. What can Michael Jackson tell me about Pepsi-Cola? He's allergic to it and doesn't drink it. I've told people that on one TV commercial, that is, that he never touches the stuff."

For the future, Mr. Nichol sees "the store as a brand, where branded manufacturers will be facing more severe pressures...You're going to see innovations—more changes in retail models. It will be either change or perish."

He also points to changes in the supplier end of the business: "Years ago, the value of Cott Beverages stock was $12 million; today, it's over $400 million. They no longer waste any time on branded product. Their mission is to develop a third major soft drink company that supplies primarily private label. Who is going to be the new Cotts of the future?

"The movement toward EDLP," he continues, "by manufacturers is the greatest thing that's happened to private label. We're doing everything we can do to encourage manufacturers to go EDLP, because that will put us in a position where we'll never have national brands priced under our private label. We'll always have that differential on the shelf...We're now riding on the crest of a huge wave that will come crashing down on the States."

26

Sub-Branding for New Departments

Traditionally, private label products have prospered in the dry grocery aisle of the typical supermarket. A store's own labels often can be found in canned foods, snacks, household chemical cleaners, paper goods, pet foods, and the like. Also, private label has had strong representation in the supermarket's frozen foods area as well as in the refrigerated dairy cases. In the recent past, new departments for private label have opened, such as in the deli, the liquor section, the bakery, health and beauty care aisle, the fresh meats/seafood cases, the produce section, and even in upscale gourmet-type foods found throughout the store. With its relatively new private label sub-branding strategy, Ralphs Grocery Co., Compton, CA, is on the cutting edge of all these developments.

About 20+ years ago, however, Ralphs had no centralized corporate strategy for private label. In fact, there wasn't even a program for private label, although its presence could be traced back to the founding of the company in 1873. The semblance of a program started to take shape in the 1950s, when influential, powerful private label brokers began promoting canned goods and other items for their principals (the manufacturers). But for the most part, Ralphs (like other supermarket chains) traditionally put private label buying decisions into its grocery buyers' hands. They, in turn, handled the Ralphs label as an afterthought—after national brand product procurement was completed in their respective product categories. In sourcing private label stock, these buyers often would ask for "only the good stuff," and then close the deal with a handshake, according to Graham Lee, vice-president, Grocery Division.

Mr. Lee, who joined Ralphs in 1974 as a UPC coordinator, believes the "dawn of Ralphs modern private label program started probably in 1970, primarily with the beginning of our relationship with Daymon Associates. They convinced our management firstly that we should have a private label program, gave recommendations on the items it should encompass, then offered guidance in developing that program. They became our preferred broker and have continued up to the present, working to generate private label business for us and for their vendors."

Prior to New York-based Daymon's involvement, Ralphs had dealt with market brokers, sourcing packer label and private label products at a buyer level and more often than not leaving product quality and package design decisions up to manufacturers. A change in that strategy developed as government labeling regulations began to call for nutritional information, metric weights, and complete ingredient listings on the package. Ralphs, working with Daymon's suppliers, then established two basic criteria for its program: "The Ralphs label product must be equal to or better than the national brand quality and it must also return a better gross profit rate than the national brand." If the company perceived enough volume in a particular item, that item would then be added to the program.

In the late 1970s, when generics began sweeping across the United States, Ralphs was first on the West Coast to adopt this strategy, picking up 30 standard grade products from its old All Star packer label program, which was exclusive to Ralphs. Within two years, its new Plain Wrap program, a white label identified by a light blue band with a darker blue boarder on the top and bottom, grew to 500 items, representing almost every product category in the store: dry groceries, bakery, dairy, meat, frozen, liquor, produce, etc. The program was called Plain Wrap everywhere except on the label itself. Ralphs did carry its own name on the distribution statement.

> *But the generics phenomenon in the US began failing in the mid 1980s generally because of inconsistent quality standards, ugly labels, lack of retailer merchandising/marketing support, and an improving economy, among other factors.*

Ralphs Plain Wrap program, however, was different from most other generics. From the start, Mr. Lee notes, Plain Wrap was programmed as another private label quality level: "It had to deliver the best value in the category and had to provide an equal or better gross profit than the national brand." It also was given support—on the label with a "Guaranteed Satisfaction or Money Back" symbol, in the store with shelf signage and special aisle displays, and in newspaper/broadcast advertising as a featured special. In fact, Plain Wrap quality was improved where necessary, especially when customers expressed disappointment in a product. In some cases, other sizes in a product category were added to the line. Overall, Plain Wrap received support from management and reenforcement wherever possible.

The Plain Wrap strategy has worked, because today there are more than 200 items still sold in the line. While some retailers have followed a similar strategy, the majority have either phased out of the generics area completely, kept a few high-traffic items, or changed the strategy to a secondary private label program—giving it support.

It could be argued that Ralphs success with generics, handling it like another private label program, encouraged the company to become more aggressive with its first-line private label program, expanding it beyond the grocery area.

In 1982, the chain operator established its own in-house quality assurance test kitchen and laboratory. The following year, the chain commissioned the design firm of Don Watts in Toronto, Canada, to revamp not only its store decor but the Ralphs label, too. The designer developed a black background that highlighted a full-field treatment of product photography, which became unique to Ralphs. This approach was so effective that other supermarket chains in the US have since paid Ralphs a fee for use of the same packaging graphics (minus the Ralphs logo) for their own private label programs.

About 1988, Ralphs realized that its first-line private label program entailed more than just grocery buying. So the company established a Merchandising Division, headed by Terry Peets, senior vice-president of merchandising, thereby taking the buying function management out of the Grocery Division. This meant

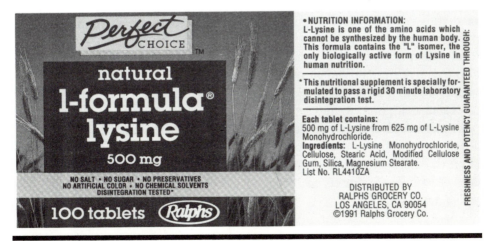

Ralphs adopts the Perfect Choice sub-brand for its health and beauty care line of products. The Ralphs logo appears at the bottom of this label.

From an unappetizing, dull packaging design, Ralphs early in the 1980s switched to a black background with the graphics punched out dramatically. This style became almost a standard in the industry, as other grocers picked up on the same graphics, under license, but with their own private label logos.

more centralized control over all perishable and non-perishable private label lines. Everybody involved in private label buying, packaging and merchandising, now reported to Mr. Peets. He, in turn, would meet with Ralphs marketing officers and Daymon monthly to set private label sales goals and develop new packaging concepts, which then would be executed at the buying level within an established strategy framework. This management restructuring also led to the establishment of a private label administrator in 1989, charged with directing private label package design and execution.

From that point, Ralphs adopted a sub-branding strategy, as it moved into other store departments, looking to develop private label lines. The first area of attack was the liquor department. This was "a novel, unique, and courageous effort of ours," says Mr. Lee. "It's very difficult to put out a bottle of vodka that doesn't look like Smirnoffs or a scotch that doesn't look like Johnny Walker. But we've done that."

The Private Stock line of liquors debuted in early 1990. It featured the familiar black background of Ralphs' first line private label program, carrying a drawing of the product, i.e., whiskey, bourbon, dry gin, etc. in a glass. The black background also was adopted somewhat in bakery and dairy items, actually designed to contrast effectively with a new store decor scheme of pastel colors. But some of these items required more flexibility. That is, black was sometimes too overpowering, especially on calorie-oriented foods. The full field of photography approach was replaced with a silhouette motif of active people on such items. Coincidentally, the branded version in this area also started to use a similar motif.

Ralphs literally could have steamrolled into other areas as well, except for the limitations of packaging: "There are so many product categories out there that are ripe for private label inclusion; but we lack the technology and physical capability of packers to reproduce the packaging." One example, Mr. Lee continues, is portion packs for puddings, apple sauce and aseptic packaging, which packers only lately are capable of handling in private label. Also, there is a problem of finding capable sources of supply.

Ralphs was looking for flexibility in its private label packaging. In January 1991, the Private Selection sub-brand appeared on meat and poultry items—all value-added quality products, promoted as such: hand-selected cuts of quality fresh beef, pork and poultry, a delicious taste (stuffed, seasoned or fully cooked with the finest ingredients added), and convenient (pre-prepared for the oven grill). Items in the line include, for example: stuffed pork chops with herb, apples and cinnamon, Cajun wild rice, or wild rice and mushrooms. Later in the year, Ralphs extended this sub-brand into a select number of grocery items, also featuring added value, bringing the count to 40+ skus overall.

One of the more ambitious moves in this strategy occurred in mid-1991 with the launch of the Perfect Choice brand, covering some 125 skus of health and beauty care products, including vitamins. Previously, Ralphs had carried only a token representation of private label in this area. This move, however, completely abandoned the black background, since black did not complement this type of product. The Ralphs logo, of course, is retained, but otherwise it is a white label identified with blue Perfect Choice lettering. The intent here as in the other lines is to present an alternative to the national brand, offering the same quality but at a better price. Ralphs, however, has a slightly different intent with Private Selection stock.

Mr. Peets describes Private Selection as "a step beyond brand quality, not necessarily gourmet, but targeted toward something better than the brands in terms of quality and/or value-added packaging." The line now encompasses items like kosher dill spears, uniquely-sized croutons in two special varieties, an Ultra Diet Thin powdered drink, mushrooms in glass jars, etc.

Ralphs has already tapped the better-than-brand-quality area in certain categories. A line of upscale pies, called Mrs. Collins, features boxed pies ranging from 32- up to 44-ounces in seven popular fruit flavors, retailing at about

$5.59 per pie. This line is positioned against the Marie Callendar pies, originated in West Coast pie shops under that name and now sold at retail as well. Interestingly, Ralphs identifies the source on the package as "The Great California Bakery Co., Los Angeles."

The company operates manufacturing facilities in bakery, dairy, ice cream and deli kitchen items. While the Ralphs and Plain Wrap identities do touch on those areas, the company also has developed special private labels, such as Mrs. Collins (mentioned above) and Chef Express, a name associated with its store deli department.

When Ralphs woke up to the potential for private label about 1970, there were some 70 items in its program. That selection today easily exceeds 2,000 items, counting all of the private label activity in its stores. The program overall takes an estimated 16% of Ralphs Grocery's total sales of $2.8 billion (fiscal year).

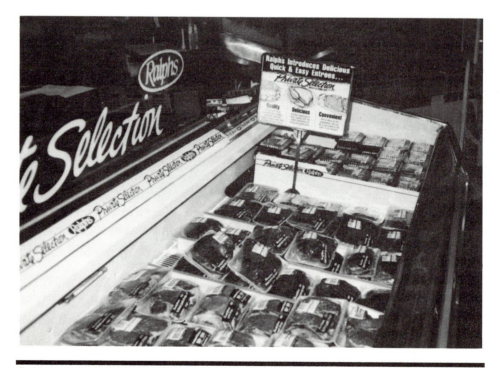

Ralphs promotes its new Private Selection brand in refrigerated meats as a quality product that is delicious and convenient.

27

Tesco's "Winning Brand"

If one was looking for a paragon in private label marketing, a very likely choice would be Tesco plc, Hertfordshire, England. Tesco does almost everything right—product research, development, and innovation; packaging strategy, marketing/merchandising efforts, etc.

Ironically, some 15 years ago, this food retailer was a disaster, operating as a price discounter. The company, in fact, called itself "terminally ill." Its own label program at one time was low-price products, commanding a respectable 20% of total turnover, but with very little attention paid to quality.

In analyzing its plight, Tesco looked closely at its competition—not only manufacturers' brands, but also principal market rivals, Marks & Spencer and Sainsbury's, each with powerful own label programs in place. This food retailer then decided to completely switch its marketing strategy, going from a price discounter to an upmarket retailer, offering a premium brand image. For its own label program, this meant repositioning the product mix from low-price, inferior quality to superior quality, better than its competitors' own label quality but at the same price or equal to that quality but at a lower price.

Execution of this plan entailed the recruitment of hundreds of "executives," charged with the task of exploring every aspect of product development—its research, its product technology, its buying and marketing aspects, and so forth. As commercial director Terry Leahy describes it: "We wanted to provide expertise around individual markets with well-paid managers who could really analyze the competition and develop and source a better product."

The strategy also involved a substantial investment in new out-of-town super stores (averaging 45,000 square feet). Today, Tesco has some 160 of these units out of a total 387 store count. The retailer hired its own store design people to help carry out this plan.

After 10 "painstaking years," Tesco has been able to push its own label share of sales to more than 50% just in packaged goods. Add to that its so-called unbranded areas, such as meat, fish, produce and the like, all part of the store's image as well, and the own label share of sales climbs to 70%. In fact, that calculates out to £4.4 billion out of £6.3 billion total sales (up 17.5%) for 1991. In 1991, its competitors are really not too far ahead: Marks & Spencer's UK and Republic of Ireland store sales total £4.9 billion—all in own label; while Sainsbury's had an estimated £5.6 billion in own label sales (two-thirds of its total £7.4 billion in total UK Sainsbury's-only store sales). This puts Tesco right in the own label UK ballgame.

Profit-wise, Tesco can report that its margin has increased from 1.3% some 15 years ago to more than 6% today. Its 1991 profits before taxes jumped by 28% to £417 million (excluding property profits).

It's no wonder then that chairman Sir Ian MacLaurin in the company's 1991 annual report paid a glowing tribute to "Tesco—A Winning Brand." Sir Ian continued: The Tesco brand now occupies a position of great strength in the marketplace. Our customers all over the country find our brand, in all its aspects, highly acceptable and it continues to gain popular recognition.

"To my mind, the concept of 'The Tesco Brand' embraces everything that customers think of when they hear the name Tesco—our people, our products, our stores."

This report indicated that "at any one time, there are 700 people within Tesco working on thousands of new product ideas. During the 1990s this development program led to over 1,000 being successfully launched.

"Every one of those new products will have been through a rigorous process of development and customer approval. Our 60 product teams, each consisting of a buyer, marketing manager, technologist, packaging technologist and home economist are responsible for developing new products, following strict quality and financial disciplines."

Mr. Leahy breaks down this support team as follows: 300 buying executives, 400 product technologists, about 100 marketing people and another 100 people involved in store design and marketing. "Our produce department," he notes, "is headed by a trading director for all produce. He has something like 25 buyers, some marketing people plus assistance from a team of 15 to 20 product technologists ... Our decision-making is completely centralized, where those people in produce have the authority and accountability (in sales and gross

Not too long ago, Tesco in this UK store positioned giant-sized mockup boxes of its Tesco brand corn flakes and washing powder soap near the entrance. This proved to be an effective attention-getter and reminder of the Tesco brand, merchandised as "extra value" items.

profits) to manage that area."

This sounds like what brand manufacturers traditionally have done in the past as far as product R & D and marketing support are concerned. The results with Tesco in charge are impressive. In 1985, Tesco undertook to fully label its food products, declaring their nutritional content, showing fat, sugar, fiber and so forth. "Nobody was doing that at the time," says Mr. Leahy. "We were the first and our method of classification has become a standard within the industry." The British government did plan such a move, but wasn't able to carry it out. Meantime, Tesco has carried this labeling over to its non-foods products in terms of what is in and on the packages, particularly any environmental effects. This effort, began in food under the Tesco Healthy Eating brand, developed into one of the retailer's most successful programs, covering some 40 products. Other sub-brand strategies at Tesco include Nature's Choice for health and beauty care products, Choices tee shirts, Long Island polo shirts, and so forth.

Tesco also has taken the initiative in shelf-stable meals, taking advantage of improved, aseptic-filled packaging. Additionally, the company has launched a range of fresh, chilled cake desserts all centrally baked at manufacturers' factories in the morning and distributed around the country that same day.

The company additionally has followed Marks & Spencer's pioneering lead into chilled, prepared ready meals—"as good as you would make at home"— based on high-quality standards. The company handles more than half its distribution with its own trucks, contracting out the rest to save on management and capital expenses.

Another area that the company has kept on top of is organic foods, beginning with produce and extending more recently into free-range eggs or chickens.

In 1986, Tesco introduced a Nutrition Center concept into its stores, some eight Centers now set up in different locations. This room within the store invites shoppers in for consumer testing. It's a unique way to conduct market research with shoppers, while also scientifically testing products to insure they meet the standards looked for by consumers and that they exceed the quality of the competition. Mr. Leahy explains: "We conduct something like 1,000 tests a year, involving more than 100 customers. So we actually sit down and do market research with more than 100,000 customers, producing a big data base on the performance of our products. It's a very practical way of doing this right in our stores."

Tesco backs this up with a huge technical center, where chemical and micro biological testing is performed, including recipe development, product evaluation and product development, all part of its quality assurance program. Up to 500 executives are on its technical staff, serving as managers and senior managers over different departments.

In marketing itself, Tesco in May 1990 launched a major TV campaign, starring actor Dudley Moore in humorous sketches that project the company as a leading quality food retailer in terms of quality, innovation, and product range. Other retailers use the media more to project a store image.

Its promotional efforts include a "Why Pay More" campaign, which concentrates on areas where own label penetration is low. Through advertising, couponing, and leaflets, consumers learn how the performance of Tesco brand is as good as the brand but less expensive. The concentrated washing powders, for example, were addressed in April 1991 in a 12-page supplement. It also featured coupons or offers of extra product on larger size products.

The Tesco strategy has been to invest heavily in creating a new set of criteria for its products—not just a copycat version of the manufacturer's brand. Mr. Leahy notes that "the margins are good, but the main benefit is sales rate. You really make this investment pay by how much you sell rather than the margin you normally charge. And you sell a lot more of the product, because it's better quality and it's been marketed better. It more closely fits the customer's needs. And that's the difference."

28

Marketing Private Label as a Measurable Difference

"The excesses of the decadent 1980s have given way to the nasty, thrifty 1990s."

Addressing this trend, Shoppers Drug Mart and Pharmaprix drugstores, two chains operated by Imasco Ltd., Montreal, Canada, have repositioned themselves with respect to their private label program. The strategy as explained by Stan Thomas, senior executive vice-president of marketing (quoted above), is basically one of changing into a marketing-driven operation, putting its "private label business into the hands of skilled marketers not buyers."

SDM Ltd's Corporate Brands Division is charged with the development and marketing of "high-quality private label products exclusive to Shoppers Drug Mart and Pharmaprix stores designed to build category market share and profitability. John Gamble, vice-president of marketing, heads up a department supported by a team of product managers and marketing assistants, some with MBAs and four to five years experience in packaged goods marketing."

Mr. Thomas elaborates: "Because our stores buy independently, we have a sales department of some 50 sales representatives and managers, calling on each of our 760 stores on regular four-to-five-week call schedules. What they do is take inventory, sell new products, handle promotions, look for opportunities, process orders, and so forth—very much like the Procter & Gamble sales representative in our stores today. This structure has allowed us to take full advantage of the market strategies that have been so successfully used by national brand companies. Just like the brands, a great deal of our time and effort is devoted to product development, product introductions, line extensions, product enhancement, etc. In all cases, we strive to be a little bit better and different from those national brands."

This executive stresses that the chain's corporate objective isn't targeted toward replacement of national brands but rather to build overall category market share and profitability. The result is a corporate brands program that encompasses more than 1,500 skus, which under the Life brand and Rialto brand, have sales projected for 1992 at $210 million ($175 million in US dollars). There is a five-year business plan "to grow our corporate brands at a rate double that of Shoppers Drug Mart sales."

A few years ago, the company decided to drop its Shoppers Drug Mart logo, which appeared on items outside the health and beauty care categories—those items covered by the Life brand. SDM switched everything, household cleaning products, paper goods, confectionery items (including snack foods) over to the Life brand identity, because, says Mr. Thomas, "it makes things a lot less confusing for the consumer and a whole lot easier for our advertising presence."

Switching logos offered the retailer an opportunity to enhance the visual appeal of its packaging as well as to update nutritional information and to emphasize particular product attributes. In the case of nuts, for example, when consumers were informed that the product is 'lightly salted' and 'a good source of protein,' sales doubled in the first year.

Mr. Thomas, speaking at a PLMA Consumerama meeting in Toronto in June 1992 noted: "The mandate I give to our private label group is first to develop a synergy with the national brands, position your products uniquely to that category. Then they must make sure those products make a measurable difference to that category, that is, they increase the share and profitability."

Results of this strategy are that SDM carries Life brand baby wipe refill packs, which outsell the tub version by three-to-one. SDM, in fact, was the first retailer selling this type of package in its market. Its baby products, formerly positioned as 'knock-off' copies of the leading brand have been reformulated, made hypoallergenic, with a unique family look—an overall differentiation that has helped boost sales and market share penetration in this category.

Just like the brands, SDM uses effective advertising and promotions to support its marketing strategy. Its national flyer reaches a weekly circulation of eight million readers, while national TV 30-second commercials, featuring stars from the TV series, "LA Law", as spokespeople, focus on specific product categories. The chain also uses national flyers to drive its everyday business, featuring the Life brand products on the front page from time to time. There are times when these products are grouped together under a promotional theme or by product categories in the flyer. Also, a semi-annual Life brand sales event is

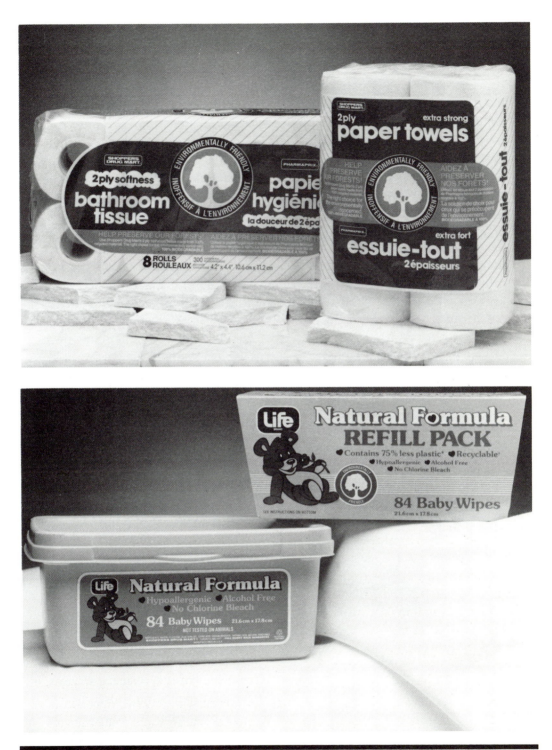

(Top) *Shoppers Drug Mart used its own store logo (as shown here) on merchandise outside the health and beauty care category. The Life brand has replaced the store logo, as part of the chain's strategy to build equity behind that brand.*

(Bottom) *Carrying the only refill pack of baby wipes, Shoppers Drug Mart captured a strong consumer following in its market. This is the new packaging for both the wipes and the refill, carrying the Life brand and SDM's bear logo motif (usually on children's items).*

orchestrated, extending over several weeks. SDM additionally uses a four-page insert devoted entirely to new Life brand products, informing consumers about the products and offering them attractive price points.

SDM promotes its private labels just like the national brand, but not with as much money. Bonus offers are made. Couponing is commonplace. Sampling of product is provided. Special packaging—pouch pack, travel-and-trial sizes are provided. The program is merchandised with shelf extenders, end-aisle displays, special sections, etc.

At that same Consumerama meeting, Barbara Brocklebank, vice-president of cosmetics at SDM related the success story of the Rialto brand program, which started in 1986 as an upscale line of pantyhose, added to the existing mix of a national brand range and the Life brand range. The new Rialto line, however, represented "a point of difference, since the Rialto brand had colors and patterns not available under the existing presentation," Ms. Brocklebank says. From that point, the program has grown to represent sales of some $30 million, of which $10 million derives from a 1990 extension of the line to Rialto Naturals.

The success of the program came when SDM offered its customers products normally found in department stores. Rather than present the Ultra pantyhose line as a private label, it was marketed as a line available exclusively at SDM. She continues: "From 1987 through 1990, we marketed a selection of fashion accessories for Mother's Day and Christmas as well, items such as scented hangers, potpourri sachets, lingerie bags and beauty accessories. We tried to give Rialto a special niche in our stores with gift items that would not ordinarily be found in a drugstore at prices that were more competitive than the department stores or the specialty boutiques."

A complete line has evolved from this effort: In 1988, the line was extended into cosmetics accessories—lip and eye pencils, cosmetic brushes, cosmetic sponges, eye makeup remover pads, etc.

A turning point (upward) for Rialto came with the launch of the Rialto Naturals program in October 1990. From its experience in

Examples of coupon savings.

cosmetics and toiletries, the company saw natural, environmentally-sound products as a growth opportunity. Ms. Brocklebank continues: "By conducting consumer research in major markets, we could project what percentage of our customers were currently either using products of this type or would consider using them, if provided. Since we had no representation of these products from our traditional suppliers, we started to develop our own range."

Launched with 40 skus, including shampoos, conditioners, hand and body lotion, soaps, bath additives, skin treatment, and specialty items, the program included some 19 trial-size products as well.

"When one looks at the launch of Rialto and the on-going support of the brand, it's easy to see why we believe we market private label as a national brand," she notes, adding: "Our logo looks like the national brand logo, our bottle design is upscale and classic, it is designed to compete against national branded products on our shelves and it's certainly more appealing than the specialty competition. In fact, our label design won a silver award in the 1991 Packaging Association of Canada competition—competing against national brands."

Even presence in the stores duplicates the national brand strategy: A special wooden fixture highlights Rialto Naturals "to expose the customer to our positioning theme—'Natural beauty that won't cost the earth.'"

Just like Life brand, Rialto Naturals is supported through flyer advertising and print campaigns, such as ads in Shopper's Drug Mart's *Images* magazine, which has an exclusive distribution of 300,000 copies furnished to its stores. Additionally, 15- and 30-second TV commercials support the line, run a minimum of eight weeks on national TV.

"To provide the maximum synergy of the Rialto image," Brocklebank indicates, "we also have developed a two-minute in-store video. We encourage our stores to run this video whenever we have any promotions running against Rialto Naturals. We also provide in-store point-of-purchase material."

Besides consumer advertising, the line is marketed to the store staff as well: A promotional calendar is developed with special offers, gifts offered with a purchase and seasonal programs such as gift baskets. (For Christmas 1992, Rialto has two gift collections carried in reusable richly patterned boxes, carrying an array of Rialto Naturals environmentally-sound, animal-friendly ingredients.)

These programs are sold to the stores by the corporate brands sales division. Training also is provided to ensure store cosmeticians are familiar with the line. Says Ms. Brocklebank: "Like the national cosmetic brands, we pay the cosmetician a commission on the Rialto products."

It all proves, she adds, "it's not only possible to market a private label like a national brand, but it's possible to go farther—to be more than a follower, to be a leader and to establish your own benchmarks and unique profile, so that other follow your leading position."

VII

Summary

29

The Art of Networking

"A New World Order"

This truly optimistic phrase, which politicians, economists, historians, and the like are now using to define today's world changes, does have some merit, no matter how fantastic it may sound to someone reflecting on the reality of world history. The New World Order defines regional free-trade agreements that have begun proliferating around the world recently. *The New York Times* (Aug. 23, 1992) lists six that have emerged since 1991, partly as a result of "the end of the cold war and the stagnation of negotiations aimed at simultaneously lowering trade barriers globally."

The latest such deal is the North American Free Trade Agreement, 1992, signed by the United States, Canada and Mexico. In 1991, three similar deals were struck in Central and South America: The Andean Pact (Columbia, Ecuador, Bolivia, Peru and Venezuela), the Mercosur agreement (Argentina, Brazil, Paraguay, and Uruguay), and a deal between Chili and other Latin American countries (Argentina and Mexico). In Europe, the European Community (E.C.) signed a trade pact in 1957, which was set into motion in 1992, lowering trade barriers among a dozen countries: Belgium, Britain, Denmark, France, Germany, Greece, the Netherlands, Ireland, Italy, Luxembourg, Portugal and Spain. Six other Western European countries (Austria, Finland, Liechtenstein, Norway, Sweden, Switzerland) along with Iceland signed a similar pact, the European Free Trade Association (E.F.T.A.) in

1960, which lately has added five other countries: Czechoslovakia, Hungary, Israel, Poland, and Turkey. In 1991, a free trade deal also was negotiated between members of the E.C. and the E.F.T.A. From 1974 up to the present, Finland and five other countries—Czechoslovakia, Hungary, Israel, Poland, and Turkey—have signed trade pacts. Freed from communism, the Baltic countries Estonia, Latvia, and Lithuania in 1992 signed an agreement with Sweden. Also in 1992, The Association of Southeast Asian Nations Free Trade Agreement was negotiated, bringing together Brunei, Indonesia, Malaysia, Singapore and Thailand; while both Laos and Vietnam have expressed interest in joining this pact as well.

While arguments are raised about built-in protectionism or the limited regional scope of these agreements, they still are viewed as positive developments that encourage trade, while allowing countries to specialize in the products that they make most efficiently, says the *Times*. Nevertheless, it's argued that diverting trade to partner allies in such alliances can be inefficient, especially when those goods can be produced more efficiently outside the pact. The truth, however, as the *Times* reports, is that "economic studies of the European Community have consistently shown that, with the conspicuous exception of farm products, the Community has created more international trade than it has diverted."

The European situation is worthy of closer scrutiny, especially its phenomenon of retailing-wholesaling alliances that have been recently established to encourage international trade and more efficient purchasing power.

The SECODIP study, referred to in the Market Research chapter, reports on eight principal European central buying organizations that have been formed since 1988: Eurogroup, Independent Distributors' Association, Co-operation Europeene de Marketing, Buying International Gedelfi Spar, Deuro Buying, Associated Marketing Services, European Marketing Distribution, and European Retail Alliance. All of these organizations provide the framework for networking on behalf of private label. Associated Marketing Services (AMS), in fact, has stated its plan to "coordinate own brand development" by examining its "partners' own label ranges to generate worthwhile additional volume for both existing and new own brand suppliers." AMS also plans to examine the "opportunity to assist in sourcing of raw materials and packing materials to reduce costs to own label suppliers." SECODIP notes, however: "Still not having an effective controlling body (hierarchy), they remain not very credible with suppliers in the scenario where orders are becoming globalized and purchasing conditions optimized." Yet despite limited results, the study allows that their "networking effect should play a full role." For AMS, in fact, it has as will be discussed below.

Since networking has been a cornerstone for private label development, these organizations are expected to help private label growth for the group members,

Pick 'n Pay Retailers (Pty) Ltd., Claremont, Cape, South Africa, introduced this line of Green products. Shown here is a pump spray that replaces the aerosol spray, featuring natural ingredients, a recyclable plastic bottle, not tested on animals, etc.

particularly when they can maintain some degree of exclusivity for their private label products. If instead they opt to develop an international or so-called global brands presence, they should prepare themselves for spending huge sums of money for advertising support, just like the global brands, Coke, et al.

It is almost poetic justice that what has spelled survival for private label in the past—its copycat or imitation strategies, following the lead of brand quality and packaging—now holds the promise for its future growth. Private labels today are assuming market leadership worldwide. The private label owners, in turn, are copying from one another. It's all part of their networking philosophy.

In the United States, the brands for decades ruled (and still do) market share. Loblaw in Canada suddenly introduced a corporate brand, President's Choice, which is now licensed to about a dozen US food retailers and wholesalers and has inspired Wal-Mart, the largest retailer in the world, to start its own upscale private label program in the food area. Now its competitor, Kmart ($34.6 billion sales) has decided to apply its 30-year-old strategy—"stores that provide good value—quality products at low prices"—to the food area. Since April 1992, this major discount department store retailer has been quietly introducing a Nature's Classics line of food items—snacks, cookies, juice, etc. On the back panel, some products tell consumers: "This premium quality product is made in the USA explicitly for Kmart Corp., Troy, MI," a message similar to Wal-Mart's on its Sam's American Choice food line.

A good example of 'private label networking' occurs in a remote part of the world—South Africa.

Impressed by the success of Carrefour's "no frills" private label line in France, Pick 'n Pay Stores, Ltd., Claremont, South Africa, in 1976—just nine years in business at the time—launched a range on "No Name" plain-white-wrap products. (The line was not positioned as a generic program, because this supermarket retailer already carried a Farm Girl program, featuring standard-grade quality, promoted as a value buy for budget-minded consumers.) The success of this new program, four years later growing to 175+ items, representing 20% of its total 4.4 billion rands volume (a South African rand equivalent to about $1 US), convinced Pick 'n Pay to redress the packaging with a striped motif plus move its store logo from the distribution statement to the front panel of the packaging.

Richard Cohen, director at Pick 'n Pay Retailers (PTY) Ltd., Bedfordview, who created this program, afterward decided to move private label from a 'walking stage' to more of a fast-walking pace, introducing a line of Pick 'n Pay Green Environment products, debuted on Earth Day, April 22, 1990, with the full range of 24 items brought in on World Environment Day, June 5, 1990. This range—again inspired by 'green programs' in other parts of the world, carried a white background, the Pick 'n Pay logo, but also featured a distinctive fresh green leaves motif. From this stage, Pick 'n Pay began jogging with private label, so to speak, copying the Marks & Spencer range (also sold in that country), by rolling out a Pick 'n Pay line of upscale food and beverage products, starting in August 1990. This new value-added range also now covers toiletries plus different convenient foods—"exceeding the quality level of branded equivalents" and priced at least 10% over the leading brands. Pick 'n Pay carries these programs throughout its chain of supermarkets and hypermarkets.

Meantime, while the European grocery trade builds alliances and expands internationally through joint ventures and acquisitions, their counterparts in the US are spreading their influence abroad as well. Wholesaler Wetterau is now investigating the potential for marketing its controlled brands in other parts of the world. Its Nature's Best, Buy Rite and Homebest labels are now being exported into the Bahamas. Mack Forsyth, director of international sales, returning from a recent trip to Russia, reports that perceptions there about private label or controlled brands are totally different. The consumers in Russia are interested first in price with quality as a second consideration. They also don't relate to label exclusivity and its value. In fact, consumers conditioned to "fresh" products markets are very suspicious of canned foods. In appraising this "virgin area," Wetterau believes that it must market its private labels just like national brands, breaking into the market with sampling, consumer education and advertising. But Mr. Forsyth thinks that eventually the private label concept can take root there as well. It can be accomplished, he feels, through a joint effort by both private label manufacturers and the Wetterau expertise in distribution. Russians are more receptive to American products, recognizing they deliver on what they promise through advertising. They are less receptive to products from Germany or Italy for historical reasons—political or business-related, feeling they have not been treated fairly in the past. He views the former Soviet Bloc countries in East Europe as being more receptive to trade with Germany, France and Italy. Countries like Czechoslovakia, Yugoslavia, Poland, etc. are more westernized in their thinking.

While networking in private label continues, there are some industry leaders who set the pace, not waiting for the brands to act. Ahold is an excellent example...

When its coffee sales became sluggish in 1989, the company's Albert Heijn supermarket chain introduced a completely new coffee line in November of that year, under the Perla brand, featuring a wide assortment of products—Arabica, extra mild and flavored blends to give consumers a better choice. Krijn Dorsman, executive vice president, reporting in the firm's annual report for that year, said: "We want to take our private labels out of the shadow of the premium brands. The Albert Heijn private labels need to be given a stronger character of their own. Perla coffee is an outstanding example." Produced by Ahold's Marvelo subsidiary, Perla has become a successful brand name in the Netherlands, through the cooperation of Marvelo and Albert Heijn. Now Marvelo is roasting and packaging a similar range of coffees under the Sensational brand for sale exclusively at Ahold's US chains, Finast and Edwards stores.

It is often these synergies within an organization or its relationships with outside suppliers that help make its private label a success. Koninklijke Ahold nv, Zaandam, The Netherlands, summed up this situation in an essay in its 1992 annual report: "The scientific approach to our profession is turning traditional grocers into state-of-the-art food marketers, using a wide array of technology to optimally serve each customer. This will mark the end of an era in which our stores were seen as a kind of way station between supplier and consumer. Today, major efforts are being made by retailers and their suppliers to enhance the shopping experience."

Ahold sees "the supermarket (as) the primary medium...the center of communication with the customer.

"In the near future, our customer will be able to watch TV programs broadcast by Albert Heijn, Finast or another Ahold company, on his own screen at home. Local television broadcasts, via cable and satellite transmissions, will gain in importance. In the stores, information on new products, special offers and recipes, for example, will be viewed by customers on small video screens attached to shopping carts. A screen on the store facade may provide information that will be visible to the customer from a distance.

"Manufacturers may take the opportunity to advertise directly through the store's video systems. Regular customers will use a 'smart card' to pay for goods, as well as to tailor the information on the shopping-cart screen to their household and personal tastes. In addition, customers will be using a phone or fax to order their groceries and pick them up soon afterward, ready and packed. Home delivery may also become a regular option...the consumer will need more personal advice on an increasingly international assortment...Besides serving as a shopping center for various customer types, our stores will also act as social meeting places."

Ahold, of course, is the market leader in The Netherlands, taking 26% market share in food, tobacco and beverage sales. The firm also controls four supermarket chains in the US. Its philosophy expressed above is now unfolding in a 112,000-square-foot Tops International superstore in Buffalo, NY, carrying 60,000 product assortments from all over the world. "The emphasis on fresh products is visible everywhere," says the company. "Food is prepared in various places in the store to cater to changing US eating habits and the ethnic diversity of the local population. In addition, the store offers an extensive range of service departments, including a cooking school that offers courses, demonstrations, lectures." These ideas are being picked up by other Ahold USA stores as well.

In June 1991, Ahold opened its first Mana supermarket in Czechoslovakia. By year end, three stores were in operation under its newly formed Euronova subsidiary, established to serve this growing chain as well as three distribution centers, operating as a wholesaler. Plans now call for several dozen stores to come under this operation via acquisitions and the country's process of privatization.

Ahold also has set up a joint venture with Jeronimo Martins & Filho S.A., a Portuguese food producer and retailer, its purpose being to develop retail food markets in Portugal. Meantime, this $12.2 billion retailer has moved its Etos health and beauty chain into Belgium.

These developments reflect back to that concept of networking and a growing international presence now emerging within the food distribution industry. Ahold is a member of two European cooperative organizations, the European Retail Alliance and AMS Marketing Services. ERA was formed in

1989, based in Brussels, for Ahold, the Argyll Group of London, and Groupe Casino of Saint-Etienne, France. AMS, based in Zug, Switzerland, was founded by Ahold in 1988 as Ahold Marketing Services. Now ERA holds a 60% interest in AMS with the balance of its shares divided among other AMS partners: Dansk Supermarked inkodob a/s (Denmark), ICA Aktiebolag (Sweden), La Rinascente S.p.A. (Italy), Migros Genossenschaft-Bund (Switzerland), Kesko Oy (Finland), and Mercadona S.A. (Spain). In 1991, AMS partners began developing their first standardized products in cooperation with manufacturers. Ahold reports: "Through standardization of product content and packaging, considerable savings are being realized in manufacturing and distribution costs. The AMS partners as well as the suppliers and customers benefit from these savings. In 1991, AMS signed cooperative agreements with more than 100 suppliers, both medium-sized and multinational."

These products could be the private label leaders of the future, fitting themselves into the new world order. To survive, however, they must promote their unique position in the marketplace—exclusive brands available only to the members' outlets, offering quality that is as good or better than any global brands marketed by multinational manufacturers.

In today's world, private label no longer challenges only national brands, but the emerging global brands as well.

Afterward

'The Best Is Yet To Come'

Imagine reflecting on the experience of a roller coaster ride, while still clinging on for dear life. This might give an impression of this writer's dilemma in trying to define and delineate the private label marketplace. The "ride" is still barreling along around corners, up and down, twisting, shaking... In other words, the business of private label is at full speed ahead, full of surprises and continuous changes. It is truly frustrating to conclude at this point, when so many interesting developments are underway.

For example, the private label industry in the United States is now mounting a national Private Label Sales Month, sponsored by key players in the business—Shurfine-Central, Federated Foods, and Marketing Management. The initial launch date is October 1992; but the full impact of this promotion will be felt in 1993 with more complete preparation for what could become one of the largest marketing promotions ever.

A&P now has the wraps still on its new America's Best private label program, which very likely will be launched early in 1993. Meantime, the grocery industry is watching Wal-Mart and Kmart with their moves into food retailing/wholesaling. The latest word is that Wal-Mart's Sam's Warehouse Club stores are now developing their own private label program as well.

New market research data also is being prepared, tracking consumer buying attitudes as well as retailer/wholesaler sales performance in private label.

The aggressive foreign expansion of Carrefour outside of France bears watching—nearly 20% of its total 100.4 billion French francs sales now in Spain, some 9% in Brazil, and fractional business in Argentina, Taiwan, and the United States—all potential growth markets. Meantime, in France, Carrefour, while integrating the Euromarche store identity into the Carrefour format, also has expanded its private label lines, the latest extension being into houseware products, helping to enhance that department's competitive edge. Private label, in fact, is an effective tool to meet specific market demands. In Argentina, for example, where escalating inflation has burdened consumers, Carrefour since March 1990 has been selling a new "Productos preciados" budget private label line, which since July 1991 has been promoted heavily.

The development of international private labels throughout Europe, the penetration of private label into Eastern Europe, the new emerging markets in Russia, China, South America, all spell excitement as this industry enters the 21st century.

Appendix

Private Label Reference Guide

This guide to private labels covers a sampling of leading retailers, wholesalers, and distributors in different countries. It also underscores the complexity of this business, where market segments tend to overlap. That is, the retailer can operate both food stores and drugstores as well as work as a food wholesaler. Or the food wholesaler can operate his own retail stores, be a part or sole owner of a cooperative, and be highly diversified, serving in retail, foodservice, institutional market segments, as well as convenience stores, military commissaries, etc. There also exists an overlapping of private label programs, where a retailer or wholesaler can be the licensee of someone else's private label program in addition to carrying his own.

Additionally, this listing shows the diversity of styles in private label marketing, that is, from a single private label program up to multi-tier programs addressing different levels of quality. These labels can be restricted to a particular retail chain operation or be distributed as a corporate brand to all the chains within an organization.

US Supermarkets

1. **The Kroger Co.,** Cincinnati, OH
   Food Stores – $19,533 million
   Convenience Stores – $864 million

Other Sales – $954 million

Total Sales = $21,351 million

Kroger operates 1,263 supermarkets (1,033 of them under the Kroger identity; other identities include Dillon, King Sooper, Fry's, etc.) in 24 states. Its convenience stores number 940 in 16 states.

Estimated private label sales = 25% of total food store sales or $4,900 million.

Estimated private label skus = 4,000+ different grocery products or 8,000+ overall.

This top US grocery chain also operates 37 manufacturing and processing facilities, producing private label products for its retail dairy cases, bakeries, delicatessens, and grocery aisles. These products also are sold under contract to outside national accounts. In addition, Kroger is a partner with the wholesaler Wetterau in wholly-owned subsidiary, Food Land Distributors, a wholesale venture.

Private Brands: Kroger, Big K (soda), Golden Crown (seltzer), Cost Cutter (generics), Country Oven (bakery), Embassy (15 dry grocery product categories in select markets), Dillon, King Sooper, Frys, other sub-brands; while some of its stores operate as members of the Topco co-operative buying program, carrying its private labels, too.

2. **American Stores Co.,** Salt Lake City, UT

Food Stores – $17,092.9 million

Drug Stores – $3,730 million

Total Sales = $20,822.9 million

American Stores operates three divisions: Lucky Stores with 429 supermarkets, Jewel companies with 510 supermarkets (Acme, Jewel, Star Market identities), and American Drug Stores with 711 drugstores, including Osco Drug, Sav-on Drug and 151 combination Jewel-Osco stores.

Estimated private label sales in food stores = 20% of total sales or $3,418.6 million.

Sku count in food stores = approximately 5,000+.

Estimated private label sales in drugstores = 7% of total sales or $261.1 million.

Sku count in drugstores = approximately 850+.

Private Brands: Jewel, Osco, Acme, Star, Skaggs Alpha Beta–all chains operated by Jewel Companies. Under Lucky Stores, private labels include Lady Lee, Harvest Day, Gold Seal, HiClass (pet food), Villa, Econo Buy (generic upscale line also carried by other chains in organizations). Osco identity also carried as health and beauty care line by different chains, although Lucky has its own Medi-Guard identity for this category. Jewel

Food recently became licensee of President's Choice controlled label program from Loblaw of Canada.

3. **Safeway Inc.,** Oakland, CA

Safeway Supermarket total sales = $15,119.2 million

Estimated private label sales = 15% of total sales or $2,267.9 million

SKU count totals 3,100 items, most of them manufactured or processed at the company's 56 company facilities (38 in the US and 18 in Canada).

Safeway operates some 1,100 stores in about 15 states. In past couple of years, Safeway has cut back its label identities from about 50 to under 30, as part of a new packaging design strategy. Completion is expected at the end of 1992.

Private Brands: Under its "finest quality" range – Safeway (non-edibles, general merchandise, and health and beauty care), Safeway Valu Pack (club packs), Bel-air (frozen foods), Captain's Choice (fish products in grocery and frozen), Cragmont (carbonated beverages), Crown Colony (spices and teas), Lucerne (milk, cheese, eggs, ice cream), Mrs. Wright's (commodity breads plus possible cookies and crackers now under its Busy Baker logo), Nature's Cupboard (all-grain breads plus other products like fruit spreads, pure old-fashion peanut butter, etc.), Edwards coffee, Smok-A-Roma (processed meats), Town House (staples like sugar, flour, cereal, canned goods, mayonnaise, jug water, etc.), Trophy (pet foods), White Magic (detergents).

Under its "good quality" range – Best Buy (cheese), Blossom Time (milk), Dairy Land (milk), Dairy Glen (milk, cottage cheese), Goldbrook (margarine), Gardenside (canned goods), Marigold (paper items like towels, plates, etc.), Ovenjoy (breads, saltine crackers, flour), Par (detergent), Piedmont (mayonnaise, vinegar, condiments), Real Roast (peanut butter), Scotch Buy (cigarettes), Snow Star (ice cream), Trader Horn (spices). Some of its private brands have been around for decades, i.e., Mrs. Wrights Baking Co. was purchased in 1929 and Lucerne Butter Co. in 1930. Scotch Buy once served as the brand for a full range of products marketed against generics.

4. **Atlantic & Pacific Tea Co., Inc. (A&P),** Montvale, NJ

Total sales = $11,590.9 million

Estimated private label sales = 23% of total sales or $2,665.9 million

Estimated private label sku count covers 1,800+ items, including 1,500+ in grocery, the balance in health and beauty care general merchandise, etc.

A&P operates a number of regional supermarket chains—A&P, Super Fresh, Kohl's, Waldbaum's, Food Emporium, all in the US and Miracle Food Mart, Dominion and A&P in Canada. Its total store count is 1,238. The company also operates two coffee roasting plants, three bakeries, two delicatessen food kitchens, an ice cream plant and under joint venture, a dairy. A&P also is 52.5% owned by Tenglemann Warenhandelsgesellschaft of Germany.

Private Brands: A&P, Super Fresh, Kohl's, Waldbaum's, Food Emporium, Miracle Food Mart, Dominion, Eight O'Clock (coffee), Bokar (coffee), Royale (coffee), Jane Parker (bakery), Wesley's Quaker Maid, Master Choice (upscale foods), Our Own (tea), Savings Plus (second quality).

5. **Winn-Dixie Stores,** Jacksonville,FL
   Winn-Dixie Supermarkets total sales = $10,074.3 million.
   Estimated private label sales = 20% of total sales or $2,014.9 million.

Winn-Dixie operates 1,207 US supermarkets in 13 states plus 13 other supermarkets in the Bahamas. It operates some 20 manufacturing and processing plants.

Private Brands: Thrifty Maid (canned fruits/vegetables), Arrow (non-food items), Sunbelt (paper goods), Crackin' Good (bakery items), Astor (grocery items), Tropical (juices), Superbrand, Sta-Fit (isotonic drinks), Premium, Prestige, WD Brand, Kountry Fresh (cereal), Dixie Darling, Prestigio (pasta), Kountry Cookin's, Feedin' Time (pet food), Vita Pep (pet food), Slick (pet food), Price Breaker (generics), Deep South (peanut butter), Deli, Ultra Fresh (health and beauty care), Fresh 'n Gentle (HBC), Nite-Time (HBC), Kuddles (HBC), Fisherman's Wharf, Chek (soft drinks), Dixie Home (tea), etc.

6. **Albertson's Inc.,** Boise, ID
   Total sales = $8,680.5 million
   Estimated private label sales = 20% of total sales or $1,736.1 million.
   Estimated private label skus = 1,600+
Albertson's operates 562 supermarkets in 17 states.

Private Brands: Albertson's, Janet Lee, Good Day, Master Treat (pet food), Maxx Pak (club pack).

7. **Publix Super Markets Inc.,** Lakeland, FL
   Total sales = $5,800 million
   Estimated private label sales = 20% of total sales or $1,160 million.
   Estimated private label skus = 2,000+
Publix supermarkets operate 392 stores in two states.

Private Brands: Publix, Breakfast Club (breads, eggs, margarine), Dairi-Fresh (milk, ice cream, yogurt), Penny Saver (detergents, window cleaner), the Deli as Publix, Danish Bakery, Pix (canned soft drinks), Ration Style

(dog food), Tasty Lite (ice milk) etc.

8. **Food Lion Inc.,** Sailsbury, NC
Total sales = $6,438.5 million.
Estimated private label sales = 18% of total sales or $1,158.9 million.
Estimated private label skus = 1,200+

Food Lion is owned by Etablissements Delhaize Freres et Cie "Le Lion," Brussels, Belgium.
Private Brand: Food Lion.

9. **Supermarket General Holding Corp.,** Woodbridge, NJ
Total sales = $5,729.6 million.

This retailer operates 146 Pathmark supermarkets, 41 Rickel home center stores, and 32 free-standing Pathmark drugstores.

Total Pathmark supermarket sales = $5,319.9 million.

Estimated private label sales = 30% of total Pathmark supermarket sales or $1,595.9 million.

Private brands: Pathmark, No Frills (generic), and Rickle (label not stocked in supermarkets).

10. **Ahold (USA) Parsippany, NJ (owned by Koninklijke Ahold nv, Zaandam, The Netherlands).**
Total sales = $5,603 million.
Bi-Lo, Mauldin, SC, taking $1,626 million with 178 supermarkets
First National Supermarkets taking $2,020 million with 109 stores.
Giant Food Stores, Harrisburg, PA taking $997 million with 55 supermarkets.

Tops Markets Inc., Buffalo, NY taking $960 million (including franchising) with 150 stores (23 franchised).

Estimated private label sales at these chains averages 15% or $840.5 million.

Estimated private label skus = 2,000+
Private Brands: Finast, Bo-Lo, Giant, Tops, Sensational.

11. **The Vons Companies, Inc.,** Arcadia, CA
Total sales = $5,350.2 million.
Estimated private label sales = 13% of total sales or $642 million.
Estimated private label skus = 1,100+

Vons operates 320 supermarket and food and drug retail stores under the names Vons, Pavilons, Tianguis, and Williams Bros. The company also operates a fluid milk and an ice cream plant plus a bakery and delicatessen kitchen.

Private Brands: Vons, Pavilions, Tianguis, Jerseymaid.

12. **Giant Food Inc.,** Landover, MD
    Total sales = $3,489.8 million.
    Estimated private label sales = 20% of total sales or $697.9 million.
    Estimated private label skus = 1,500+

This retailer operates 154 supermarkets of which 105 are food-drug stores, plus three additional stores are free-standing drugstores. The company operates a dairy processing plant, an ice cream manufacturing facility, a bakery plus other factories.

Private Brands: Giant (being converted to Super G label to create marketing flexibility in geographic areas where Giant name cannot be used), Heidi, Aunt Nellie's, Kiss, Rene, SuperDeal, etc.

US FOOD WHOLESALERS

1. **Fleming Companies, Inc.,** Oklahoma City, OK
   Total sales = $12,901.6 million.
   Estimated private label sales = 15% of total sales or $1,935.2 million.
   Estimated private label skus = 30,700+

This wholesale food distributor serves 4,800+ stores in 36 states, working through 35 divisions, backed up with more than 100 support services – store planning, financing, advertising, merchandising, etc. The 2,920 supermarkets served represent estimates sales of $23,900 million. Fleming is the largest IGA supplier in the US, while also supplying accounts like Piggly Wiggly, Big T, Thriftways, Big Star, Shop 'N Bag, Sentry and United Super. Additionally, it franchises price impact store formats like Food 4 Less, Magamarket, Checkers and Super 1 Foods. The company also exports to: Mexico, South and Central America, the Caribbean, Japan and other Pacific Rim countries, those sales close to $200 million. Joint venture formed with Grupo Gigante (one of Mexico's largest food and general merchandise retailers) to develop price impact stores in Mexico.

Private Brands: TV(True Value), Montco, Bonnie Hubbard, Shop 'n Bag, Hyde Park, Rainbow (budget line), Piggly Wiggly, Marquee (health and beauty care), IGA, Sentry, Sunrise (second quality), Value Pack (club pack), Shop 'n Bag, P.S. (Personnally Selected meat), Merit, Glee, Holsum, Foodtown/Bi-Rite.

2. **Supervalu,*** Minneapolis, MN
   Total Sales = $10,632.3 million.
   Estimated private label sales = 15% of total sales or $1,594.8 million.

Estimated private label skus = 2,500+

Operating through 17 wholesale food divisions, this company serves 2,650 retail stores in 31 states and also operates 105 supermarkets and superstores, under names like Cub Foods, Scott's, Twin Valu and Hornbacker's. Supervalue also operates Preferred Products Inc., a food packaging and processing facility (peanuts, rebagged candy/nuts, sweet coconut) in Chaska, MN. In its retail food operation, covering sales by its owned food stores, the company reports private label taking 7% of their total sales ($2 billion) or $140 million. Private label share in retail support sales ($9,841 million) are more difficult to track, going to independently owned food stores.

*At this writing, Supervalu Inc. and Wetterau Inc. announced letter of intent for a merger.

Private Brands: Flav-O-Rite (food), Chateau (non-foods), IGA, Elf (second label), "for Pet's Sale" (dog food), Shoppers Value (price sensitive items), Preferred (candy), Rite Choice, Sub Scusine, Shop 'n Save, Supervalu.

3. **Scrivner, Inc.,** Oklahoma City, OK

Total sales = $6,000 million.

Estimated private label sales = 8% of total sales or $480 million.

Estimated private label skus = 3,000+

This voluntary wholesaler serves some 4,870 independent stores in 28 states. It also operates 170 corporate stores under such names as Festival, Market Basket, Food Saver, Thompson Food Basket, Super Duper, Boogaarts, etc. The company is owned by Franz Haniel Cie Gmbh, Duisburg, Germany, a diversified company with $10,351 million in sales.

Private Brands: BestYet, Our Value, Red & White, IGA, Gateway Quality, Nature's Finest (produce), Super Tru (meats), Exceptional Value.

4. **Wetterau, Inc.,** Hazelwood, MO

Total sales = $5,712.5 million.

Estimated private label sales = 11% of total sales or $628.4 million.

Estimated private label skus = 6,000+

Working through 15 divisions, this food wholesaler serves 2,897 retail stores in 29 states, including affiliated retailers like IGA, Foodland, and Save-A-Lot stores, as well as unaffiliated retailers. Additionally, the firm serves some 1,700 institutional customers. The company operates chains like Shop 'n Save, Save-A-Lot, Laneco stores, and Food Lane supermarkets. Wetterau also operates Hazelwood Farms Bakeries, a leading producer of frozen dough products. Its Foodland International Corp. (second largest US voluntary food group) licenses wholesalers to use the Foodland name on stores and private label merchandise.

Private Brands: IGA, Nature's Best, Foodland, Homebest (household products, health and beauty care, and general merchandise), Topmost (pet-related foods and other items), Bi-Rite (second label), ALLways Rite (second label), Why Pay More? Also, Foodland manages the Clover Farm, Best Mart and Kwik-Way brands.

SELECTED US DISCOUNT CHAINS

1. Wal-Mart Stores, Inc., Bentonville,AR

Total sales = $43,886.9 million.

Estimated private label sales = 15% of total sales or $6,583 million.

The world's largest retailer operates 1,720 Wal-Mart stores and 208 Sam's Club stores in 42 states plus has a 50% interest in CIFRA, Mexico. Wal-Mart also owns McLane distribution centers, serving convenience stores and grocery store retailers as well as its own 20 food stores (The Phillips Companies).

Private Brands: Sam's American Choice (foods, non-foods, beverages), Wal-Mart (paint, paper goods, auto supplies), Equate* (health and beauty care), Renegade (fishing accessories), J-Bend (plumbing supplies), Sports Afield (soft goods, hunting togs), Workman's Choice (tools and hardware), Ozark Farms (peanuts), Ol Roy (dog food), Bobbie Brooks (women's casual wear).

*Equate is licensed from Perrigo, a manufacturer.

2. Kmart Corp., Troy, MI

Total sales = $34,580 million.

(General Merchandise sales = $25,548 million; specialty retail sales = $9,032 million)

Estimated private label sales = 40% of general merchandising or $13,832 million.

Estimated private label sales in specialty retailing, covering only Pace Warehouse and PayLess Drug = 15%+ or $1,354.8 million.

Private Brands: Kmart (health & beauty care), K grow (tools, plants), Focal (film video cassettes), Jaclyn Smith (fashion womens apparel and accessories), Fox Hollow (preppy separates), Noah's Ark (children's wear), Ketch/Envoy/Private Club (men's shirts), Body Co. (Bodywear), Cycle Club (sports wear), Nature's Classics (snacks, other food items), The Performer (paint/rust remover by Dutch Boy), Sheer Intrique (pantihose fashion hosiery), At Home with Martha Steward (home furnishings collection), Sentress (sanitary pads), Little Ones (baby wipes, wash cloths), Kat's Delight (cat food, canned), Gentle 'n Easy (enema relief), Fit 'Ems (diapers), XLE tires, generic packaging, etc.

In specialty retailing: Payless and PACE.

SELECTED US COOPERATIVES

1. Topco Associates, Inc., Skokie, IL

Total sales (Estimated) = $3,000 million+ — all private label

Estimated private label skus = 16,000+ skus

This marketing/procurement organization is a co-op owned by 25 "blue chip" food retailers, covering some 40 states. Roughly 50% of its product mix is in grocery items, the balance in perishables (produce, meat, dairy, fish, etc.)

Private Brands: Food Club, Kingston, Top Crest (grocery, non-foods and general merchandise), Top Care (health and beauty care), World Classics (upscale foods), GreenMark (environmental line), Mega (secondary economy line), Maxxi (secondary economy line), and ValuTime (upscale generic). Topco also manages some private brands for its member programs, under their private labels.

2. Shurfine-Central Corp., Northlake, IL

Total sales = $715 million — mostly private label

Estimated private label skus = 9,000+

This co-op is owned by 36 shareholders (medium-size food wholesalers), serving more than 10,000 independent retailers in 46 states, who together account for $25,000 million in retail sales. Accounts also include convenience stores, the military, institutions, etc. Shurfine exports product to : Sweden, Japan, Malaysia, and Singapore, while distributing its stock in Mexico, Central and South America, as well as the Middle East.

Private Brands: Shurfine (its flagship line including 60%+ of stock), Shurfresh (perishables), Ultimate Choice (grocery/perishable), Project Green (environmental line), Price Saver (secondary, economy foods/non-foods), Saver's Choice (economy line also).

3. IGA, Inc., Chicago, IL

Total sales = $675.9 million — all private label.

Estimated private label skus = 3,200 (dairy, bakery, snacks, frozen foods, grocery, meats).

IGA is a huge voluntary retail network, whose participants represent more than $16,200 million in sales worldwide. It is owned by 21 food wholesale companies, who work through more than 3,750 affiliated supermarkets in 49 states plus Australia, Canada, Japan, Korea, and Papua New Guinea. The US portion alone represents retail sales of $11,500 million.

Private Brands: IGA, TableRite (meats), TableFresh (produce).

4. **Western Family Foods Inc.,** Portland, OR

Total Sales = $370 million — all private label

Estimated private label skus = 6,400+

This buying/market organization serves food wholesalers plus wholesalers under the Shurfine program, covering some 23 states, while also exporting goods to Japan.

Private Brands: Western Family, Western Family Advantage Pack (club packs), Shurfine program, Valley Fare (secondary label), Shur Saving Shurfine program, Valley Fare (secondary label), Shur Saving (secondary label), Market Choice (secondary label), Cottage (secondary label).

OTHER COUNTRIES—SELECTED RETAILERS

CANADA

Loblaw Companies Limited (71% of its stock owned by George Weston Limited), Toronto.

Total Sales = $8,533 million (Canadian dollars)

Retail sales take 63% or $5,380 million; balance of sales derive from operation as a wholesaler to franchised independent and independent accounts.

Corporate brand sales = 35% of retail sales or $1,883 million.

Estimated corporate brands skus = 3,000+

Loblaw operates 341 corporate stores plus serves 1,156 franchised independent stores. Its stores include: Loblaws, Zehrmart, Fortino's Supermarkets, Westfair Foods.

Corporate Brands: No Name, President's Choice, PC Club Pack, PC G.R.E.E.N., PC Too Good to Be True!

UNITED KINGDOM

J. Sainsbury p.l.c., London

Total sales = £9,202.3 million.

Sales include £8,159.2 million in UK and £1,043.1 in US. Sainsbury takes lion's share of sales at £7,892.3 million in UK. Its other operations include: Homebase DIY stores in UK at £257.6 million 964 units) and Shaw's Supermarkets in US (73 units).

In 313 stores under Sainsbury's name, retailer carries 7,000 product lines under its Sainsbury's label, representing two-thirds of its sales. Shaw's label covers some 800 skus and Homebase label some 300+ skus.

Own Brands: Sainsbury's, Homebase, Shaw's.

Marks & Spencer p.l.c., London

Total turnover (excluding sales taxes) - £5,774.8 million.

M&S has 100% own label in M&S stores: 48.4% in food, 38.8% in clothing, 11.2% in homewares, and balance of sales in financial activities. M&S operates in nine countries. Its principal activity is retailing under the Marks & Spencer operation. Company also operates clothing stores: Brooks Brothers and Kings Super Markets (both in the US), and D'Allaird's and Peoples in Canada.

Own Brands: St Michael, Kings, Brooks, etc.

SWITZERLAND

Migros, Zurich

Total sales = Sfr. 14,532.5 million.

Estimated private label sales = 95% of those sales or Sfr. 13,806 million.

This federation of 12 cooperatives has the backing of at least 13 manufacturing plants — foods, beverages, cosmetics, cleaning agents, meat processing etc. The group operates with 549 stores plus another 90 Migros Stores-on-Wheels.

Private Brands: M-Sano bread, M-Plus cleaning agents, M-Power batteries, Frey chocolates/confectionery items, Golden Hair hair care, Sun Look sun protection, Famioly (economy line) health and beauty care, Aproz mineral water/soft drinks, Midor bakery items, etc.

Markant AG, Pfaffikon

This partnership of medium-sized wholesale and retail business was started as a German cooperative in 1983. The merger of Selex and Tania created Markant Handles — und Industriewaren—Vermittlungs AG in 1988. Its partners, covering at least eight European countries, represents sales exceeding 40,000 million Deutsche Mark. Because of the complexity of this partnership, only the Germany operation is examined here.

In Germany, more than 100 Markant customers from the private wholesale and retail sector participate. They include some 8,000 retailers and supermarkets (names like Ihre Kette, A & O, IFA, Vivo, Katra, Vege, Gefra, Meyer, etc.), some 400 consumer markets and self service stores, plus drugstores, discount stores, DIY outlets etc. Markant's service arm, Selex Handelsgesellschaft mbh, Offenburg, manages commodities and food, including private labels of which the group averages about 5 to 10% of their sales.

Private Brands: Juwel (pet food), Globetrotter (tobacco), Omega (canned foods), Rio Brand (imported commodities), Erntegold (canned vegetables), Selex (detergents), Landsknecht (canned ready-to-eat food), Selmi (milk), Frischgold (fresh foods), Dorati (sweets/cakes), Hanse Wappen (coffee/cocoa), Kon-Tiki (rice), Apte (pasta, mayonnaise), Dorati (cookies, biscuits, snacks), etc., covering some 400 skus.

In addition, Markant's Tania Handles GmbH, Wiesbaden, has private labels in the non-foods area, such as: MacLoy (leather goods), Patrick Lion (sportswear), and Peppi or Tramp (children's clothes), covering hardware, textile, and leather goods.

FRANCE

Carrefour, Lisses

Total sales = 100,377 million French francs (FF)

Estimated private label sales = 15% of hypermarket sales in France (approximately 66,000 million FF total or 10,000 million FF in private label).

Carrefour reports sales in France of 69,811 million FF, including its 133 Carrefour hypermarkets, 137 Ed "hard discount" stores plus other operations. Overall, Carrefour operates 490+ stores in six countries.

Private Brands: Carrefour, tex, Ed, etc.

THE NETHERLANDS

Koninklijke Ahold nv, Zaandam

Ahold The Netherlands sales = Dfl 10,264 million ($6,004 million)

Ahold United States sales = Dfl 9,577.8 million ($5,603 million)

Total sales = Dfl 19,841.8 million ($11,607 million)

Company operates Albert Heijn supermarkets, the market leader with 965 stores plus 173 franchised stores or 1,138 stores total. They break down into: 448 Albert Heijn stores, 330 Gall & Gall liquor stores, 152 Etos health and beauty care stores. Albert Heijn chain (minus its franchised stores) generates Dfl 7.641 million. Estimated private label share is about 30% of those sales or Dfl 2,292.

In the US, Ahold operates: Bi-Lo, Giant Food Stores, First National Supermarkets, Tops Markets. Some 15% of its total sales or $840 million is in private label.

Private Brands: Albert Heijn, Perla (coffee), Albi (detergents), Brouwers (beer), etc. In US: Bi-Lo, Giant, Finast, Tops, Sensational.

Glossary

Charts on Market Research

CHART 1A

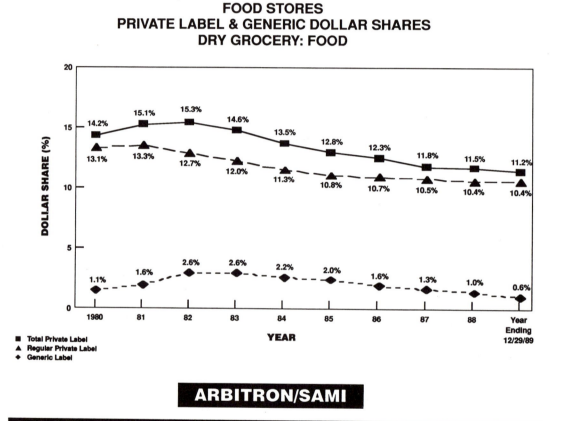

**FOOD STORES
PRIVATE LABEL & GENERIC DOLLAR SHARES
DRY GROCERY: FOOD**

ARBITRON/SAMI

SAMI chart, taken from PLMA Special Report, July 1990, tracks only warehouse product withdrawals; direct store product deliveries not included. Copyright owned by Information Resources Inc., Chicago, IL.

CHART 1B

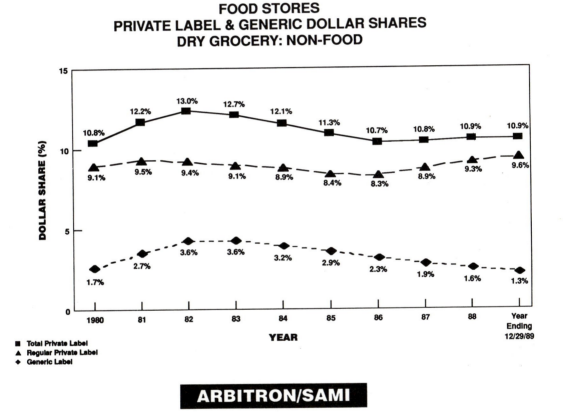

FOOD STORES
PRIVATE LABEL & GENERIC DOLLAR SHARES
DRY GROCERY: NON-FOOD

ARBITRON/SAMI

SAMI chart, taken from PLMA Special Report, July 1990, tracks only warehouse product withdrawals; direct store product deliveries not included. Copyright owned by Information Resources Inc., Chicago, IL.

CHART 1C

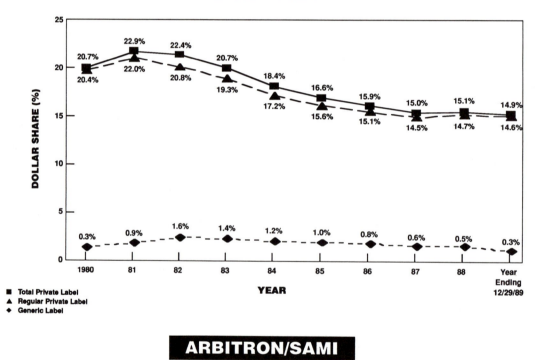

FOOD STORES
PRIVATE LABEL & GENERIC DOLLAR SHARES
FROZEN FOODS

■ Total Private Label
▲ Regular Private Label
♦ Generic Label

CHART 1D

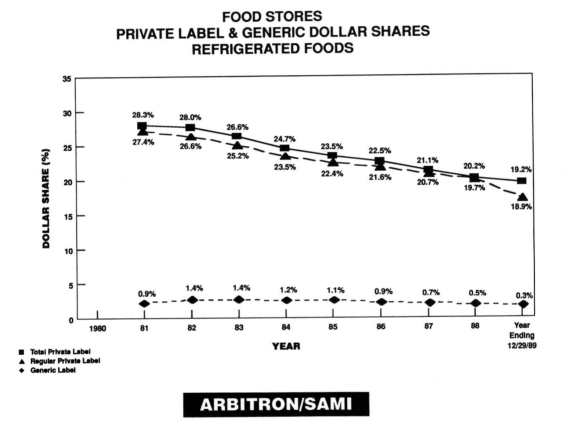

FOOD STORES
PRIVATE LABEL & GENERIC DOLLAR SHARES
REFRIGERATED FOODS

SAMI chart, taken from PLMA Special Report, July 1990, tracks only warehouse product withdrawals; direct store product deliveries not included. Copyright owned by Information Resources Inc., Chicago, IL.

CHART 1E

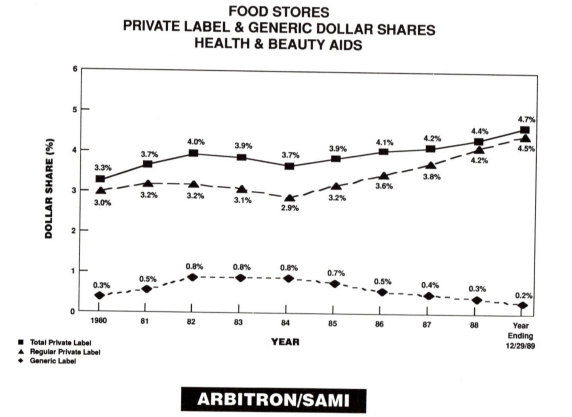

FOOD STORES
PRIVATE LABEL & GENERIC DOLLAR SHARES
HEALTH & BEAUTY AIDS

■ Total Private Label
▲ Regular Private Label
◆ Generic Label

ARBITRON/SAMI

SAMI chart, taken from PLMA Special Report, July 1990, tracks only warehouse product withdrawals; direct store product deliveries not included. Copyright owned by Information Resources Inc., Chicago, IL.

CHART 2A

InfoScan

US SUPERMARKET REVIEW
VENDOR MULTI-CATEGORY REPORT – 1991

	Dollar Sales Ending 12/29/91	Dollar Sales 52-Week Ending 12/29/91 vs 52 Weeks Ago	Category Dollar Share 52-Week Ending 12/29/91	Category Dollar Share 52-Week Ending 12/29/91 vs 52 Weeks Ago	% Price Differential 52-Week Ending 12/29/91	Est. Average Activity Weighed Distribution
Total Private Label	25,774MM	2.21	*	*	23.02	99.5
Milk	5,432MM	–2.77	64.06	0.84	17.83	84.6
Fresh Bread Rolls	1,556MM	2.09	27.87	0.12	28.87	94.7
Cheese	1,370MM	5.35	24.75	1.43	22.96	96.7
Ice Cream	911,960M	5.26	27.83	0.47	26.38	91.3
Frozen Plain Vegetables	815,909M	–4.23	46.48	–2.07	22.89	96.6
Carbonated Beverages	620,345M	6.97	6.70	0.29	22.59	87.1
Vegetables Shelf Stable	604,716M	–1.16	28.12	–0.36	25.86	99.3
Sugar	603,940M	–2.10	41.63	–0.80	21.93	87.2
Frozen Juices	573,684M	–4.80	30.99	0.65	28.74	98.1
Juice Shelf Stable	540,860M	8.06	13.32	0.29	20.93	99.5
Juice Refrigerated	518,066M	3.87	18.88	0.04	27.80	90.9
Fruit Shelf Stable	449,757M	2.87	30.61	0.14	20.32	99.1
Deli Luncheon Meats	374,595M	–3.25	13.43	–0.50	20.13	78.1
Chips & Snacks	350,154M	5.02	7.18	0.12	22.23	75.1
Food & Trash Bags	345,349M	–2.92	25.57	0.33	22.56	98.3
Cold Cereal	318,428M	33.4	4.58	0.94	18.17	93.0
Breakfast Meats	284,679M	2.11	15.41	0.21	21.83	82.1
Cookies	276,165M	12.05	8.57	0.83	22.27	87.1
Cottage Cheese	273,283M	–3.61	39.01	0.55	24.69	86.5
Diapers	272,920M	16.97	11.35	1.18	14.25	85.9

CHART 2A (continued)

	Dollar Sales Ending 12/29/91	Dollar Sales 52-Week Ending 12/29/91 vs 52 Weeks Ago	Category Dollar Share 52-Week Ending 12/29/91	Category Dollar Share 52-Week Ending 12/29/91 vs 52 Weeks Ago	% Price Differential 52-Week Ending 12/29/91	Est. Average Activity Weighed Distribution
Pickels/Relish/ Olives	268,164M	8.53	25.60	1.62	24.44	85.2
Cups and Plates	250,314M	0.70	28.83	1.21	17.79	86.6
Spices/Seasonings	238,565M	4.53	17.44	0.07	26.55	95.3
Butter	233,990M	−2.81	40.34	−0.08	24.14	91.4
Coffee	230,649M	−5.82	7.92	0.14	24.10	81.9
Tomato Products	227,747M	1.84	25.91	0.08	22.40	98.6
Shortening & Oil	212,549M	4.22	15.24	0.84	18.34	98.6
Toilet Tissue	184,321M	−13.38	8.15	−0.63	22.73	92.9
Seafood Shelf Stable	182,600M	−2.11	10.71	0.24	24.63	88.3
Yogurt	179,240M	10.25	14.75	1.00	25.32	79.9
Crackers	177,376M	11.70	6.32	0.55	25.02	88.6
Pastry/Doughnuts	176,931M	6.86	16.89	0.00	20.34	51.8
Peanut Butter	176,446M	5.03	17.20	−0.73	18.22	97.8
Dog Food	169,412M	7.74	5.83	0.47	19.46	88.1
Foils & Wraps	169,152M	3.17	28.81	1.86	18.24	95.6
Bottled Water	168,594M	2.38	15.12	0.22	21.74	82.8
Potatoes/Onions	166,432M	0.37	23.41	0.52	24.95	93.0
Paper Towels	162,322M	−3.72	11.55	−0.24	25.41	91.9
Creams	161,104M	3.80	35.01	−1.02	18.73	76.8
Frozen Novelties	160,604M	10.88	10.64	0.75	24.60	63.8
Jellies and Jams	155,107M	3.57	19.74	−0.04	23.75	93.9
Sour Cream	146,509M	−1.20	35.04	−0.82	22.28	86.0
Pasta	146,275M	5.01	13.10	0.33	29.59	92.9
Soup	144,529M	9.51	5.29	0.16	23.98	75.4
Frankfurters	137,228M	0.09	9.29	0.18	24.18	63.8
Powdered/ Condensed Milk	134,523M	−0.06	34.33	0.41	13.94	96.2
Margarine/Spreads	132,837M	5.08	8.75	0.36	25.42	95.9
Tea	127,043M	10.71	13.08	0.76	17.74	94.5
Internal Analgesics	124,071M	21.38	12.50	1.33	30.87	95.1
Cat Food	115,829M	2.98	5.62	0.31	17.78	77.8
Vitamins	113,497M	7.47	30.16	0.21	27.30	78.9

CHART 2A (continued)

	Dollar Sales Ending 12/29/91	Dollar Sales 52-Week Ending 12/29/91 vs 52 Weeks Ago	Category Dollar Share 52-Week Ending 12/29/91	Category Dollar Share 52-Week Ending 12/29/91 vs 52 Weeks Ago	% Price Differential 52-Week Ending 12/29/91	Est. Average Activity Weighed Distribution
Dinners	112,315M	10.61	4.96	0.35	23.43	96.8
Bleach	103,385M	9.12	18.36	2.33	20.84	98.4
Baking Needs	101,985M	6.17	11.22	0.46	23.61	87.9
Snack Nuts	100,215M	−7.42	16.03	−1.22	20.66	84.2
Pies and Cakes	99,079M	19.61	27.73	3.66	22.85	39.8
Facial Tissue	96,420M	−8.61	11.64	−1.15	19.22	90.9
Laundry Detergent	95,851M	4.56	2.76	0.15	21.75	81.6
Rice	90.385M	12.26	9.15	0.54	18.12	89.5
Biscuits/Dough	86,994M	9.70	11.37	0.22	26.69	73.8
Paper Napkins	85,483M	−1.32	20.63	0.54	16.12	93.9
Hot Cereal	84,510M	13.72	7.73	0.86	21.12	83.1
Mustard & Ketchup	84,192M	14.47	13.16	1.47	21.46	94.9
Dry Bean/Vegetables	83,481M	−12.14	43.61	−1.32	23.27	61.1
Frozen Pizza	79,322M	12.31	6.32	0.34	23.67	49.3
Frozen Fruit	74,820M	0.94	50.95	0.75	18.44	83.3
Cigarettes	74,060M	39.83	0.94	0.24	11.66	25.9
Dried Fruit	70.207M	2.16	14.97	0.38	15.73	82.7
Entree/Side Dish	70,034M	0.06	18.28	−0.60	19.66	26.1
Mayonnaise/Various Dressings	66,716M	7.21	6.79	0.22	19.71	90.5
Household Cleaners	64,934M	7.84	4.06	0.22	20.94	94.0
Other Refrigerated Products	64,751M	1.80	11.40	−1.17	22.79	67.4
Syrup/Molasses	63,157M	5.81	11.72	0.52	23.00	93.4
English Muffins	62,088M	4.60	17.28	0.99	31.41	68.7
Dish Detergent	60,975M	8.82	5.38	0.56	17.56	84.4
Popcorn/Popcorn Oil	60,580M	2.60	10.44	−0.07	24.27	87.2
Frozen Seafood	59,362M	−10.68	7.69	−0.52	25.60	50.3
Coffee Creamer	57,667M	8.30	28.33	1.88	19.88	97.7
Mexican Food	54,369M	6.99	7.61	−0.04	20.57	68.4
Pizza Refrigerated	52,963M	−0.25	27.56	−6.63	21.22	24.5
Vinegar	51,262M	12.90	27.98	2.08	17.73	90.3
Hosiery	50,582M	−3.98	11.0	0.12	27.13	55.3

CHART 2A (continued)

	Dollar Sales Ending 12/29/91	Dollar Sales 52-Week Ending 12/29/91 vs 52 Weeks Ago	Category Dollar Share 52-Week Ending 12/29/91	Category Dollar Share 52-Week Ending 12/29/91 vs 52 Weeks Ago	% Price Differential 52-Week Ending 12/29/91	Est. Average Activity Weighed Distribution
Cold & Sinus Tablet/Cough	46,882M	34.59	7.19	0.97	28.43	84.5
Candy/Mints	46,809M	−3.31	1.88	−0.13	16.37	46.0
Flour/Meal	44,389M	−0.71	10.47	0.04	21.57	88.4
Sanitary Protection	43,369M	−11.70	5.00	−0.66	17.62	78.6
Drink Mixes	42,852M	17.63	5.33	0.44	18.90	57.4
Moist Towelettes	42,603M	10.55	20.13	1.20	20.37	89.1
Fabric Softner Sheet	41,554M	2.25	12.85	0.95	20.08	92.9
Cat Litter	40,795M	7.32	10.54	−0.08	20.17	81.7
Baking Nuts	34,667M	4.93	13.04	0.25	17.03	26.1
Mouthwash	33,087M	21.85	9.99	2.41	30.91	86.2
Baking Mixes	32,722M	−1.33	3.09	−0.11	20.32	66.4
Bakery Snacks	31,735M	−5.48	4.08	−0.23	23.95	46.6
Spaghetti Sauce	31,018M	4.17	2.99	0.04	24.03	59.3
Baked Beans	30,957M	4.11	8.64	0.39	25.34	82.8
Cotton Balls	30,168M	5.94	26.52	1.72	29.00	90.4
Gravy/Sauce Mixes	29,847M	25.75	4.82	0.74	23.18	80.3
Coffee Filters	29,659M	13.48	25.51	1.14	29.83	76.7
Salad Dressings	29,524M	12.40	2.45	0.11	22.97	36.5
Instant Potatoes	28,463M	0.04	11.52	−0.32	17.65	81.0
Frozen Meat	28,404M	−4.97	6.52	−0.40	17.35	29.6
Marshmallows	27,633M	14.30	32.20	2.25	19.75	78.0
Bread/Bkd. Goods Refrigerated	27,570M	15.55	42.04	1.46	25.06	20.3
Gelatin/Pudding Mix	27,547M	7.38	4.81	0.25	20.46	33.9
Sauces	27,432M	18.61	3.22	0.20	23.01	62.6
Sponges	27,078M	3.32	12.63	0.14	24.87	52.3
First Aid Treatment	26,978M	6.88	34.11	1.95	36.54	89.4
Cocoa Mix	26,496M	12.69	9.28	0.59	19.31	71.8
Frozen. Dessert/Topping	26,106M	12.05	4.84	0.18	21.51	65.2
Sausage	24,858M	7.01	6.04	−0.04	26.65	21.5
Fabric Softner Liquid	24,664M	−0.73	5.75	−0.03	18.40	92.9
Cold/Allergy Liquid/Powder	23,826M	40.99	13.58	1.78	24.12	77.7

CHART 2A (continued)

	Dollar Sales Ending 12/29/91	Dollar Sales 52-Week Ending 12/29/91 vs 52 Weeks Ago	Category Dollar Share 52-Week Ending 12/29/91	Category Dollar Share 52-Week Ending 12/29/91 vs 52 Weeks Ago	% Price Differential 52-Week Ending 12/29/91	Est. Average Activity Weighed Distribution
Frozen Dinners/Entrees	21,625M	−8.37	0.53	−0.04	26.86	31.2
Frozen Pies	21,562M	1.18	5.14	−0.13	24.03	52.2
Frozen Chicken	21.082M	59.82	3.14	1.24	22.51	40.3
Meat – Shelf Stable	19,926M	12.56	4.75	0.52	20.56	31.9
Razors	19,482M	8.10	5.37	0.12	27.03	72.3
Frozen Pot Pies	17,983M	4.38	6.77	0.31	29.92	37.7
Natural Foods	17,368M	24.68	3.94	0.43	12.59	35.2
Dental Accessories	17,096M	16.15	7.79	0.53	37.33	69.8
Frozen Breakfast Foods	17,093M	39.62	2.23	0.43	24.60	53.8
Frozen Pastry/ Baked Goods	17,045M	25.18	4.22	0.70	23.63	38.5
Dessert Toppings	16,187M	13.38	8.59	0.75	15.33	82.9
Shampoo	13,727M	−0.80	2.02	0.06	23.24	80.1
First Aid Accessories	13,519M	12.90	10.49	1.07	24.76	61.4
Cough Syrup	13.275M	19.30	7.69	0.89	21.93	65.1
Stuffing	12,824M	21.01	5.04	0.68	19.75	53.1
Dry Fruit Snacks	12,714M	1.41	3.44	−0.14	18.20	35.2
Laxatives	12,587M	30.88	8.07	1.14	23.66	58.3
Pancake Mix	11,793M	10.56	8.56	1.38	16.90	67.8
Antacids	11.792M	7.03	4.34	0.04	21.90	56.4
Breadcrumbs/Batters	11.508M	18.37	5.66	0.25	29.07	44.1
Foil Pans	11.501M	6.12	9.68	0.39	37.24	14.6
Ice Cream Cones/Mix	11.127M	14.89	17.48	1.44	16.43	30.2
Frosting	10,325M	−9.29	4.89	−0.52	14.85	59.8
Nasal Spray	9,356M	32.51	8.87	1.32	29.49	61.2
Misc. Remedies	8,793M	22.55	4.12	0.65	27.94	56.8
Seafood – Refrigerated	8,552M	−10.51	7.00	−0.86	25.97	8.8
Eye/Contact Lens Care	8.071M	35.35	2.63	0.65	27.46	48.9
Hand & Body Lotion	7,987M	7.38	3.64	0.34	25.32	68.7
Frozen Dough	7,040M	10.43	11.06	1.78	20.83	30.4
Toothpaste	6,813M	39.23	0.91	0.22	25.66	46.1
Frozen Coffee Creamer	6,696M	−5.82	22.79	0.84	18.18	47.1
Frozen Side Dishes	6,439M	−13.56	1.26	−0.23	23.05	33.4
Deodorant	5,915M	21.02	0.87	0.16	21.14	50.1

CHART 2A (continued)

	Dollar Sales Ending 12/29/91	Dollar Sales 52-Week Ending 12/29/91 vs 52 Weeks Ago	Category Dollar Share 52-Week Ending 12/29/91	Category Dollar Share 52-Week Ending 12/29/91 vs 52 Weeks Ago	% Price Differential 52-Week Ending 12/29/91	Est. Average Activity Weighed Distribution
Air Fresheners	5,904M	3.11	1.66	−0.15	20.22	31.3
Bath Products	5,269M	10.89	4.76	0.32	33.63	40.1
Feminine Needs	5,046M	15.17	2.47	−0.23	19.55	41.8
Mexican Sauces	4,988M	60.66	1.00	0.28	22.77	23.1
Croutons	4,599M	23.19	5.44	0.43	17.08	20.2
Frz. Prepared Vegetables	3,893M	−20.30	2.17	−0.18	22.95	17.0
Refrigerated Pasta	3.889M	21.29	2.13	0.11	27.89	7.2
Misc. Health Treatment	3,862M	9.35	21.71	0.86	18.18	51.3
Desserts – Refrigerated	3.820M	14.36	1.57	0.06	23.86	18.0
Canned Ham	3,531M	−21.73	2.49	−0.19	22.70	7.1
Denture Products	3,485M	39.72	2.94	0.85	18.63	45.3
Frozen Egg Substitutes	3,466M	61.66	3.42	1.06	16.48	19.0
Pickles/Relish – Refrigerated	3,466M	1.04	2.66	−0.07	25.90	14.5
Spreads – Refrigerated	3,178M	15.79	10.05	1.41	10.67	5.6
Personal Soap Product	3,063M	12.73	0.26	0.03	20.42	16.4
Suntan Products	3,013M	20.40	3.67	0.69	19.71	13.3
Cheesecake	2,974M	−2.38	56.52	7.92	17.44	8.1
Rug/Upholstery Cleaner	2,689M	−12.06	1.17	−0.20	19.24	30.8
Misc. Remedy Tablets	2,660M	−15.42	4.16	−1.20	21.51	26.2
Facial Moisturizer/ Cleanser	2,654M	13.74	0.91	0.00	28.62	17.9
Hair Conditioners	2,495M	−12.14	0.87	−0.06	23.18	34.9
Furniture Polish	2,053M	−1.15	1.47	0.06	15.59	19.2
Salad Dressing – Refrigerated	2.030M	12.85	2.05	0.23	22.31	7.1
Diet Aids	1,892M	30.22	0.64	0.16	25.61	13.9
Pest Control	1,850M	−10.59	0.61	−0.11	15.40	9.6
Oriental Food	1,749M	17.39	0.69	0.07	17.70	19.1
Floor Cleaners	1,741M	−16.07	2.26	−0.11	27.50	9.0
Diet Pills	1,717M	24.77	5.32	1.59	31.04	22.4
Frozen Pasta	1,636M	94.82	2.30	0.54	30.02	6.2
Rice/Popcorn Cakes	1,486M	104.82	1.00	0.45	18.83	5.5
Starch	1,437M	−22.26	1.91	−0.37	16.96	24.5

CHART 2A (continued)

	Dollar Sales Ending 12/29/91	Dollar Sales 52-Week Ending 12/29/91 vs 52 Weeks Ago	Category Dollar Share 52-Week Ending 12/29/91	Category Dollar Share 52-Week Ending 12/29/91 vs 52 Weeks Ago	% Price Differential 52-Week Ending 12/29/91	Est. Average Activity Weighed Distribution
Beer & Ale	1,412M	−12.80	0.02	0.00	12.48	3.1
Foot Care Products	1,218M	17.06	1.16	0.15	32.49	17.4
Hair Spray	1,141M	−36.26	0.38	−0.18	24.80	20.0
Shaving Lotion	1,011M	8.48	1.55	0.14	27.08	16.1
Gum	962,066	−30.35	0.18	−0.08	13.65	11.8
Meat Pies	745,516	139.14	4.00	2.41	27.54	0.8
Misc. Health Tablets	676,007	27.11	1.21	0.21	32.04	5.1
Cocktail Mixes	649,236	0.14	0.90	−0.03	19.91	11.6
External Analgesic Rub	581,411	32.32	1.34	0.34	32.11	11.8
Hair Styling Gel/ Mousse	512,650	−4.08	0.33	0.00	27.12	7.2
Shaving Cream	486,438	−9.44	0.51	−0.05	15.01	10.6
Oral Hygiene	432,346	116.23	1.66	0.78	17.68	9.3
Lunches – Refrigerated	336,112	871.98	0.17	0.15	17.35	1.8
Baby Food	185,541	−23.15	0.02	0.00	0.00	2.2
Frozen Cookies	118,562	427.56	14.64	12.36	12.41	1.1
Egg Substitutes	54,633	*	37.51	37.51	23.75	1.6
Misc. Hair Care Products	10,289	20.04	0.10	0.01	35.99	0.2
Non Fruit Drinks – Shelf Stable	516	−99.63	0.00	−0.32	0.00	0.0

Source: Information Resources Inc., 1992

CHART 3A

InfoScan

US SUPERMARKET REVIEW
VENDOR MULTI-CATEGORY REPORT – 1991

	Unit Sales 52-Week Ending 12/29/91	Unit Sales 52-Week Ending 12/29/91 vs 52 Weeks Ago	Category Unit Share 52-Week Ending 12/29/91	Category Unit Share 52-Week Ending 12/29/91 vs 52 Weeks Ago
Private Label	22,884MM	3.37	*	*
Milk	3,171MM	1.49	62.04	1.08
Fresh Bread & Rolls	2,095MM	0.26	40.23	–0.01
Carbonated Beverage	1,388MM	3.82	18.90	0.46
Vegetables – Shelf Stable	1,182MM	2.93	33.51	0.45
Cheese	840,688M	9.85	30.35	2.75
Plain Vegetables	809,713M	–4.04	52.50	–1.52
Juices	627,088M	6.47	37.44	1.76
Fruit – Shelf Stable	523,228M	–0.30	33.61	0.21
Tomato Products	498,868M	6.50	29.41	1.08
Ice Cream	461,771M	6.76	34.70	1.12
Juices – Shelf Stable	432,406M	2.69	15.30	0.25
Yogurt	374,660M	13.07	21.80	1.54
Sugar	374,145M	–0.58	40.85	–0.52
Soup	367,028M	5.17	8.94	0.25
Juice – Regular	326,042M	16.05	21.82	0.73
Chips & Snacks	315,272M	1.78	9.61	–0.32
Deli Luncheon Meats	298,856M	–5.54	19.50	–0.49
Cat Food	281,255M	1.19	7.68	0.30
Bottled Water	266,947M	3.66	23.47	0.83
Paper Towels	263,170M	1.99	15.31	0.36
Margarine/Spreads	227,844M	5.26	15.08	0.93
Seafood – Shelf Stable	226,089M	1.40	13.55	0.59
Dinners	224,143M	11.69	9.97	0.99
Food & Trash Bags	221,432M	1.66	31.02	0.86
Pickles/Relish/Olives	204,892M	5.76	29.35	2.23
Cottage Cheese	198,110M	1.49	41.83	1.46

CHART 3A (continued)

	Unit Sales 52-Week Ending 12/29/91	Unit Sales 52-Week Ending 12/29/91 vs 52 Weeks Ago	Category Unit Share 52-Week Ending 12/29/91	Category Unit Share 52-Week Ending 12/29/91 vs 52 Weeks Ago
Cookies	195,319M	5.10	11.21	0.61
Pasta	190,487M	9.05	14.36	0.66
Spices/Seasonings	189,880M	2.56	21.56	0.45
Toilet Tissue	181,512M	−8.98	9.34	−1.02
Powdered/Condensed Milk	176,594M	4.87	38.25	1.82
Cold Cereal	171,274M	28.22	6.90	1.47
Biscuits/Dough	170,980M	8.75	21.80	1.61
Crackers	168,973M	5.91	10.24	0.71
Creams	168,882M	6.24	37.80	0.29
Cups and Plates	166,367M	3.90	27.83	1.76
Breakfast Meats	165,727M	2.34	18.57	0.44
Sour Cream	162,840M	2.19	39.01	−0.23
Dog Food	160,696M	11.15	7.84	1.27
Butter	157,143M	0.02	42.36	−0.11
Foils & Wraps	137,662M	4.27	35.48	2.75
Pastry/Doughnuts	127,523M	5.06	21.54	−0.02
Facial Tissue	121,920M	−9.15	15.68	−1.49
Frozen Potatoes/Onions	120,152M	2.18	26.63	2.30
Shortening & Oil	115,802M	3.54	19.36	0.65
Bleach	107,329M	8.58	26.97	3.15
Dry Bean/Vegetables	104,431M	1.89	45.55	0.17
Frankfurters	101,457M	2.42	11.90	0.51
Jellies and Jams	100,860M	0.80	22.52	0.04
Coffee	95,333M	−2.33	9.74	0.03
Baking Needs	93,447M	3.75	13.40	0.61
Mustard & Ketchup	92,489M	11.38	17.81	1.90
English Muffins	91,137M	2.34	32.67	1.25
Frozen Novelties	88,755M	11.07	13.01	0.99
Paper Napkins	80,146M	−2.37	22.44	0.46
Mexican Food	79,650M	7.10	10.60	0.20
Rice	77,106M	7.41	10.54	0.45
Peanut Butter	72,865M	−11.89	19.02	−2.18
Baked Beans	72,827M	13.71	12.27	1.34

CHART 3A (continued)

	Unit Sales 52-Week Ending 12/29/91	Unit Sales 52-Week Ending 12/29/91 vs 52 Weeks Ago	Category Unit Share 52-Week Ending 12/29/91	Category Unit Share 52-Week Ending 12/29/91 vs 52 Weeks Ago
Other Reg. Products	70,800M	−0.07	15.80	−0.84
Household Cleaners	69,098M	4.61	7.63	0.52
Hot Cereal	66,352M	7.20	12.37	1.26
Tea	64,133M	9.41	14.73	0.86
Gravy/Sauce Mixes	61,158M	25.84	8.07	1.59
Mayonnaise/ Various Dressings	55,462M	2.75	9.61	0.49
Frozen Fruit	53,865M	0.81	55.31	0.89
Candy/Mints	53,375M	−4.67	2.00	−0.11
Gelatin/Pudding Mix	52,955M	6.52	6.31	0.56
Vinegar	52,413M	6.54	36.73	2.84
Frozen Pizza	50,382M	10.04	8.34	0.56
Internal Analgesics	49,360M	13.49	19.23	1.61
Popcorn/Popcorn Oil	49,295M	4.33	15.41	0.38
Drink Mixes	49,097M	18.75	3.67	0.54
Flour/Meal	46,990M	5.18	12.62	0.53
Dried Fruit	46,630M	−1.28	16.38	0.44
Bakery Snacks	46,500M	−10.02	6.25	−0.63
Laundry Detergent	44,733M	6.33	4.67	0.64
Dish Detergent	44,595M	8.69	7.40	1.04
Frozen Pot Pies	44,117M	2.90	13.50	1.33
Syrup/Molasses	42,108M	3.53	17.01	0.82
Coffee Creamer	42,028M	5.66	37.20	2.33
Snack Nuts	41,718M	−13.97	15.94	−1.68
Marshmallows	41,207M	15.09	36.56	3.24
First Aid Treatment	40,656M	3.17	64.91	2.28
Diapers	37,596M	21.25	14.91	2.03
Pies and Cakes	36,295M	14.68	27.77	3.19
Baking Mixes	35,186M	−3.13	3.48	−0.17
Sponges	31,348M	0.53	13.64	0.31
Hosiery	31,150M	−6.02	18.07	0.33
Entree/Side Dish	30,793M	1.61	15.16	−1.05
Sauces	29,583M	16.09	5.08	0.39
Vitamins	28,795M	3.47	39.30	0.40

CHART 3A (continued)

	Unit Sales 52-Week Ending 12/29/91	Unit Sales 52-Week Ending 12/29/91 vs 52 Weeks Ago	Category Unit Share 52-Week Ending 12/29/91	Category Unit Share 52-Week Ending 12/29/91 vs 52 Weeks Ago
Fabric Softener Sheet	28,471M	2.93	17.33	0.94
Coffee Filters	28,448M	13.26	30.19	2.59
Frozen Desserts/Topping	28,174M	10.09	7.77	0.29
Salad Dressings	26,326M	8.36	3.33	0.33
Cotton Balls	25,946M	2.56	34.64	2.25
Instant Potatoes	25,925M	−2.07	12.73	−0.55
Cold & Sinus Tablet/Cough	25,874M	29.13	10.38	1.31
Cat Litter	25,625M	4.58	15.66	0.46
Spaghetti Sauce	24,166M	7.38	3.90	0.28
Pizza – Refrigerated	23,930M	2.98	32.03	−4.19
Meat - Shelf Stable	22,245M	7.18	5.87	0.70
Frozen Pastry/Baked Goods	21,881M	20.89	6.83	1.26
Frozen Seafood	21,508M	−6.34	8.37	0.09
Sanitary Protection	20,415M	−6.74	6.40	−0.76
Moist Towelettes	19,584M	8.78	22.85	1.24
Cigarettes	19,318M	18.56	0.96	0.19
Frozen Breakfast Foods	18,800M	27.04	4.11	0.73
Baking Nuts	18,707M	−3.08	13.73	0.08
Cocoa Mix	18,623M	12.86	12.46	0.80
Frozen Pies	18,429M	4.79	9.26	0.47
Mouthwash	17,616M	17.07	15.76	3.69
Frozen Dinners/Entrees	16,604M	−1.66	0.76	−0.02
Fabric Softener Liquid	16,080M	−2.68	9.23	−0.14
Dental Accessories	15,825M	12.93	12.43	1.03
Bread/ Baked Goods – Refrigerated	15,295M	11.84	33.42	0.36
Dessert Toppings	13,082M	10.41	10.54	0.97
Stuffing	12,982M	18.19	7.77	1.26
Breadcrumbs/Batters	12,630M	16.40	8.67	0.52
Razors	10,958M	0.57	8.30	0.38
Sausage	10,779M	11.61	6.91	0.23
Pancake Mix	10,168M	4.17	10.27	1.61
Frozen Coffee Creamer	10,088M	−11.75	25.40	0.27
Ice Cream Cones/Mix	9,936M	10.76	20.01	1.63

CHART 3A (continued)

	Unit Sales 52-Week Ending 12/29/91	Unit Sales 52-Week Ending 12/29/91 vs 52 Weeks Ago	Category Unit Share 52-Week Ending 12/29/91	Category Unit Share 52-Week Ending 12/29/91 vs 52 Weeks Ago
Frozen Chicken	9,442M	57.43	3.84	1.51
Frosting	9,137M	−7.73	5.26	−0.55
Cold/Allergy Liquid/Powder	8,575M	38.85M	20.98	3.02
Natural Foods	8,538M	18.08	4.30	0.37
Air Fresheners	8,333M	−1.21	3.34	−0.41
First Aid Accessory	8,062M	10.03	14.42	1.63
Frozen Meat	7,933M	−10.34	4.06	−0.46
Dry Fruit Snacks	7,623M	2.19	3.53	−0.22
Shampoo	6,863M	−8.58	2.43	−0.14
Frozen Side Dishes	6,772M	−15.79	2.12	−0.26
Foil Pans	6,355M	8.31	8.76	0.49
Frozen Dough	6,243M	12.43	14.40	2.20
Cough Syrup	5,318M	17.82	11.64	1.46
Laxatives	5,314M	24.21	12.96	1.51
Toothpaste	4,983M	32.60	1.31	0.34
Croutons	4,826M	21.08	7.04	0.77
Misc. Remedies	4,302M	15.09	7.08	0.98
Eye/Contact Lens Care	4,232M	34.60	6.14	1.66
Pickles/Relish – Refrigerated	4,210M	−6.67	6.22	−0.32
Hand and Body Lotion	4,204M	1.70	5.28	0.39
Antacids	4,191M	31.47	4.02	0.88
Nasal Spray	4,169M	31.17	16.11	2.74
Feminine Needs	4,026M	14.39	6.60	0.87
Mexican Sauces	3,580M	49.05	1.21	0.35
Frozen Prepared Vegetable	3,544M	−18.15	2.50	−0.08
Deodorant	3,472M	19.70	1.23	0.22
Personal Soap Product	3,038M	−1.39	0.41	0.02
Desserts – Refrigerated	2,968M	7.74	2.19	−0.05
Bath Products	2,612M	10.61	6.35	0.81
Misc. Health Treatment	2,475M	3.14	41.38	1.29
Seafood – Refrigerated	2,390M	−15.19	5.40	−0.07
Spreads – Refrigerated	2,168M	10.50	10.78	1.51
Rug/Upholstery Cleaner	2,136M	−12.71	2.35	0.44

CHART 3A (continued)

	Unit Sales 52-Week Ending 12/29/91	Unit Sales 52-Week Ending 12/29/91 vs 52 Weeks Ago	Category Unit Share 52-Week Ending 12/29/91	Category Unit Share 52-Week Ending 12/29/91 vs 52 Weeks Ago
Refrigerated Pasta	1,998M	26.24	2.78	0.21
Frozen Egg Substitutes	1,916M	65.46	3.84	1.26
Denture Products	1,669M	35.65	4.42	1.32
Oriental Food	1,549M	8.92	1.00	0.06
Hair Conditioners	1,461M	−17.97	1.13	−0.18
Starch	1,365M	−20.77	2.04	−0.46
Furniture Polish	1,342M	−6.62	2.35	0.07
Rice/Popcorn Cakes	1,332M	77.88	1.51	0.63
Facial Moisturizer/Cleanser	1,326M	10.85	1.28	0.03
Gum	1,292M	−30.30	0.17	−0.06
Beer & Ale	1,210M	11.00	0.12	0.01
Misc. Remedy Tablets	1,124M	−26.36	6.77	−2.35
Frozen Pasta	1,072M	98.67	2.60	0.78
Salad Dressing – Refrigerated	1,057M	13.97	2.11	0.28
Foot Care Products	995,104	6.97	2.90	0.30
Suntan Products	974,806	13.14	6.49	1.02
Cocktail Mixes	929,520	−1.88	2.93	−0.03
Cheesecake	866,790	6.31	54.26	7.51
Pest Control	792,370	−9.84	0.88	−0.12
Hair Spray	696,115	−33.56	0.41	−0.18
Floor Cleaners	665,636	−20.16	2.67	−0.16
Diet Pills	582,946	27.29	9.15	2.93
Diet Aids	522,551	58.99	0.57	0.11
Shaving Lotion	499,327	2.51	2.88	0.25
Shaving Cream	446,229	−9.73	0.70	−0.07
Baby Food	394,061	−26.28	0.02	0.00
Canned Ham	348,922	−29.02	1.59	−0.30
Oral Hygiene	316,458	84.36	3.59	1.55
Lunches – Refrigerated	299,322	939.08	0.26	0.23
Misc. Health Tablets	277,164	33.43	2.05	0.50
Hair Styling Gel/Mousse	237,793	−4.38	0.38	0.00
External Analgesic Rub	227,286	27.41	1.85	0.49
Meat Pies	152,541	51.14	2.93	1.16

CHART 3A (continued)

	Unit Sales 52-Week Ending 12/29/91	Unit Sales 52-Week Ending 12/29/91 vs 52 Weeks Ago	Category Unit Share 52-Week Ending 12/29/91	Category Unit Share 52-Week Ending 12/29/91 vs 52 Weeks Ago
Frozen Cookies	49,567	713.87	12.79	11.46
Egg Substitutes	27,482	*	32.80	32.80
Misc. Hair Care Products	2,258	20.00	0.15	0.02
Non Fruit Drinks – Shelf Stable	847	−99.16	0.00	−0.32

Source: Information Resources Inc., 1992

Index

N

O